Programming for Absolute Beginners

Using the JavaScript Programming Language

Jonathan Bartlett

Apress®

Programming for Absolute Beginners: Using the JavaScript Programming Language

Jonathan Bartlett
Tulsa, OK, USA

ISBN-13 (pbk): 978-1-4842-8750-7   ISBN-13 (electronic): 978-1-4842-8751-4
https://doi.org/10.1007/978-1-4842-8751-4

Managing Director, Apress Media LLC: Welmoed Spahr
Acquisitions Editor: Steve Anglin
Development Editor: James Markham
Coordinating Editor: Mark Powers

Cover designed by eStudioCalamar

Cover image by Fullvector on Freepik (www.freepik.com)

Distributed to the book trade worldwide by Apress Media, LLC, 1 New York Plaza, New York, NY 10004, U.S.A. Phone 1-800-SPRINGER, fax (201) 348-4505, e-mail orders-ny@springer-sbm.com, or visit www. springeronline.com. Apress Media, LLC is a California LLC and the sole member (owner) is Springer Science + Business Media Finance Inc (SSBM Finance Inc). SSBM Finance Inc is a **Delaware** corporation.

For information on translations, please e-mail booktranslations@springernature.com; for reprint, paperback, or audio rights, please e-mail bookpermissions@springernature.com.

Apress titles may be purchased in bulk for academic, corporate, or promotional use. eBook versions and licenses are also available for most titles. For more information, reference our Print and eBook Bulk Sales web page at http://www.apress.com/bulk-sales.

Any source code or other supplementary material referenced by the author in this book is available to readers on GitHub (https://github.com/Apress). For more detailed information, please visit http://www.apress.com/source-code.

Printed on acid-free paper

Most good programmers do programming not because they expect to get paid or get adulation by the public, but because it is fun to program.

—Linus Torvalds

Table of Contents

About the Author

Jonathan Bartlett is a software developer, researcher, and writer. His first book, *Programming from the Ground Up*, has been required reading in computer science programs from DeVry to Princeton. He has been the sole or lead author for eight books on topics ranging from computer programming to calculus. He is a senior software developer for McElroy Manufacturing, spearheading projects in web, mobile, and embedded software. He is now the author of several Apress books including *Electronics for Beginners* and more.

About the Technical Reviewer

Germán González-Morris is a polyglot software architect/engineer with more than 20 years in the field, with knowledge in Java(EE), Spring, Haskell, C, Python, and JavaScript, among others. He works with web-distributed applications. Germán loves math puzzles (including reading Knuth) and swimming. He has tech-reviewed several books, including an application container book (Weblogic), as well as titles covering various programming languages (Haskell, Typescript, WebAssembly, Math for coders, and regexp). You can find more details at his blog site (`https://devwebcl.blogspot.com/`) or Twitter account (`@devwebcl`).

Acknowledgments

I want to take a moment and thank everyone who helped me write this book. First, I want to thank those who read and appreciated my first programming book, *Programming from the Ground Up*. The encouragement I received from that book has given me the encouragement to continue writing and educating throughout the years.

Next, I want to thank my homeschool summer co-op class for being guinea pigs for this material. Your questions, your successes, and your difficulties all informed the writing of this book. You were both my motivation to write in the first place and the first proving ground for the material.

I would also like to thank my family, my friends, and my church, all of whom are essential parts of my life. Thanks especially to my wife who puts up with me when I am too focused on my writing to notice what the kids have been up to or to put a stop to whatever trouble they have found themselves in!

CHAPTER 1

Introduction

The modern world is filled with computers. Computers run our phones, our cars, and even our refrigerators. Computers manage our businesses, our calendars, and our social lives. With the world relying on computers for so many functions, it is important to know how these devices work. Even if you never need to program a computer yourself, chances are that, at some point in your life, you will be involved with software development. You may be an accountant who needs to tell a computer programmer how you want your purchasing system set up. You may be an engineer who needs to describe your engineering process so that a programmer can automate it. In all such tasks as these, it is important to know something *about* how computers are programmed, even if you are not personally writing the software.

1.1 What You Will Learn

When programming computers, a programmer uses a **programming language** to tell the computer how to do something. Because computers are not intelligent beings, they can't understand ordinary human languages. Computers understand a type of language called **machine language**, which will be discussed further in Chapter 5. Machine languages are very different from the kind of languages ordinary people use. Therefore, programming languages were developed to meet programmers halfway—they are more humanlike than machine language and more machinelike than human language.

Numerous programming languages have been developed over the years. Some that you may have heard of include Java, JavaScript, Ruby, Python, C#, Go, Rust, and Swift. Although each language looks different, they are all trying to do the same task of helping you to interface with the machine in a way that is friendlier and easier to manage than machine language. In fact, most programming languages are geared around very similar concepts, and some of them even look similar. Therefore, learning any programming language will help you more easily learn any other programming language. I have rarely

1

© Jonathan Bartlett 2023
J. Bartlett, *Programming for Absolute Beginners*, https://doi.org/10.1007/978-1-4842-8751-4_1

hired people for my development team who already knew the programming language that my team uses. If someone learns one programming language and practices until they are good at it, then the effort to learn a new language is fairly minimal.

You may wonder why, if the languages are so similar, there are so many programming languages to choose from. The fact is, when engineering anything, trade-offs have to be made. Sometimes in order to make one type of task easier, another type of task has to be made harder. In my kitchen I have both a mixer and a blender. Both of them operate on the same basic principles—you put food into the main container area, an electric motor turns, and some attachment combines the food together. While these tasks are very similar and operate on the same principles, there are many types of food in the world and many ways that they need to be mixed, such that the mixer works better for some tasks and the blender for others. Similarly, with programming languages, some of them are better suited to different tasks. Also, the choice of programming language is dependent on the programmer. Just as different types of cars suit the preferences and tendencies of different types of drivers, so do different programming languages suit the preferences and tendencies of different types of programmers. Because of these reasons, there are numerous programming languages available for nearly any task you might want to perform.

The programming language covered in this book is called JavaScript. I like to teach JavaScript as a first language for several reasons. First of all, JavaScript was developed to be a first language. One of the goals of the language was to make it easy for new programmers to get started quickly. Even though JavaScript was designed to make programming easier for new programmers, it is not any less powerful as a language. Second, JavaScript has become the *de facto* programming language for website interfaces. If you use a website that does anything besides link to other web pages, JavaScript is probably involved. Therefore, learning JavaScript will have immediate practical benefits in learning how the Web operates. Third, the tools for programming JavaScript are available on every computer. You don't need to download any special tools to program JavaScript. If you have a computer with a web browser, you can program JavaScript! Finally, JavaScript is very similar to other popular programming languages such as C#, Java, and Swift. Therefore, knowing JavaScript will not only be immediately beneficial for programming websites, it is also a language that makes it easy to transition to other popular systems.

This book is for the first-time programmer. No prior programming experience is assumed. This book does assume that you have a basic understanding of how to use your computer and browse the Internet. That is all that you need!

You will learn not only the basics of computer programming but also a more general knowledge of how computers and data work. You will learn where computers came from, how they work, how computers work with data, how data is transmitted, and how web pages work. This book will not go in-depth in all of these subjects, but it will give you a basic working framework that will help you better understand ideas that you may encounter elsewhere.

1.2 How to Use This Book

This book follows several conventions to help you along your programming journey. First, this book will introduce you to new terminology. In order to highlight the important words, terms will be printed in **bold print** the first time that they are used. You can find a complete list of terms in Appendix A. These terms are important, and you should memorize their meanings.

When this book lists out computer programs, parts of computer programs, or anything that should be typed in directly (and precisely), it will be offset from the text and written in a special font to help you see that it is a computer program. Computer programs will look like this:

```
window.alert("This is an example of a computer program.");
```

When discussing smaller pieces of code within a paragraph, code that is under discussion will look like this.

Now, there are many different types of computers, each with different operating systems and software loaded on them, with each of those having different versions. There are also numerous different web browsers, each with different features available and slightly different ways of working. This book attempts to walk you through setting everything up on each operating system. If there is anything in this book that depends on the specific operating system or browser that you are using, Appendix B has the steps for several different systems, including Windows and Mac operating systems. This book will refer you to the appropriate section of the Appendix when needed. Though this book works with any modern web browser (basically anything released after 2008), I recommend that you use Google Chrome. As of the time of this writing, Google Chrome is the easiest browser to work with as a programmer. That being said, you should be just fine with any web browser, including Brave, Firefox, Safari, Chrome, Opera, or Edge.

This book contains several practice questions and practice activities. The goal of these questions and activities is to provide you with a hands-on way of understanding the material. By doing the questions and activities, the text will become much more meaningful and understandable. More importantly, they might show you the places where you did not fully understand the text. Many people have a tendency to skip over things if they don't understand them well. Practice questions and activities give you a chance to slow down and make sure you know which parts you understood and which parts you need to read again and spend time thinking about. Practice questions build on each other, so by doing them all in the order given, you can see exactly where you are having problems.

At the end of every chapter is a review section which covers the most important concepts of each chapter. After that is a section to help you practice applying your knowledge to problems. These questions require you to further engage your brain and really think about what you learned in that chapter and what it means.

Appendix A contains an extended glossary of terms used in this book, plus others you are likely to encounter when reading about programming. This chapter will help you find your bearings as you read and talk with other people about programming. I would suggest that, concurrent with your readings, you also take the time to look through the glossary for words that you may have heard but did not understand at the time.

Also, if you run into problems when writing code, Section B.6 has several suggestions for getting you back on the right track.

1.3 For Younger Programmers

This book is primarily geared for people who are coming to computer programming as a new career, college students, or even high school students. However, it can also be used for middle school students with some modification. Middle school students, generally, are not cognitively ready for all of the material after Part 3. This doesn't mean it can't be covered or read, but it might be good to pick and choose material that is appropriate to student interests and abilities. If parts are difficult to understand, they can be returned to at a later time.

All right, are you ready? Let's get started!

PART I

Computers, Data, and Communication

The purpose of this part is to help you understand how computers work on the inside. While it is possible to learn programming without learning how your computer works, in the long term, knowing what is going on inside the computer will help you write better programs. This part covers the basics of how computers communicate, how they store data, and how computer programming works at the lowest level.

CHAPTER 2

A Short History of Computers

The history of computers is weird and wonderful. What started as an abstract philosophical quest ended up setting the course for society for over a century and continues to be one of the most profound parts of modern life. The goal of this chapter is to trace an outline of where computing started, where it has been, and where it is now.

2.1 The Prehistory of Computers

Humans have always had tools. Humans have built fires, made spears, and built houses from the beginning. At first, however, technology was limited to standing structures or tools that were extensions of yourself—like knives or bows and arrows. Very little early technology was powered and free-functioning. It was manually powered by human effort. Therefore, since the power of a machine was limited to what humans could drive, only small machines could be devised.

The ability to power a machine led to huge advances in technology. The earliest power source was probably water, where water could turn a wheel to grind wheat or operate a sawmill. These water-based power sources, however, were fairly limited in the types of devices they could drive. Such technology was mostly limited to standing wheel-based inventions.

This was essentially the state of technology from about 300 BC to the early 1700s AD. At this point in history, technology had two main limiting factors. The first was limitations of power availability, and the second was the need for customized parts. The industrial revolution solved both of these problems. The steam engine allowed the creation of powered machines anywhere. Powered machines were no longer tied

© Jonathan Bartlett 2023
J. Bartlett, *Programming for Absolute Beginners*, https://doi.org/10.1007/978-1-4842-8751-4_2

to being near streams but could now go anywhere, since the power could be generated from fire and stored water. Eventually this even allowed the creation of trains, since the power could move with the vehicle.

The other invention of the industrial revolution was interchangeable parts. This allowed a standardization and maintenance of equipment that was previously unattainable. Instead of having each part be a unique piece, the parts became standardized which allowed for the machines to become more specialized. It is one of the more curious paradoxes of technology that as the *pieces* of technology become less unique, the more advanced and unique the systems created from those parts can become. Standardization allows for users of technology to stop having to think about all of the low-level decisions and focus on the larger, more meaningful decisions. This also allows for better communication *about* systems, because the parts can be more readily described. If I can give you a schematic that lists premade parts, it is much easier to design and communicate that design than if I also had to describe how each individual part was supposed to be made.

So the introduction of available powered machinery and standardized parts in the industrial revolution led to an explosion of specialized machines. We then had machines to perform any number of tasks that a person could want to do. The next step was the introduction of machines which were directed not by people directly controlling the machine but by coded instructions. The earliest of these machines was the Jacquard Loom, which used punched cards to signify a pattern woven into a fabric. The cards had punched holes to signify to the machine the raising or lowering of the particular thread causing it to be visible or hidden in the pattern. Thus, the loom could be programmed to make a pattern by specifying at each point whether each thread should be raised or lowered.

Later inventions applied this concept to mathematics. Calculating machines had been around for a long time, with Blaise Pascal's mechanical calculator having been invented in the mid-1600s. However, this required the power of physical manipulation to actually accomplish the addition. Most mathematical tasks are not single-step like addition but require a process of several steps, sometimes repeating steps, before finding an answer. Charles Babbage invented a more advanced machine to perform navigational calculations. In this machine, the user entered the input, and then the machine used that input to run a series of steps which eventually yielded results. Babbage eventually designed a machine that could take a list of arbitrary instructions much like a modern computer, but he was never able to build that design.

Once humans had the ability to power a machine, create a machine that operated on external instructions, and use those instructions to perform mathematical functions, they had all of the pieces in place to create a computer. However, the revolution that brought about computing took place not from an invention, but from a problem in philosophy.

2.2 The Idea of a Computer

What separates modern computers from the calculating machines of the past is that modern computers are **general-purpose computers**. That is, they are not limited to a specific set of predesigned features. I can load new features onto a computer by inputting the right program. How did we get the idea of creating such a general-purpose machine?

It turns out that a question in philosophy led to the creation of general-purpose machines. The question was this—was there a way to create an unambiguous procedure for checking mathematical proofs? This seems like an odd question, but it was a big question in the nineteenth century. There had been many "proofs" where it was unclear if the proof actually proved its subject. Thus, philosophers of mathematics tried to find out if there was a way to devise what was then called an "effective procedure" for checking the validity of a mathematical proof. But that leads to another question—what counts as an "effective procedure" anyway? If I list out the steps of a procedure, how do I know that I've given you enough details that you can accomplish this procedure exactly as I have described it? How can I tell that my instructions are clear enough to know that the procedure that I have listed can be unambiguously accomplished?

Alan Turing and Alonzo Church both tackled this problem in the 1930s. The results showed that one could define unambiguous procedures with the help of machines. By describing a machine that could perform the operation, one can be certain that the operation of the procedure would be unambiguous. In addition, Turing described a set of operations which could be used to mimic any other set of operations given the right input. That is, Turing defined the minimum set of features needed for a computing system to become truly programmable—where the programmer had an open-ended ability to write whatever software he or she wanted. Machines and programming languages that are at least as powerful as Turing's set of features are known as **Turing-complete** or **Universal** programming languages. Nearly every modern programming language in common usage is Turing-complete.

It is interesting to note that the creation of computing came from a question in philosophy. Many are eager to dismiss the role of philosophy in academics as being impractical or unimportant. But, as we see here, like all truths, philosophical truths have a way of leading to things of deep practical importance.

And what happened to the original question—can you develop an effective procedure for checking proofs? The answer is, strangely, no. It turns out that there are true facts that cannot be proven via mechanical means. But to learn that answer, we had to develop computers first. Of course, that leads to another interesting intersection between computers and philosophy. If there are true facts that cannot be mechanically proven, how could we know that? The only way must be because our minds cannot be represented mechanically. This puts a limit on the potential capabilities of artificial intelligence and shows that even though computer programmers have developed some very clever means of pretending to be human, the human mind is simply outside the realm of mechanism or mechanistic simulations.[1]

2.3 The Age of the Computer

Shortly after Turing described the necessary feature set for computers, people began to build them. Probably the first Turing-complete machine was Konrad Zuse's Z3 computer, built in 1941. Although the Z3's operating principles were somewhat similar to modern computers, the Z3 was still largely a mechanical device. The first general-purpose, digital electronic computer was the ENIAC in 1946 and was about a thousand times faster than its mechanical predecessors. It should be noted that the ENIAC was the size of a very large room, but it had roughly the same processing power as a scientific calculator. Its main jobs included performing calculations for the production of the hydrogen bomb and calculating tables for firing artillery.

The next generation of computers introduced what is normally termed the **von Neumann architecture**, which means that the computer had a single memory area which held both programs and data. This is based on the fact that both a program and the values that the program generates can both be represented by numbers. Therefore, the same memory can be used both for the program that tells the computer what to do

---

[1] If you want to dive deeper into this subject, you can see my article in MindMatters, "Why I Doubt That AI Can Match the Human Mind," available at https://bit.ly/3FOtOsS. You may also want to check out my YouTube video, "How to Build an Artificial Intelligence Using the Doctrine of Man," available at https://youtu.be/FzXW7p3AG1Y.

and for the data that the program generates and operates on. This makes the computers much easier to program and use, which led to the ability to sell computers commercially. The first commercially available computer to implement this idea was the Manchester Mark 1. The first mass-produced computer was the UNIVAC I, followed shortly after by IBM's 650. These computers were still massive in size but contained less memory storage space than a single graphic on a modern computer. The UNIVAC I was the first computer to have an external tape storage, and external disk storage (similar to modern hard drives) followed soon after.

The next move for computer hardware was toward miniaturization. The original computers used large devices called vacuum tubes to perform data processing (see Figure 2-1, left column). These vacuum tubes would allow or not allow current to flow based on whether other wires had current flowing through them or not. Combinations of many of these tubes could allow for data to be stored as current flow, for mathematical operations to be performed on such data, and for the data to be moved around.

After the vacuum tube came the invention of the transistor (see Figure 2-1, middle column). Transistors generally have three wires, where the middle wire controls whether the electricity can flow between the other two wires. As with vacuum tubes, transistors can be wired together to create digital computer memory, digital computer logic operations, and digital information pathways. Transistors, while they performed the same basic functions as the vacuum tube, were able to do so in a much smaller package and operating on a lot less power. Transistors allowed much smaller devices to be built which also required almost 1,000 times less power. The Metrovick 950, released in 1956, was the first commercial computer that operated on this principle.

Miniaturization continued with the advent of **integrated circuits** or what are often called **microchips** or just **chips** (see Figure 2-1, right column). An integrated circuit basically allows for miniaturized transistors to be stored on a small, single plate of silicon. When integrated circuits were first introduced, they only had a few transistors. Today, integrated circuits come in a variety of sizes, and the ones used for desktop computing can hold billions of transistor equivalents on a 2-inch square chip. Integrated circuits basically brought computers as we know them into the world. However, when they were first introduced, they were primarily used by very large businesses.

In the 1960s, Douglas Engelbart led a research team to look at the future of computing. In 1968, Engelbart presented what has been termed "the mother of all demos," which predicted and demonstrated nearly all aspects of modern personal computing, including graphical interfaces, networking, email, video conferencing, collaborative document editing, and the Web. This served as an inspiration for a number of companies to start pushing to make this vision of computing a reality. Engelbart had accomplished it in a lab, but others were needed to make it a commercial reality.

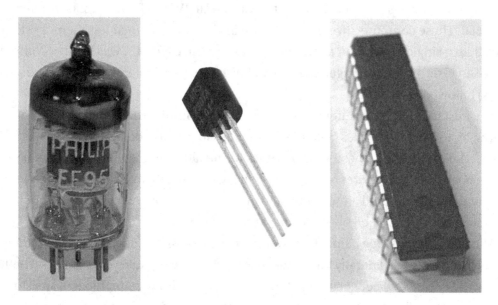

Figure 2-1. *Advancements in Computer Hardware Miniaturization*

The picture on the left is of a vacuum tube (photo courtesy of Tvezymer on Wikimedia). Vacuum tubes are still around today, primarily for audio applications. The picture in the middle is of a transistor. Transistors were much smaller, required fewer materials to produce, and used much less power but still did largely the same job as vacuum tubes. The picture on the right is a modern microchip used in appliances (photo courtesy of Vahid alpha on Wiki-media). Such a microchip contains the equivalent of a few hundred thousand transistors.

The first recreational personal computer was the Altair, and the first commercial personal computer was the Apple I which came out in 1976, after which a flood of personal computers entered the market. IBM eventually entered the market, with Microsoft providing the software for the computer. The interfaces for these computers were usually text-only. However, eventually Apple released the Macintosh, which inaugurated the age of graphical user interfaces. Shortly after, Microsoft released Windows, which brought the graphical interface to the IBM side of the personal computer world.

2.4 Computers in the Age of Networks

Thus far, computers had been largely isolated machines. You could share files through disks, but, by and large, computers operated alone. When you link together two or more computers, it is called a **network**. Though networking technology had been around for quite a while, it had not been cheap enough or popular enough to make an impact for most personal computer users.

For most users, networking started with office file sharing systems, usually using a type of local networking called **Ethernet** which runs networking services over specialized networking cables. People would use applications that were installed on their own computers but store the files on a **server** so that the other members of the office could access it. A server is a computer on the network that provides one or more services to other computers and users on a network. A software program that accesses a server is often called a **client**. Many office networks eventually added **groupware** services to their networks—local email and calendar sharing systems that allowed the office to work together more efficiently. While smaller organizations were focused on local services such as file sharing and groupware, larger institutions were also at work linking networks together. This allowed organizations to share information and data between each other more easily.

At the same time, a few home computer users started reaching out to each other through the phone system. A device called a **modem** allowed a computer to access another computer over standard telephone lines. Services called **bulletin-board systems** (known as a BBS) started popping up which allowed people to use their computers to access a remote computer and leave messages and files for other users.

These developments laid the groundwork for the idea of the **Internet**. At the time it was developed, there were many different, incompatible networking technologies. Organizations wanted to connect their networks to other organizations' networks but were finding it problematic since everyone used different types of networks. In the 1970s and 1980s, DARPA, the Defense Advanced Research Projects Agency, developed a way to unify different types of networks from different organizations under a single system so that they could all communicate. This network, known as ARPANET, became very popular. Other large, multi-organizational groups started using the design of ARPANET to create their own network. Since these networks all used the same basic design, they were eventually joined together to become the Internet in the late 1980s.

The 1990s witnessed the rise of Internet Service Providers, or ISPs, which provided a way for computer users to use the modems that they used to use for bulletin-board systems to connect their computers to the Internet. Instead of using a modem to connect to a single computer, like they did with bulletin-board systems, the ISP allowed a user to use their modem to connect to a whole network. This began the mass public adoption of the Internet by both individuals and organizations of all stripes.

In the early days of the Internet, the speed of the network was very slow, and only text could be transmitted quickly. Eventually, modems were replaced with more advanced (and faster) ways of connecting to the Internet, such as DSL, cable, and fiber. This allowed more and more complex content to be transmitted over the Internet. Also, because these technologies do not tie up a phone line, they can be used continuously, rather than intermittently. In addition, wireless technologies, such as **WiFi** and cellular-based networking, allowed users to connect to the Internet without being tied down by cables. These developments together led to the near-ubiquitous availability of the Internet that we have today.

So, today, nearly all computer software is built with the network in mind. In fact, much of the software that people use on a daily basis operates not on an individual computer, but over a network. This allows for users to access software programs no matter where they are or what computer they are using. It has also changed software development so that the focus of computer software is no longer on individuals and individual tasks but on organizing groups of people.

2.4.1 Review

In this chapter, we covered the basic history of computers. We have learned the following:

- Humans have used tools to accomplish tasks from the beginning.

- Early tools were limited by available power options.

- Advances in power technology allowed for the improvements and industrialization of tools.

- Standardization of parts allows for more complex machines to be built and serviced.

- Electricity allowed for the movement of power to any needed location.

- The ability to control a machine via instructions, such as the Jacquard Loom, allowed for the creation of more general-purpose tools which could be specialized by providing the right sets of instructions.

- Alan Turing and Alonzo Church identified the logical requirements for making general-purpose computations.

- Several early computers were built around the idea of a general-purpose calculating machine.

- Advances in electronics allowed for storage of millions of transistors onto a single microchip.

- The availability of microchips led to the era of personal computing.

- The increased usage of computers in organizations eventually led to the need to have better means of communication between computers.

- Networks were invented to allow computers to be hooked together to share file and messages.

- The isolated networks around the world were eventually unified into a single Internet-work, known as the Internet.

- The growth of the Internet combined with the ability to access the Internet wirelessly has made the Internet a primary factor in computer usage.

- The ubiquity of the Internet has led programmers to start designing applications with the network in mind first, rather than as an afterthought.

2.4.2 Apply What You Have Learned

1. Take some time to think about the history of technology and the Internet. What do you think is next on the horizon for technology?

2. The pace of technology appears to have been accelerating over the past century. What do you think has caused this acceleration?

3. Pick your favorite piece of technology mentioned in this short history and research it. What inspired the person who developed it? What other inventions came after it? Was it successful? Write a few paragraphs describing the technology you have chosen, how it functioned, and how it impacted the future of technology.

CHAPTER 3

How Computers Communicate

Before we start our study of computer programming, we are going to begin by studying the way that computers communicate. The Internet is basically a giant communication system. Communication systems operate using **protocols**. A protocol is a predefined sequence of steps used to ensure proper communication.

We actually use protocols every day. Think about what happens when you answer the phone. What do you say and why do you say it? Think about what happens when you answer the phone (see Figure 3-1). This signals to the person calling us that we have picked up the phone and we are ready to start talking. If we didn't say "hello," the person might think that we accidentally accepted the call without knowing it or that we are not quite ready to talk yet. Then, at the end of the call, we usually say something like, "Thanks for calling! Goodbye!" This signals to the other person that we are done with the conversation. If we didn't tell them goodbye, they might think that we are still on the line and continue talking. If they heard silence, they may presume that either we were not speaking because we were upset or that there was a technical problem. Therefore, we end our conversations with a "goodbye" to let the person we are talking to know that the conversation is over.

This is the essence of a protocol. A communication protocol is a sequence of steps or possible steps that enable two parties to communicate or interact and know the status of the communication or interaction. Because computers cannot think or feel, computers rely on very rigid and exact protocols to allow them to communicate with each other. In fact, computers use hundreds of different protocols to communicate different types of data in different ways. Most of the time, there are actually multiple protocols happening at once.

© Jonathan Bartlett 2023
J. Bartlett, *Programming for Absolute Beginners*, https://doi.org/10.1007/978-1-4842-8751-4_3

Figure 3-1. *Even Answering the Phone Has a Protocol*

Think about writing a letter. When you write a letter, there is a basic protocol that governs the form of a letter—at minimum it should have a date, a greeting, and a closing. However, if you decide to mail the letter, you have to send it through the mail service, which has its own protocol. To send the letter through the mail, you need to take the letter, fold it up, and put it in an envelope. What you write on the envelope is governed by another protocol designed by the US Postal Service. Their protocol requires a return address on the top left corner of the envelope, a destination address in the middle of the envelope, and a stamp in the top right corner. Now you have two protocols happening simultaneously—the letter-writing protocol and the envelope-addressing protocol. These protocols are *layered*, which means that one of the protocols runs fully inside of the other protocol. In computer jargon, we would say that the envelope protocol *encapsulates* the letter protocol. The envelope protocol takes the results of the letter protocol, packages it up, and puts its own protocol on top.

3.1 The Layers of Internet Communication

On the Internet, there is a similar layering of protocols occurring. The difference is that on the Internet, there are many more layers interacting at once, and they all have funny names like HTTP, TLS, TCP, IP, IEEE 802.3, SMTP, and FTP. The International Standards Organization developed a way to help you think of these layers called the **OSI Model**, which identifies seven different layers of protocols that may need to be active when communicating on a computer network. To understand what these layers are doing, let's look at the questions that have to be answered in order for one computer to talk to another.

Let's say that we have a chat application that sends messages to another computer. What must happen to get that message to another computer?

1. The computers must be physically connected to the Internet. "Physical" can include both wired connections and wireless connections. This is called the **physical layer**.

2. The computers must know how to move data on those physical connections. It is not enough for the wires to be connected; they must also know the protocols for sending messages on that physical medium. Each computer has to be able to identify other physically connected computers, be able to signal to them that they are sending data, and know which computer they are sending it to, among other details. This is called the **data link layer**.

3. Once the computers know how to talk to the other computers they are physically connected to, they need to be able to talk to computers which they are only indirectly connected to. For instance, most locations get their Internet connection by connecting a **router** to their DSL or cable line, and then the other devices in the home connect to that router. The devices in the home are all connected physically and communicate using the data link layer. However, only the router is physically connected to the Internet Service Provider (ISP). The other computers must adopt a protocol in order to tell the router to relay their messages on to the rest of the network. The rest of the network, likewise, must be able to follow the same protocol. In addition, in order

to speak to other computers on the network, you must be able to identify them, so it also includes at least some sort of naming or numbering system for the computers on the network. This layer, which interconnects computers which are only indirectly connected to each other, is called the **network layer**.

4. Now that we can move data across the Internet, there is another issue. Other networks might not be as reliable as we want them to be. Since we have no control over how reliable the other networks are, we must adopt a protocol for making sure all of the data arrives at the other side of the network safely and allows us to retransmit any missing data that did not make it to the other side. This layer is called the **transport layer**.

5. Once we know how to reliably move data through the network, we need to be able to signal to a computer that we want to start talking to it and let it know when we are finished with our communication. This is called the **session layer**.

6. Now that we have a connection to a remote computer, and the remote computer is accepting data, sometimes we need to adjust or rework some aspect of that communication. This is called the **presentation layer**. For instance, oftentimes we want encrypted communication between computers. The message, when it is sent, goes through a layer of encryption. The encryption and decryption of the message happens at the presentation layer. Other times (though this is rare), two computers have different ways of representing data, and, therefore, the message has to be translated between the computers. This would also happen at the presentation layer.

7. Finally, now our application can reliably send data to a similar application on the other computer. Of course, for our applications to speak to each other, they must both use their own protocol. This layer of communication between applications is called the **application layer**.

As you can see, there is a lot going on when you send a message from one computer to another through the Internet! Thankfully, since this is built in layers, we rarely have to think about all of the things that are going on at the different layers. For instance, when you mail a letter to a friend, you never have to think about the different mail sorting facilities, postal routes, or delivery times of the post office. That is a system that is already in place, and you must simply drop your letter in the mailbox and let the system do the rest. That is the same with communication on the Internet. However, it is good to know what is happening behind the scenes, both so you can better understand the capabilities of the system you are using and so you can better identify issues when something goes wrong!

	Layer	What it Does	Example
7	Application Layer	the main content of the message	HTTP
6	Presentation Layer	handles encodings and encryption	TLS
5	Session Layer	controls the conversation flow	TCP
4	Transport Layer	ensures reliable sending in a noisy network	TCP
3	Network Layer	provides a logical addressing mechanism and bridges different physical configurations	IP
2	Data Link Layer	low-level communication protocol for the physical medium	Ethernet
1	Physical Layer	how the machines are physically connected	Category 5 Cable

Figure 3-2. *Overview of the OSI Model*

Computers haven't always been connected through the Internet, and the OSI Model was developed when the Internet was not the primary means of communication. In fact, at the time, nearly all communication was on private networks. Since its development, certain technologies have become fairly standard in each layer. Figure 3-2 shows common technologies used at each layer.

For the physical layer and data link layer, the two primary technologies are **Ethernet** for wired connections and **Wi-Fi** for wireless connections. In addition, your connection to the Internet, whether it is through cable, DSL, or fiber, also uses its own physical and data link layers. The network layer is handled by the **Internet Protocol**, usually abbreviated as **IP**. The number that identifies each computer on the Internet is known as the computer's **IP address**. On the Internet, the transport and session layers are usually combined and handled through a protocol called the **Transmission Control Protocol**, abbreviated as **TCP**. Because TCP and IP are almost always seen together, they are often collectively labeled as **TCP/IP**. The only common presentation-layer protocol is the **Transport Layer Security** protocol, usually abbreviated as **TLS** or **SSL** (based on its original name, the Secure Sockets Layer). TLS handles the job of encrypting and decrypting data on a secure connection, to prevent other people from being able to listen in on your communication.

Thankfully, however, we rarely need to know much about these layers. In fact, this is one of the main reasons such layers were invented—so that all an application programmer really needs to interact with is the application layer. It is still good to know that these other layers exist, as occasionally you might interact with them. In addition, knowing the basics of how the network works is part of being a programmer.

The layer that most computer programmers deal with directly is the application layer. There are several application-layer protocols that operate on the Internet. The Internet is best known for **HTTP**, which is the protocol used to access websites. Second to HTTP is probably **SMTP**, which is the protocol used to send email. **POP** and **IMAP** are two protocols often used to *receive* emails if you use a separate email program. These protocols make up a large majority of people's use of the Internet.

3.2 Communicating Using HTTP

As mentioned earlier, when you access a website, the protocol you are using is HTTP, which stands for "HyperText Transfer Protocol." Web pages are considered "hypertext," and the file format that web pages use is called the "HyperText Markup Language" or HTML. We will dive further into the details of HTML in Chapter 6. For now, we will just consider the protocol used to access HTML documents and not concern ourselves with the contents.

The first thing to know about HTTP is that it is fundamentally about *documents*. Websites might look fancy, but really they are a collection of interactive documents. Therefore, when you go to a website, your browser connects to the remote computer (called the **server**) and requests a document. When you click on a link, what usually happens is that the link tells your browser the location of a new document to fetch. Your browser then retrieves that new document and shows it to you. These documents are identified and located by a piece of text called a "Universal Resource Locator" or **URL**.

A typical URL looks something like what is shown in Figure 3-3.

protocol   hostname   path

https :// www.bplearning.net /example/about.html

Figure 3-3. *Typical URL Structure*

Each URL has three main parts—the application-layer protocol, the hostname (the server's name or IP address), and the document path. Optionally, there is also a fourth and fifth part, the **query string** and the **anchor**, which provide additional information to the server and/or the JavaScript on the page itself. In a URL, the protocol is everything up until the colon. In this case, it is "https," which is the normal protocol used on the Internet for encrypted connections. If the connection is an unencrypted connection, the protocol would just be "http." The two slashes after the protocol indicate that the next piece of the URL is the **hostname**. In this case, the hostname is `www.bplearning.net`. We will discuss hostnames in more depth in Section 3.4. The slash after the hostname is the beginning of the path. The path includes the starting slash and is essentially the rest of the URL. Sometimes the path is extremely short. For instance, when you first go to a website, the path is usually just /. It can also be very long, like `/orders/123/products/5`. The way to think about a path is that each piece of the path is like a folder on your computer, and the path is the list of folders someone has to go through to find a document. That isn't exactly what is happening on the server, but it is a helpful way of thinking about it.

For an example, open up your browser. Find the location bar in your browser. (For more information on finding the location bar in your browser, see Section B.1.) Put `https://www.bplearning.net/example/` into the location bar and press the enter key. This will bring up an example website that I built for this book. Depending on your browser, it might show you the whole URL, or it might remove the protocol from the URL to make it easier to read. Some browsers will also remove the path unless you actually click in to the location bar itself.

Now, click on the link titled "About." Once the page finishes loading, take another look at your browser's location bar. The location bar should now read `https://www.bplearning.net/example/about.html`. That URL is used to find the server and tell the server what document it should give you and the protocol for the communication channel.

Now we will look at how the browser actually retrieves the document. Data transmission on the Internet using HTTP is not quite as mysterious as it may seem.

The main steps are as follows:

1. Establish a connection with the server.

2. Tell the server what the path to the document is.

3. Tell the server any additional information about the communication.

4. Send a blank line.

5. Receive the file.

Once the connection with the server is established, here is what the protocol looks like to request the "about" page:

```
GET /example/about.html HTTP/1.1
Host: www.bplearning.net
Connection: close
```

The first line, called the request line, does most of the work. It has three components. The first component is called the **HTTP verb**. This tells the server what action you are trying to do. You are retrieving the document, so you use the GET verb. Other verbs include DELETE for remotely destroying documents and POST for sending data to a document on the server. The next component is the path, which tells the server how to find the document. The last component is the protocol version—you are using HTTP version 1.1.[1]

The next few lines are called the request headers. They are a list of options that you send to the server to clarify in more detail what you want and how you want it delivered. The first request header line that we send tells the server what hostname you are looking for. This may seem redundant, since we already connected to the server that we want. However, modern web servers are actually built to serve requests for any number of hostnames which may be sharing the same server. Therefore, even though you are connected to the server for `www.bplearning.net`, you still have to tell it what site you were really looking for. The next header line is optional, but it tells the server to close

---

[1] Note that, starting with HTTP protocol version 2, the protocol will no longer be based on textual commands, so you won't be able to use HTTP 2 via the keyboard alone. However, servers will likely maintain backward compatibility with HTTP/1.1 indefinitely.

the connection after it gives you the document. Otherwise, it will sit and wait for you to request something else. Then, to signal that we are at the end of our request headers, we send a blank line. There is also an optional request *message* (called the request body) that we can send at this point, but that is beyond the scope of our discussion. The requests we will be discussing in this chapter will not have a request body.

When the server receives the blank line, it knows that you are done asking for your document, and it attempts to process your request. It then responds with something that looks like this:

```
HTTP/1.1 200 OK
...Possibly other data here...
Server: Apache
Content-Type: text/html; charset=UTF-8
...Possibly more data here...

....Document Gets Put Here....
```

The response is very similar in format to the request. The first line is the response line. It lists the protocol version that the server is responding with, followed by a status code and status message. 200 is the status code that means everything went just fine and there is a document coming. Other common status codes include 404 which means that the document could not be found, 500 which means that the server ran into an error, 301 and 302 which mean that the document has moved locations, and 400 which means that the request did not follow the proper protocol or sent bad data. After the response line is a series of response headers. These communicate additional information about the server and the response. The headers shown here are just an example—most servers give back several more headers as well and usually in no particular order. The two headers shown tell us the type of document we have retrieved (in this case, an HTML file, which is what Content-Type: text/html means) and the name of the server software that the server is running (Apache in this case). The server then sends a blank line telling us that it is done sending the headers, and the rest of the communication will be the document we asked for. The document we get back is an HTML file. It may look strange, but that is exactly what the browser receives from the server. It includes all of the data that the browser needs to display as well as the instructions for how to display it on the screen and how you can interact with it.

3.3 Connecting with a Remote Server Manually

Depending on your computer and computer setup, you may have the tools installed to access a web server manually. If not, Appendix C has some instructions for setting up the necessary tools on your computer. Most Mac and Linux computers have these tools already installed. For this, you will need to go to the command line of your computer. For information about what the command line is and how to get to it for your computer, see Appendix B.2. If for some reason you are not able to get the commands in this section working, don't worry, they are not required for any other part of the book but merely here to show you what is going on under the hood. Feel free to skip to the next section if needed.

We will start by using the telnet command to directly talk to servers without using our browser, so we can see exactly what is taking place under the hood. Once you are on the command line, type the following to connect to the bplearning.net server using HTTP:

```
telnet www.bplearning.net 80
```

You are now talking directly with the web server yourself! Now you just need to follow the HTTP protocol to get what you need. Type in the request that we mentioned earlier (note that the request ends with a blank line):

```
GET /example/about.html HTTP/1.1
Host: www.bplearning.net
Connection: close
```

The server will then respond with its response line, response headers, and response message as outlined above. However, it won't be the page we requested. It will, instead, be a *redirect* response. The reason for this is that the website only allows secure requests, and HTTP by itself is unencrypted. Therefore, we have to communicate using HTTPS (HTTP over a secure/encrypted connection) rather than just HTTP.

You may be wondering what the 80 is doing in the original telnet command. That is the *port* that the HTTP server listens on by default. Servers use "port numbers" to know what service is being requested, as each service listens on a different port number. Port 80 is the standard port number used for HTTP communication. For our

HTTPS communication, we will be connecting to port 443, which is the standard port for HTTPS.[2]

The command to communicate via HTTPS is openssl, which does essentially the same thing as telnet but establishes a secure connection first (openssl actually does a lot more, but we won't concern ourselves with its other functionality). Since the standard port for HTTPS is 443, not 80, we will have to connect using that port. In order to connect using openssl, we have to issue the following command (the command is lengthier because openssl has so many options and other capabilities):

```
openssl s_client -crlf -quiet -connect www.bplearning.net:443
```

From here, you can issue the same request as above. Since encryption happens on the presentation layer, no changes are needed to the protocol that we type, which happens entirely at the application layer. The openssl command handles all of the presentation-layer encryption for us.

The response this time is the full document you requested (as well as the HTTP headers).[3]

You have now communicated directly with a server using the HTTP protocol. You have spoken your first bit of computer-ese!

3.4 How Computers Are Located on the Internet

One thing that we haven't talked about yet is how computers are located on the Internet. We mentioned earlier that the URL contains a hostname that names the computer. You might wonder how is a server found if you just have its hostname? It turns out that there is a lot involved in that process!

---

[2] The standard port numbers are essentially arbitrarily chosen. The Internet Assigned Numbers Authority (IANA) is responsible for assigning which services are supposed to listen on which port. Port assignments for services essentially depend on when services were developed and which ports were unassigned when the service was standardized. Technically, there is nothing preventing a server from listening on a wrong port or running a different protocol on a standard port, but then the browser won't know how to access it.

[3] If you already know HTML, then, depending on the response length, you might notice that there are a few extra letters and numbers in the response that aren't in the HTML file itself. This is due to the "transfer encoding," which sometimes sends the HTML in chunks. Those numbers and letters tell the browser how much data is coming in the next "chunk." However, since we haven't covered HTML yet, you probably didn't notice the extra numbers and letters in the response. In any case, for our purposes, they can be ignored.

We talked in Section 3.1 about the different protocol layers in the Internet. Layer 3 is the network layer, and, on the Internet, the network layer is handled by the Internet Protocol (IP). The Internet Protocol mandates that each computer on the Internet is identified by a series of numbers, known as the computer's **IP address**. However, we don't normally refer to computers by that series of numbers for two reasons. The first reason is that humans aren't good at remembering numbers. It's much easier to remember google.com than it is to remember 64.233.160.138. The second reason is that it is good to separate out *physical issues* from *logical issues*. In other words, the IP address tells the network what physical location on the Internet you want to go to. However, the user doesn't care where that is. The user just wants to go to Google's website. Therefore, by creating a *name* for Google's website (i.e., google.com), the user can access the site even if its physical location on the network changes. The IP address is similar to a phone number, and the hostname is like the name of the person you want to reach.

However, when you want to connect to a server for a website, the computer must know the destination IP address to make the connection. How does the computer know what the IP address is for the website you want to visit?

The computer finds the destination IP address through the **Domain Name System** (DNS). DNS is a system that translates hostnames to IP addresses, kind of like the way a phone book translates a person's name into a phone number. However, DNS is a *distributed* system, so, rather than just one big phone book, there are millions of them organized into a hierarchy. Each server (i.e., "phone book") in this system is called a nameserver. So, when you tell your browser you want to go to www.bplearning.net/example/about.html, before it makes a connection to the server, it must first figure out *where* www.bplearning.net is located. In order to do that, it breaks the hostname down into pieces, separated by a dot. In our case, there are three pieces—www, bplearning, and net. The browser starts with the rightmost piece, called the top-level domain name (TLD). Each browser is preprogrammed with a set of "root" nameservers. The browser begins by asking the root nameservers if they know who maintains the DNS records (i.e., who handles the phone book) for .net domains. The root nameserver responds with the IP address of the nameserver or nameservers that handle requests for those domains. Next, the browser goes to the .net nameserver and asks it who maintains the DNS records for the bplearning.net domain. The .net nameserver will point to yet another nameserver who handles the bplearning.net domain. Finally, the browser will go to the bplearning.net nameserver and ask it if it knows what the IP address of www.bplearning.net is. The bplearning.

net nameserver will respond with the IP address of `www.bplearning.net,` and with that IP address, your computer will be able to establish a connection to the `www.bplearning.net` server.

This usually happens in a fraction of a second, so we don't notice that the computer is doing all of this work behind-the-scenes. In addition, the computer usually skips the steps that it has performed recently and just remembers what results it got back last time so that it doesn't have to do the same query over and over again.

3.4.1 Review

In this chapter we covered the basics of Internet communication. We have learned the following:

- Protocols define how communication happens.

- The Internet is built on a layering of many protocols, each with a specific function or set of functions.

- HTTP is an application-level protocol, used for transmitting interactive documents to users browsing the web.

- A URL is a piece of text that gives the browser all of the information it needs to locate a document on the Internet.

- A URL is composed of a protocol (usually HTTP or HTTPS), a hostname, and a path.

- The hostname on the URL is translated into an IP address using DNS nameservers.

- The path of the URL is sent to the server to identify the document being requested.

3.4.2 Apply What You Have Learned

1. Go to your favorite website. Click through the different pages. Pay attention to how the URL changes on each page. Does every click change the URL? Which ones change the URL and which ones don't?

2. Some websites have very structured, easy-to-understand URL paths, and some of them don't. When a website uses structured URLs, it is often easy to predict what the URL will be for something you are looking for. Go to Wikipedia.org and click around. Look at what the URLs look like. Now, try to guess what the URL to the Wikipedia entry on JavaScript will be. Put it into your browser and see if you are correct.

3. Go to Amazon.com and click around. Are the URLs as predictable and easy to understand as those on Wikipedia? Do you think you could guess the URL of a book the same way you could guess the URL for JavaScript in Wikipedia?

4. Go to the command line and try to retrieve the web page for JavaScript from Wikipedia directly using the HTTP protocol.

CHAPTER 4

How a Computer Looks at Data

Chapter 3 covered the basics of how computers transmit data to each other over the Internet. This chapter expands on that, covering how documents are stored within the computer. Much of the information in this chapter, like the last one, is more background information than practical knowledge. The JavaScript programming language automates a lot of the data handling for you, so you don't have to worry about it. Nonetheless, it is important to know what the computer is doing for you!

We think of computers as systems which are capable of anything, but in reality computers are very limited. In many areas of engineering, engineers achieve the most powerful results by *limiting* the possibilities, which makes the remaining available possibilities more potent. Engines are made by taking the energy from combustion reactions and channeling them in a specified direction to operate the engines. Instead of letting the energy go in every direction (which is what it normally does), it is only allowed to go in specific directions. The driver of the car can go anywhere he or she wants to, but only because the combustion within the engine is directed to a very limited number of directions. Computers are powerful precisely because they are similarly limited.

Computers, at their core, perform two functions—they process numbers and they transmit numbers. This may seem counterintuitive. After all, when you type on your keyboard, doesn't it produce letters on the screen? Doesn't your computer do graphics and sound? In reality, all of these things are controlled by numbers. The color of each pixel on your screen is a number. Each letter you type has a corresponding number. Each sound is a long sequence of numbers. The computer may *look* like it is doing lots of different things, but it is really doing only two things—processing numbers and transmitting numbers.

© Jonathan Bartlett 2023
J. Bartlett, *Programming for Absolute Beginners*, https://doi.org/10.1007/978-1-4842-8751-4_4

The first part of this chapter will cover how data is stored on a computer using numbers. The second part of this chapter will cover how those numbers can be arranged into a **file format** which can be read by software applications like web browsers.

4.1 What Computer Memory Looks Like

To understand how the computer views memory, imagine a room filled with numbered lockers that are all the same size. These lockers are similar to computer memory in that each are numbered sequences of fixed-size storage locations. For example, if you have 2 gigabytes of computer memory, that means that your computer contains roughly 2 billion fixed-size storage locations or, to use our analogy, 2 billion lockers. Each location has a number, and each location has the same fixed-length size. The difference between a locker and computer memory is that you can store different kinds of things in a locker, but you can only store a single number in a computer memory storage location.

On modern computers, each storage location can store a single number between 0 and 255. Such a number is called a **byte**. You may be wondering why computers use the range between 0 and 255, and not something more natural, like 100 or 1000. The reason is that the range of 0 to 255 *is* natural to a computer. In math, we usually represent numbers using the decimal system which has ten digits—zero through nine. Computers, however, use the binary system which only has two digits—zero and one. Each digit is called a **bit**, which is short for *binary digit*. If you write down numbers, when you get to ten you have run out of digits, so you add another digit to keep counting, making a two-digit number. In binary, you run out of digits at two.

Figure 4-1 lists the numbers zero through eleven in decimal and in binary.

Decimal	Binary	
0	0	The first two numbers look the same
1	1	
2	10	Since we only have two digits in binary, we have to add another place.
3	11	Just like in decimal, the digit on the right will increase again.
4	100	However, we already have to go to yet another place!
5	101	
6	110	
7	111	
8	1000	
9	1001	
10	1010	Since the decimal numbers have ten digits, it is only when we get to ten that we need another place.
11	1011	

Figure 4-1. *Numbers Displayed in Decimal and Binary*

If you carry this out, you will find that the number 255 is the maximum number that you can get with 8 bits. It looks like 11111111 in binary. In short, the reason why a computer byte stores numbers between 0 and 255 is because a byte is made up of 8 bits.

It is important to note that the numbers in the left column and right column are the *same numbers,* just represented differently. The reason we use decimal numbers is probably due to the fact that our culture started counting with its fingers. A few cultures, such as the Yuki, started counting using the spaces between their fingers and therefore only have eight digits in their system. The numbers in each of these cases are not different—only the way they are displayed!

Two other systems that are regularly encountered in computer programming are the **octal** system and the **hexadecimal** system. The octal system uses only the digits 0–7, but the hexadecimal system actually *adds* digits to our current ones. Hexadecimal uses letters to add additional digits. So, in hexadecimal, the letters A–F represent the decimal numbers 10–15, and 10 in hexadecimal is the same as the number 16 in decimal.

Figure 4-2 shows a combined list of the numbers 0–16 in decimal, binary, octal, and hexadecimal:

Decimal	Binary	Octal	Hexadecimal
0	0	0	0
1	1	1	1
2	10	2	2
3	11	3	3
4	100	4	4
5	101	5	5
6	110	6	6
7	111	7	7
8	1000	10	8
9	1001	11	9
10	1010	12	A
11	1011	13	B
12	1100	14	C
13	1101	15	D
14	1110	16	E
15	1111	17	F
16	10000	20	10

Figure 4-2. *Numbers 0–16 in Decimal, Binary, Octal, and Hexadecimal*

The reason why octal and hexadecimal are often used in computing is that a single octal digit represents exactly 3 bits, and a single hexadecimal digit represents exactly 4 bits. Two hexadecimal numbers together represent 1 byte. Therefore, octal and hexadecimal are essentially used as a shorthand for writing binary numbers. An example of this is in screen colors. Each dot on your screen is represented by 3 bytes—1 byte for the red component, 1 byte for the green component, and 1 byte for the blue component. In many tools, these are all smashed together as a six-digit hexadecimal number. For instance, red is represented by FF0000, green is represented by 00FF00, blue is represented by 0000FF, a greenish blue would be 00FFFF, and a darker shade of greenish blue would be 009999.

In any case, computer memory is a long sequence of millions or billions of bytes, one after another. Each byte has an address, which is basically like a locker number, so you can refer to specific memory locations on the computer. We won't be accessing bytes by their memory addresses ourselves, but that is how the computer works at the lowest level.

Now, it might seem very limiting to only be able to deal with numbers that are between 0 and 255. The reason this is not a problem is because this is only how the machine works at the lowest level. Programming languages group several of these bytes together to represent much larger numbers or other kinds of data altogether. Representing numbers that have a decimal point is a harder problem, but it is usually done by designating some number of bits to be the number without a decimal point and some number of bits to be the location of the decimal point in the number. Even though you won't have to deal with these details in JavaScript, it is good to keep in mind that, at the lowest level, everything you deal with is just a sequence of numbers between 0 and 255.

Going forward, we will assume that the computer can handle whatever size number we throw at it. This isn't entirely true, but it is true enough for our purposes.

☞   PRACTICE QUESTIONS

- How do you write the decimal number 12 in binary?

- How many bits are represented by a single hexadecimal digit?

- Since black is the absence of color, how do you think you would represent black in the hexadecimal system discussed in this section?

- What about white, which is the mix of all colors?

4.2 Using Numbers to Represent Data

So, if all we have to work with are numbers, how do we store other types of data? The answer is that we must convert our information into a series of numbers. Let's say we want to describe a person. What information might we want to store? We might want to store the following:

- Height

- Weight

- Hair color (black, blonde, brown, red, white, etc.)

- Eye color (blue, green, hazel, etc.)

Some of these values are actually numbers, like height and weight. We just have to decide what units we are using. Let's use inches for height and pounds for weight. Hair color and eye color are not numbers, but computers only have numbers to work with. So, what do we do? We choose numbers to represent the possible values. We might say that, for hair color, black is 0, blonde is 1, brown is 2, red is 3, and white is 4. There doesn't have to be any reason that a color gets a particular value. The important thing is to make sure that whatever number we assign, we consistently use that same number to represent that hair color. Next, we can choose numbers to represent eye color. For eyes, we can say blue is 0, green is 1, and hazel is 2. It doesn't matter that our numbers overlap with the same numbers we used for hair color, as long as we know which one we are dealing with.

We can now represent a person with a sequence of four numbers—their height, weight, hair color, and eye color. Using this system, I would be 72, 275, 2, 2. Someone identical to me, but with blue eyes, would be 72, 275, 2, 0. Notice how important the order of the numbers is. If we didn't know what order the numbers were in, we wouldn't be able to understand the data. It isn't that the numbers are in order of importance— we could just as easily have arranged it as weight, eye color, height, hair color—the important thing is that we *know* what order to expect the numbers and *follow that convention* every time we use the data. Otherwise, we might wind up mistaking someone's weight for their height or their eye color for their hair color.

When you have a predefined set of data to describe something, it is called a **data format**. It might not seem like a data format is that big of a deal. However, when communicating with other programs, they may have their data in a different pattern than you do with yours. Imagine another program which stored the same data but used feet instead of inches for the height. Or, let's say that it had five numbers for each person, with the fifth being their age. In each of these cases, if you loaded data from this other format, you would have to convert the data from the data format you are given to the data format you need for your own program. This may include transforming certain pieces of data (e.g., feet to inches), ignoring certain pieces of data (since our format doesn't include an age), calculating data (if one program needs an age or another program sends the date of birth), or any other number of possibilities. These are called **data transformations** and account for a very large portion of programming tasks.

☞ PRACTICE QUESTIONS

1. Describe yourself using the data format described in this section.

2. Write out in plain language what someone with the following numbers looks like:

   69, 150, 0, 1

4.3 Sequences in Data

The data format we explored in Section 4.2 is only helpful if we have a fixed number of things to store. Because each piece of data is identified by its position in the sequence, if we changed the number of items in the data, we would also change what they meant. Let's say you wanted to store the ages of a person's children. The problem is that we don't know how many children a person might have. They might have none or 20. One way to solve the problem is to have a count of the number of children first and then the children's ages. This way we would know when the children's ages stopped. For instance, we could modify our format to be height; weight; number of children; age of child 1, age of child 2, etc.; hair color; and eye color. By storing the number of children *before* the list of children, even though each record would have a slightly different length, we would still know where each piece of data is in the record because we know how many children we need to be looking for.

Let's say that our friend Fred has three children, ages 12, 10, and 5. His record might look like this: 70, 200, 3, 12, 10, 5, 1, 1. The number 3 tells you that the next three records will be children's ages. After that, you go on to the rest of the record.

Another way of storing repeated values is to use what is called a **sentinel** value. A sentinel is a value that tells you that you are at the end of a list. Therefore, rather than storing the number of children, we could decide that we are going to use a sentinel value. Since no children have a negative age, we could use a -1 to indicate that we are at the end of the list, rather than having a count. Under this scheme, Fred's record would look like this: 70, 200, 12, 10, 5, -1, 1, 1.

Such sequences of data are commonly referred to as **arrays**. An array is simply a sequence of data that is packaged together into a single set. In this example, the children's ages are treated as an array.

☞ **PRACTICE QUESTIONS**

1. What would Fred's record look like if he had six children, aged 21, 19, 14, 12, 10, and 5, using the format that counts his children?

2. What would that record look like using the format that has a sentinel value?

3. Why is it important that the sentinel value not be a possible data value?

4.4 Using Numbers to Represent Letters

Now that we know a little about how computers represent data using numbers, we can now talk about one of the most common things for computers to store—text. One thing that was missing from our description of a person in the previous section was the person's *name*. How would you represent a name, or any text, using only numbers?

Before we look at how computers store whole blocks of text, let's start by looking at how a computer might store an individual character. Since computers store everything as numbers, computers do the same thing for letters. Just like we used the number 0 to represent blue eye color, we could come up with a number to represent each letter in the alphabet. However, what we display on the screen is not just the letters of the alphabet. There is also punctuation, upper- and lowercase letters, symbols, and even digits. It might seem odd that a digit needs a representation as a number, but when you mix them in with the list of "characters that need to be typed or displayed," it makes sense. Since there is nothing preventing you from typing a 0 as part of a piece of text, it is something that must be represented along with everything else.

Each character that might be displayed has a corresponding number that represents it. The most common system for representing characters by numbers in a single byte is called the **ASCII** code, which was developed in the 1960s. In ASCII, the decimal numbers 65–90 represent the uppercase letters A–Z, the decimal numbers 97–122 represent the lowercase letters a–z, the decimal numbers 48–57 represent the digits 0–9, and the space is represented by the decimal number 32. A more complete ASCII table is available in Appendix D.

That is how you represent a single character, but how should a whole block of text, like someone's name, be represented? If you think back to the previous section, how did we represent a sequence of things? We used an array, and a block of text can be thought of as an array of characters. As an array, it can either be represented as a length followed by the list of characters or as a list of characters with a sentinel value. In ASCII, the decimal number 0 is a special character called the **null** character, which is used as a sentinel for a list of characters. An array of characters is often referred to as a **string**, and a string that is represented using a null for its sentinel value is often called a **null-terminated string**.

Let's go back to our person data format before we added the children. Let's say we wanted to store the name of the person to the record. The record would store the name, height, weight, hair color, and eye color. We can use a null-terminated string for the name. Therefore, my name, "Jon," would be encoded as 74, 111, 110, 0. Then, my whole record would be as follows:

```
74, 111, 110, 0, 72, 275, 2, 0
```

You can tell where my name ends and the rest of the record begins by the sentinel.

Now, let's add children, using -1 for the sentinel value. We'll pretend I have two children, Jim and Bob. In the next record, we will use the format name, height, weight, hair color, eye color, name of child 1, age of child 1, ... , -1. It looks like this:

```
74, 111, 110, 0, 72, 275, 2, 0, 74, 105,
109, 0, 14, 66, 111, 98, 0, 12, -1
```

☞ PRACTICE QUESTIONS

- Look at the record above. Based on the format, what is Jim's age?
- Create a new record for me if I had another child named Mary Ann, aged 6.

As you can see, in order to process data, computers have to be very exact about what kind of data goes where, how long it is, and whether it repeats. In order for two programs to communicate, or even for two functions within the same program to communicate, they must both agree on the format of the data. Now, in modern programming languages such as JavaScript, the representation is much nicer than a string of numbers. JavaScript, for instance, allows you to say "Jim" instead of 74, 105, 109, 0, but underneath it actually does the same thing. "Jim" is a string of characters. In most programming languages, putting quotations around a string of characters indicates that those characters should be treated as a string of text. Generally, if you see 234 in a program, it means the *number* 234, but "234" means the string of characters 2, 3, 4 (which would be represented by the numbers 50, 51, 52 in ASCII).

Modern programming languages and programs use an encoding called **UTF-8** instead of ASCII, but for most purposes, when using the English language, they are equivalent. For more information about character encodings and UTF-8, see Appendix D.

4.5 What Is a File Format?

So far, we have discussed how computers store things in memory using data formats. Data formats are used because everything is represented by numbers, so we need a format to know what the numbers *mean*. A *file format* is exactly like a data format, except that it is stored on a disk rather than in memory.

Have you ever tried to open up a document in the wrong application? What happened? Usually, if you open up a document in the wrong application, it either gives you an error, or it gives you a lot of junk. As we have seen, since programs are just dealing with numbers, they have to know what the data format is to make sense of the data. Without knowing that format, the file is gibberish.

Computers often distinguish between different file types by the name of the file. Most files have a **filename extension** which tells you the type of file it is. For instance, Adobe Portable Document Format files usually end in .pdf. There are many different graphics formats, each with their own extension, such as .jpg, .jpeg, .png, or .gif. MP3 audio files have the extension .mp3.

However, on the Internet, the URL does not always contain an extension and for various technical reasons sometimes even contains a *different* extension from the type of file it is sending you. In addition, sometimes there is more than one format with the same extension. Therefore, to remove ambiguity, the Internet signals a file format differently, using **content types**, also called MIME types. If you remember back to communicating with a server using HTTP in Chapter 3, after we sent our request, it sent back a response line, response headers, and a response document. One of the response headers that gets sent back from the webserver is the Content-Type header. In our example, the server gave back a content type of text/html. Content types have two parts, a type and a subtype. In this case, the type is "text" and the subtype is "html." Since the type is "text," how do you think it stores its data? All text documents store their data as a long sequence of characters. In a text document, the *only* type of data allowed is characters. Most files that do not have a "text" type are called **binary** files, which only means that it contains data that is not text.

Notice, however, that there is a subtype, "html." This indicates that text files themselves can have formats. That is, we can organize a text file such that it is easy for a computer to locate specific kinds of data. For instance, spreadsheets often use CSV (comma-separated value) files. The CSV file format uses a comma to separate data that go into different columns and a return character to separate data that go into different rows. Figure 4-3 shows a sample CSV file with three columns and four rows.

```
Name,Age,Height
Jon B,36,72
Fred F,44,70
Jennifer Q,50,60
Jim Z,22,68
```

Figure 4-3. *An Example CSV File*

Since a CSV is a text document, this whole file would be stored as a string of characters. A spreadsheet, when loading the document, might convert columns 2 and 3 into numbers, but, on a disk, since it is a text document, it is stored as a string of characters. The format says that when the spreadsheet loads the file, it should split the row into columns based on where the commas occur and split the file into rows based on where the line breaks are. So, because it is a text format, all of the details of the file are easily viewable and understandable by people, since it is just a string of characters. However, it is in fact a *data format* because the different pieces of the file have significant meanings—in this case, the commas and the newline characters.

In Chapter 6 we will look at the HTML file format.

☞ PRACTICE QUESTIONS

To see the difference between text files and binary files, open up different file types with your text editor. For information on what a text editor is and how to use one, see Appendix B.3.

1. Open up your text editor according to the instructions in B.3.

2. Open up a file on your computer with one of the following extensions: `.jpg`, `.jpeg`, `.png`, `.pdf`, `.mp3`, `.doc`, `.xls`. If your computer is not showing you the file extension, Section B.3 describes how to make them visible.

3. Since you are using a text editor, it will attempt to treat each number in the file as if it were a character. This is what makes all of the funny characters—your text editor doesn't know how to deal with the non-text characters.

4. Now open up a file on your computer with one of the following extensions: `.txt`, `.csv`, `.html`, `.rtf`. If you don't have any of these types of files, you can easily create a `.rtf` file using any word processor. Just tell the word processor to export your document in "Rich Text Format," and it will produce an appropriate file with an extension of `.rtf`.

5. Even if you don't *understand* the file, it should at least be viewable—you should recognize the characters that it is using.

6. Note that the extensions themselves don't do anything—they are merely there to help you know what is in the file, what program to use to open the file, and what icon to display for the file. Your operating system keeps a list of default programs to use for various file extensions. If you change a file extension of a file, the computer will likely open up the wrong program for that file!

4.5.1 Review

In this chapter, we covered some of the details about how computers look at and process data. We have learned the following:

- Computers store everything using numbers.

- In order for a computer to understand what those numbers mean, they must be in a predefined data format.

- Lists of data are often stored by storing the length before the number of data items or by using a sentinel value to indicate the end of a list.

- Display characters, including letters, digits, punctuation, and spaces, are stored using numbers to represent each character.

- Blocks of text are stored as sequences of display characters called *strings*.

- Just like other sequences, the size of a string is given either by a length or by a sentinel value at the end, usually the number zero (not the text digit "0"), called the *null* character.

- A file format is just a data format stored on a disk.

- Filenames have a *file extension* to indicate what the format of the data is.

- A text file is a file format where the entire file is stored as one long string.

- Text files often have a specific structure themselves.

- CSV files are an example of a text file with a specific structure—they use the newline character to separate records and commas to separate fields.

- HTML files are text files with their own structure.

4.5.2 Apply What You Have Learned

1. Let's say that we wanted to store data on a computer about a car. What pieces of data might we want to store? How would we want to represent it in the computer using numbers?

2. Write the name of your favorite car using ASCII numbers.

3. Try to create your own CSV-formatted file with a text editor. Be sure to make the file extension .csv when you save it. Now, if you have a spreadsheet program on your computer, try to open up the file with your spreadsheet program. What happens?

4. Take your spreadsheet program and create a spreadsheet. Add colors and styles to the spreadsheet cells. Now, save or export the spreadsheet to a CSV file. Open up the file in the text editor. What does it look like? Open the CSV file again in the spreadsheet. What changed?

5. Write a document in your word processor. Write three or four lines of text, with each line being formatted slightly differently (font size, italic, etc.). Save this file as an RTF (also called "Rich Text Format," extension `.rtf`) file. An RTF file is a text format for word processors. Open up the file with your text editor. What does it look like? Can you find your original text? Can you decipher what those other characters might mean? Now, in the text editor, make a change to some of your original text and open it in the word processor. What happened?

CHAPTER 5

How Computers Work

Now that we know a little bit about where computers come from, how they communicate, and how they store data, we can learn how computers work. Chapter 1 discussed the difference between a machine language, which allows a programmer to give a computer instructions that it directly understands, and a programming language, which is a more humanlike way of programming the computer. Programming languages, since they are not native to a computer, eventually have to be translated into machine language instructions. Therefore, because they have to be translatable into a machine language, programming languages have to be more rigid and exact than a human language.

Most programmers never need to use machine language. However, it is good to at least understand conceptually what a machine language looks like, as it will help you understand the exactness required in programming. The biggest problem that new programmers run into is that, when they write programs, they expect the computer to do what they *mean*, which is often different from what they actually told it to do.

When I was young I was in a class where the teacher had two people sit back-to-back, so they couldn't see each other. Then, one person was supposed to make a paper airplane and describe to the other person exactly how to fold the paper so that the other person could make one as well. If you've ever tried something like this, you know how hard it is to communicate exact instructions to someone when you can't watch them try to interpret what you are saying and have no visual clues as to what you mean. Almost invariably, the other person folds the paper wrong and gets useless garbage at the end. The point is that even when we think we are being exact, even when we are trying to be exact, it is often the case that instructions that we give are not as precise as we think they are. Computers, however, require exact precision when instructing them.

Knowing how machine language works will give you a feel for the exactness required to program a computer. Therefore, before we begin our study of programming, this chapter will give you a feel for how the computer actually does its processing at the machine language level.

© Jonathan Bartlett 2023
J. Bartlett, *Programming for Absolute Beginners*, https://doi.org/10.1007/978-1-4842-8751-4_5

The examples in this chapter may seem tedious. They *are*. Few people program in machine language anymore because *it is* quite tedious. Don't worry, though, programming languages were invented specifically to remove the tediousness of machine language. The point here is to introduce you to the way a machine thinks so that you will better understand the exactness required and start thinking in the ways that the computer needs you to think. In my entire programming career, I have never needed to program in machine language. However, knowing how machine language works has helped me immensely to align my imagination and thinking to better understand how to make my programs work.

5.1 Parts of a Computer

You can conceptually break a computer into four main pieces:

- The **Central Processing Unit** (CPU)

- The computer's **memory** (also known as Random Access Memory, or RAM)

- An **input/output system**

- A **data bus** which moves the data between these different parts

The computer's CPU is where most of the data processing happens. The CPU itself is divided into two components—the **control unit** and the **arithmetic and logic unit** (ALU). The control unit manages the process of computing itself. The control unit maintains a piece of data called the **instruction pointer** which holds the location in memory of the next instruction to perform. The control unit looks at an instruction, determines what is needed to process that instruction, and then manages all of the components needed to make that instruction happen. This might include things like writing and fetching data to and from the memory, reading and writing data to the input/output system, and telling the arithmetic and logic unit to perform computations. The arithmetic and logic unit performs basic calculations, such as add, subtract, multiply, and divide, directly. It also performs logical comparisons, such as comparing if two values are equal or if one value is greater than another. Although some processors have more basic calculation features than others, all of them are computationally equivalent. Even if you only had a processor that could add and subtract, you could write additional code that would use addition and subtraction to be able to multiply and divide. A computer equipped with only minimal instructions can perform any computation necessary—it just takes more work from the programmer. The ALU can also contain temporary storage locations, called registers, which are used to perform the computations and store the results.

The computer's memory is where a computer stores data that is being actively used for processing. The computer's memory is *not* the same thing as its hard drive. The hard drive is actually external to the computer and is connected through the input/output system. The hard drive is where data can be permanently stored. Computer memory is where data is stored while it is being used. To conceptualize the difference, if you turn off your computer suddenly, the information stored in memory is wiped away. In Chapter 4, we discussed how computer memory was laid out. It is divided into billions of storage locations, where each location can hold a number between 0 and 255. The locations themselves are numbered so that they can be identified and accessed easily.

The input/output system in a computer is tasked with communicating with the outside world. The main computer itself is incapable of interacting with people. Keyboard input, screen output, hard drives, network adapters, and all of the other things that we think of when we interact with our computer are all actually on the "outside" of the computer, connected through the input/output system. There are several standards for input/output systems, the most common of which is the **Universal Serial Bus** (USB). USB defines a standard way of connecting input/output devices to a computer. This allows USB drives, USB cameras, USB keyboards, and a myriad of other devices to all connect to your computer. Without the input/output system, computers would be impossible to use, as there would be no way for us to give it data or programs or see the output of computations.

The data bus handles moving data between each of these systems. It is an important, but often overlooked, feature of computer systems. For instance, if you have a really fast CPU and a lot of memory, neither of these do much good if the data bus is slow in moving the memory to the CPU. Buses are connected together by hubs, which direct traffic to and from each device. Many modern computer architectures have two separate hubs. The fastest hub, which connects directly to the CPU, is often called the northbridge. It connects the CPU to the memory and the graphics card. The other hub, often called the southbridge, connects from the northbridge to the rest of the input/output systems.

5.2 A Simplified Paper Machine Simulation

For the rest of this chapter, we will be playing with a "paper machine." That is, we will use a pen and paper to simulate what a CPU would be doing when running a program.

The purpose of the machine and machine language introduced here is to help you understand the *concept* of a machine language. The machine language we will cover is not an actual machine language used on any computer, but it is very similar, and it should help you understand and learn real machine languages should you ever wish to. Because of this, you do not need to memorize anything from here to the end of the chapter. You do, however, need to follow the instructions and do the activities because they will help you understand what it is that the computer is doing.

To perform the simulation, you will need several blank sheets of paper, a pen, and a pencil with an eraser. You also might want to use a ruler to help you make straight lines. Be sure to use a pencil when it says to, because you will be doing a lot of erasing.

These first steps should be done in pen.

On the top of the first sheet of paper, title the paper "Computer Memory." Now, make an 8x8 grid of squares to fill the whole sheet of paper. Number each square in the top-left corner of the square, starting with 0 and going through 63. These are the addresses of the memory locations. Be sure to leave enough room to write a value in each box. Each memory location can receive a number between 0 and 255. If there is no value written in the square, then the value is assumed to be zero (so right now your memory is all zeroes). This sheet of paper will represent a very tiny computer memory. (Real computer memories would take about half a billion sheets of paper.) As we progress in our simulation, the values in the squares will change.

On the top of the second sheet of paper, title the paper "Control Unit." Now, make an empty box at the top-left of the paper, and label the box "Instruction Pointer." Now make four columns on the rest of the paper, titled "Meaning," "Opcode," "Operand 1," and "Operand 2."

On the top of the third sheet of paper, title the paper "Arithmetic and Logic Unit." Make 16 boxes in this area and label them "Register 0" through "Register 15."

At the end of this process, you should have three sheets of paper that look like Figure 5-1.

In the next section, we will have a machine language program to process, which should be done in pencil. You will copy the program (Figure 5-3) into memory. Then to run the simulation, you will use the steps detailed in Figure 5-2.

In this machine language, each instruction consists of three parts—the **opcode**, operand 1, and operand 2. The opcode is the actual function being performed. The list of opcodes and what they mean are at the end of the chapter. Each opcode has a very specific job. An opcode might tell you to load a value from memory into a register, add register values together, compare register values, etc. Operand 1 and operand 2 will behave differently based on what opcode is being used. The description will tell you how to use each one.

The way an operand is used is called a mode. Sometimes an operand will specify a register number (called *register mode*). This means that the number in the operand refers to a register in the Arithmetic and Logic Unit. If the operand was 6, using register mode would mean that the operand was referring to register 6. Sometimes an operand will specify a memory location (called *memory mode*). This means that the number in the operand refers to a memory location in Computer Memory. If the operand was 6, using memory mode would mean that the operand was referring to memory location 6. Sometimes an operand will specify a value (called *immediate mode*). This means that the number in the operand is used as the number itself. If the operand was 6, using immediate mode would mean that the operand was just referring to the number 6 itself. Finally, there is a mode called *indirect mode*. In this mode, the operand refers to a register, but the register is used to refer to a memory location. So, if the operand was 6, using indirect mode would mean that the operand was referring to a memory location stored in register 6. If register 6 had the value 23, then in indirect mode memory location, 23 would be used as the operand.

As an example, let's say that the instruction was 20, 5, 10. This means that 20 is the opcode, 5 is operand 1, and 10 is operand 2. Now, let's look up opcode 20 in the opcode tables at the end of the chapter (Section 5.5). It says that this opcode means "Load Immediate." In the table, it says that operand 1 uses *register mode* and therefore refers to a register. Since operand 1 is 5, operand 1 is interpreted to mean register 5. The table says that operand 2 uses *immediate mode*, and therefore the number itself is used. Since operand 2 is 10, operand 2 is simply the value 10. In the description, it says that we are supposed to load the value specified by operand 2 into the register specified by operand 1. Therefore, we would pull out the "Arithmetic and Logic Unit" sheet, erase what is in register 5, and write in the value 10.

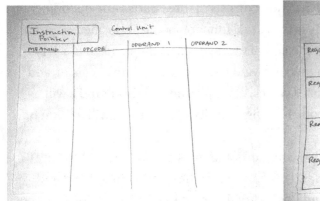

Figure 5-1. *Machine Simulation Setup*

These steps should all be done *in pencil*. Before you begin a simulation, be sure to double-check that you copied the memory locations *exactly*.

Before you start the steps below, set the box labeled Instruction Pointer to 0. Then, repeat the steps below until you get to a halt instruction (0, 0, 0). Each time through the steps will allow you to execute one instruction.

1. Take the Control Unit sheet and look at your Instruction Pointer.

2. Look at the Computer Memory sheet at the location indicated by the Instruction Pointer. For instance, if the Instruction Pointer says "0," then you would retrieve the first value in Computer Memory. If the Instruction Pointer says "15," you would get the last value on the second row in Computer Memory.

3. Copy the value from the Computer Memory into the first empty line of the Control Unit sheet under the heading "Opcode."

4. Now, look back at the Computer Memory, and copy the next value into the Operand 1 column of the Control Unit, and the value after that into the Operand 2 column of the Control Unit. So, if the Instruction Pointer said 15, then you would copy the value in memory location 16 to Operand 1 and the value in memory location 17 to Operand 2. The Control Unit now has the full instruction to execute.

5. Add 3 to the value in the Instruction Pointer (erase the old value). If the value was 15, you would erase that and write 18. This will prepare us to read the next instruction the next time through. We add 3 because each instruction uses three bytes (opcode, operand 1, and operand 2).

6. Look up the value that you wrote in the "Opcode" column in the list of opcodes (these are provided in Section 5.5). Write the name associated with the opcode in the column labeled "Meaning."

7. In the opcode table, there is a description that tells you what to do with each opcode. Perform the task as specified in the description. If it is the "Halt" opcode (0), the simulation is finished.

8. Go back to step 1 and do it again.

Figure 5-2. Simulation Steps

In the next section, we will do a full simulation.

☞   DOING THE SIMULATION IN A CLASS SETTING

This simulation is easy to do in a class setting and was actually originally developed for use in a class. To do this, you need to use markerboards or chalkboards rather than sheets of paper. Appoint one student to be the Control Unit. This student is responsible for performing the steps outlined above, but they cannot leave the control unit area or write on another student's board.

Appoint another student to be the Data Bus. This student is responsible for transferring all needed data to and from the Computer Memory. The Control Unit will direct which values the Data Bus needs to fetch or store. The Data Bus only takes instructions from the Control Unit.

Appoint another student to handle the Arithmetic and Logic Unit sheet. They will perform any computation requested by the Control Unit on its registers and can give to the Control Unit any value that has been computed in its registers.

I have found that doing the computations interactively greatly increases the ability of students to visualize what is happening inside the computer and makes them better programmers long-term.

5.3 A Short Program: Multiplying by 2

Now we will perform a program to multiply a number by 2. If you look through the opcode tables at the end of this chapter (Section 5.5), you might notice that there is no opcode for multiplication. However, basic arithmetic tells us that we can multiply by repeated adding. Therefore, we will need to fetch a number, add it to itself, and then store the value back to a register or memory. In our program, memory location 62 will hold the value that we want to multiply (in this case, the number 12), and, at the end of the program, memory location 63 will hold the value that we calculate.

```
var multiply_by_two = function(x) {
   return x * 2;
};
```

Figure 5-3. *Multiply a Number by 2 in JavaScript*

5.3.1 Setting Up the Simulation

To begin the simulation, the code and the data are both written into memory. Copy the values from Figure 5-4 into your Computer Memory sheet.

0	1	2	3	4	5	6	7
22	0	62	21	1	0	133	0
8	9	10	11	12	13	14	15
1	25	63	0	0	0	0	0
16	17	18	19	20	21	22	23
0	0	0	0	0	0	0	0
24	25	26	27	28	29	30	31
0	0	0	0	0	0	0	0
32	33	34	35	36	37	38	39
0	0	0	0	0	0	0	0
40	41	42	43	44	45	46	47
0	0	0	0	0	0	0	0
48	49	50	51	52	53	54	55
0	0	0	0	0	0	0	0
56	57	58	59	60	61	62	63
0	0	0	0	0	0	12	0

Figure 5-4. Machine Language Program to Multiply a Number by 2

Before you decide to quit programming altogether, let me remind you that the point of this exercise is not that we would ever actually program this way but rather to give you a glimpse into how the computer looks at processing. The very reason that computer programming languages were invented was so that we would not have to deal with this stuff on a daily basis. So, to allay your fears, Figure 5-3 shows what this would look like in JavaScript.

You still may not understand what exactly this does or why it is written that way, but hopefully it gives you hope that it will be more understandable than a bunch of numbers written out.

Now, to run the program, you need to look at the steps in Figure 5-2. We will go through them step-by-step so you know how to do it.

5.3.2 Running the Simulation

Now, let's go through the program step-by-step to see what is happening. This will all be done *in pencil*. Look at Figure 5-2. The first thing it says is to double-check that the memory locations were copied over correctly. Do this now. Next, it says to write a 0 in the box labeled Instruction Pointer. Do so now. Now we can proceed to the numbered steps.

Step 1 says to look at the instruction pointer. It should read 0.

Step 2 says to look at the memory location indicated by the Instruction Pointer. Since ours says 0, we will look at memory location 0.

Step 3 says to copy the value at that memory location to the first line of the Control Unit sheet under the heading Opcode. The value at memory location 0 is 22, so we will write 22 in the first line of the Control Unit sheet in the Opcode column.

Step 4 says to copy the next value in memory to the column labeled Operand 1. The next memory location is memory location 1, and it has the value 0. Therefore, we will write the number 0 to the Operand 1 column. We then copy the next value in memory (memory location 2) to the Operand 2 column. Memory location 2 has the value 62 in it, so write the number 62 in the Operand 2 column. This is our first instruction: 22, 0, 62.

Step 5 says to add 3 to the value in the Instruction Pointer. The instruction pointer currently has a 0 in it, so 3 + 0 is 3. Erase the 0 and write 3 in the box. This will allow us to read the next instruction the next time we go through the steps. However, it is important to do this now rather than at the end of the steps, as some instructions may further modify this value.

Step 6 says to look up the value in the Opcode column in the list of opcodes in Section 5.5. The opcode is 22, so go through the list of opcodes to find opcode 22. The opcodes are not listed in numerical order, so you will need to look through all of them until you find the right one. The opcode is "Load Memory." Therefore, write "Load Memory" in the column labeled Meaning.

Step 7 says to perform the steps listed in the opcode table for this opcode. You will notice that the opcode table says that Operand 1 refers to a register and Operand 2 refers to a memory location. Therefore, we will be working with register 0 and memory location 62. The description says to load the value in the memory location specified by Operand 2 into the register specified by Operand 1. Therefore, we will load the value in memory location 62 into register 0. Memory location 62 has the value 12 in it, so we will write 12 in register 0 on the Arithmetic and Logic Unit sheet.

Step 8 says to go back to step 1 and repeat for the next instruction.

Now we are back to step 1. Therefore, we need to look at our Instruction Pointer again. This time it is set to 3. Step 2 says to look at the memory location indicated by the instruction pointer. It contains the number 21. Step 3 says to copy that number to the next line on the Control Unit sheet under the Opcode column. Therefore, write the number 21 into the Opcode column. Step 4 says to copy the next two memory locations to the Opcode 1 and Opcode 2 columns. The next two memory locations have the numbers 1 and 0 in them, so write 1 in the Opcode 1 column and 0 in the Opcode 2 column. The instruction we copied is 21, 1, 0.

Step 5 says to add 3 to the Instruction Pointer. Therefore, write 6 in the Instruction Pointer box, erasing the previous value.

Step 6 says to look up the value that is written in the Opcode column in the list of opcodes in Section 5.5 and write the name of the opcode in the Meaning column. The meaning of the opcode is "Load Register." Step 7 says to do what the description of the opcode says to do. The description says to copy the value of the register specified in Operand 2 into the register specified by Operand 1. Operand 1 is 1 and Operand 2 is 0. Therefore, look at register 0. It currently contains the number 12. So write 12 into the box for register 1.

This instruction has given us two copies of the same number—one in register 0 and one in register 1. This is good because multiplication by 2 is just adding the same number twice. Therefore, what type of instruction do you think will come next? Look through the list of instructions to see which one you think we will do next. Step 8 says to repeat the process for the next instruction, so let's do that now.

If you go through steps 1–4 again, you will have the next instruction copied over, which is 133, 0, 1. Step 5 then tells us to add 3 to the Instruction Pointer, so write a 9 in the Instruction Pointer box. Step 6 says to look up the Opcode (133) in the list of opcodes and write down its meaning. Write "Add" in the Meaning column. Step 7 says to do what the description of the opcode says. It says to add the two registers specified by Operand 1 and Operand 2 and store the result in the register specified by Operand 1. Operand 1 is 0 and Operand 2 is 1. Therefore, we will add the value in register 0 to the value in register 1. Register 0 has 12 in it, and register 1 also has 12 in it. Added together, this makes 24. The instruction says to store the value in register specified by Operand 1. Operand 1 is 0, so we will store the result in register 0. Therefore, erase what is currently in register 0 and write 24 in it.

Register 0 now has the value we want (24 is 12 * 2), but the goal was to get it stored in memory location 63. So what do you think the next instruction might do? Step 8 says to repeat the process to find out.

Following steps 1–4 will give us the next instruction: 25, 63, 0. Step 5 tells us to increase the Instruction Pointer to 12. Step 6 tells us to look up the meaning of opcode 25 in the opcode list and write it down in the Meaning column. This gives us "Store Memory."

Step 7 tells us to perform the instructions associated with the opcode. This says to store the value in the register specified by Operand 2 into the memory location specified by Operand 1. Operand 1 is 63 and Operand 2 is 0. Therefore, we will take the value in register 0 (which is 24) and write it in memory location 63, erasing what is currently there. Therefore, write 24 into memory location 63.

Step 8 says to go back to step 1 and process the next instruction.

Performing steps 1–4 will give us our next instruction—0, 0, 0. Step 5 says to increase the Instruction Pointer to 15. Step 6 says to look up the opcode, which tells us that opcode 0 is "Halt." Step 7 says that if we reach a Halt instruction, we should end the simulation.

Now we are done! If you remember from the beginning of this section, the goal was to take the value stored in memory location 62, multiply it by 2, and store it in memory location 63. Memory location 62 has a 12 in it, and memory location 63 has a 24 in it. It took a lot of work, but that is exactly what the computer does when it processes instructions. The instructions have to be so simple because computers themselves cannot think; they can only process. Because the instructions are so simple, it takes quite a few of them to perform even simple tasks. However, this simplicity also allows the computer to perform billions of them every second.

5.4 Adding a List of Numbers

Now we are going to do a more complicated program—we are going to add a list of numbers. In order to do this, we need to be able to know when we are at the end of our list of numbers. We will use a sentinel value to indicate that we are at the end of the list of numbers. (See Chapter 4 for more information on sentinel values.) We will use the number 255 as the sentinel to represent the end of the list of numbers.

What the program will do is add up all of the numbers starting in memory location 57 until it hits the sentinel value and then store the result in memory location 56.

The program is shown in Figure 5-5.

0	1	2	3	4	5	6	7
20	0	0	20	3	255	20	1
8	9	10	11	12	13	14	15
57	20	5	1	23	2	1	21
16	17	18	19	20	21	22	23
4	3	37	4	2	65	33	4
24	25	26	27	28	29	30	31
133	0	2	133	1	5	64	12
32	33	34	35	36	37	38	39
0	25	56	0	0	0	0	0
40	41	42	43	44	45	46	47
0	0	0	0	0	0	0	0
48	49	50	51	52	53	54	55
0	0	0	0	0	0	0	0
56	57	58	59	60	61	62	63
0	10	12	3	255	8	2	0

Figure 5-5. *Machine Language Program to Add a List of Numbers*

Now, before we go through the program step-by-step, let's think about what needs to happen to do this procedure. First, we will need a place (probably a register) to hold the current results of the sum as we go through the numbers. As we go along, we will need to check each number to see if it matches our sentinel value, 255. We need to get the computer to do something *different* if it hits the sentinel value than if it doesn't. Finally, we will need a way to repeat steps, since we don't know how many times we will be doing the calculation.

The way to accomplish all of this is with comparisons and conditional jumps. That is, we will compare two numbers and, based on the results of that comparison, potentially change the instruction pointer to tell the computer to run different code. Since we look at the instruction pointer to retrieve the next piece of code, if an instruction modifies the instruction pointer, then we will do a *different* task than we would otherwise have.

The other feature we will look at is indirect mode. Since we will be looking at an unknown number of different values, we cannot put the location of the value to load in our code. Therefore, what we will do is use a register to hold the address of the first value and then use indirect mode to tell the computer to load the value from the address stored in the register. From there, we can add one to the value in the register to have it point to the next location in memory.

So now, let's run through the simulation using the steps in Figure 5-2. Instead of going through each step like we did in the previous program, I am going to assume that you now know how to work the steps. Each paragraph is the entirety of the eight steps. I will focus on the meaning of each instruction rather than all of the steps to perform it. Performing the steps is your job, but be sure to do all of the steps *in the right order*. Also, in order to make what is happening more understandable, as we go along we will be writing names on our registers so we know what they are doing. The computer doesn't use this—this is entirely for our own purposes so we know what each register is being used for.

The first instruction is 20, 0, 0. This says to load register 0 with the number 0. Register 0 will hold the sum of all of the numbers. You might go ahead and label register 0 as "sum," so you can remember what it is for. Remember, the computer doesn't care what it is for—the computer just does what you tell it. But *you* need to remember what it is for, so you can understand the program.

The next instruction is 20, 3, 255. This says to load register 3 with the number 255. This is our sentinel value and will be used for comparison. You might label register 3 with the word "sentinel."

The next instruction is 20, 1, 57. This says to load register 1 with the number 57. This is the beginning of the locations that we will be reading the values from. Note that we are storing the *number* 57 into register 1, not the contents of memory location 57. That will come later. Label register 1 with the word "pointer," since it will point to the location in memory that we are reading values from.

The next instruction is 20, 5, 1. This says to load register 5 with the number 1. This is the number that we will use to increment the memory location pointer. Label register 5 with the word "increment."

Take note of what the instruction pointer currently is. It should be at 12. All of the previous instructions were "setup" instructions that were meant to get the ball rolling. The next instruction will really start the process. You should label memory location 12 with the words "main process start" to remind yourself that this is where the core of the process will happen.

The instruction here at memory location 12 is 23, 2, 1. This says to look in register 1 and use that value as the memory location to look in. Right now, register 1 has the number 57 in it. Therefore, look in memory location 57 and put that value in register 2. Label register 2 with the words "current value." It should have the value 10 in it.

If you think back to what we are trying to do, the next thing we need to do is determine whether or not the current value is our sentinel value or not. Therefore, we have to compare our current value (register 2) with our sentinel value (register 3). However, since in this machine language comparisons overwrite one of the values being compared with the results of the comparison (look at the Compare instruction in the tables), we have to first copy one of the values to a new register so it doesn't get destroyed. Therefore, the next instruction reads 21, 4, 3. This says to copy the contents of register 3 (the sentinel value) to register 4. Label register 4 with the words "sentinel comparison." It should have the value 255 in it.

The next instruction is 37, 4, 2. When you look up that instruction, it says to compare the value in register 2 (the current value) with the value in register 4. If they are equal, it will store the number 0 into register 4. If the value in register 2 is greater than the value in register 4, it will store a 2 in register 4. Finally, if the value in register 4 is greater than the value in register 2, it will store a 1 in register 4. This way, at the end of the comparison, register 4 will contain the result of comparing the current value with the sentinel. Since register 4 had the value 255 and register 2 has the value 10, the value in register 4 should be erased, and, in its place, you should write the number 1 since 255 is greater than 10.

Now that we have the comparison, what do we do with it? The next instruction is 65, 33, 4. This instruction says to look at register 4. If the value is 0, then change the instruction pointer to 33—otherwise, do nothing. This is a conditional jump. Basically, it says if the previous comparison of our current value to the sentinel showed that they were equal (gave the value 0), then go to the end of the program (which is at memory location 33). Since register 4 contains a 1, nothing happens and we go to the next instruction like normal.

The next instruction is 133, 0, 2. This adds the contents of register 2 (the current value) to register 0 (the sum so far) and stores the result in register 2. Since register 0 currently is at 0, it should now be 10 + 0, or 10.

Now we need to do the same thing to the next value. But how do we get to the next value? Since register 1 holds the pointer to the next value, we just need to increase register 1 by 1, which is stored in register 5 (the increment). The next instruction is 133, 1, 5. This says to add the contents of register 5 (the increment) to register 1 (the pointer) and store the result in register 1.

Now we are all set to do the same computation on the next value. We just need to go back to the right place in our code to do it all over again. The next instruction is 64, 12, 0. The instruction for 64 is an "unconditional branch." This means that we directly modify the instruction pointer to be 12. Therefore, on the next instruction, you will go back to memory location 12 to get the next instruction. We labeled this earlier with the words "main process start." Label this location in memory (30) "main process end."

```javascript
var add_numbers = function(num_list) {
    var sum = 0;
    for(var i = 0; i < num_list.length; i++) {
        sum = sum + num_list[i];
    }
    return sum;
};
```

Figure 5-6. *Add a List of Numbers in JavaScript*

Now, I'm not going to walk you through all of the next steps, as you will just be going back through the same steps repeatedly. However, think about what happens when you do load in the value 255 from memory? At that point, our comparison above will notice that the value in register 4 (sentinel comparison) is equal to the value in register 2 (current value) and will therefore store the value 0 in register 4. Then, the next "Jump if Zero" instruction will actually work—the value in register 4 *will* be zero, so we will modify the instruction pointer to point to the location specified in the instruction (which is 33).

At that point, we will load the instruction at memory location 33, which is 25, 56, 0. This stores the value of register 0 (the current sum, which is now the final sum) into memory location 56. Memory location 56 should now contain the sum of the relevant values (i.e., 25).

The next instruction is 0, 0, 0, which tells the simulation to stop. We are now finished, and memory location 56 holds the value of the sum of memory locations 57, 58, and 59.

Just as before, this is much easier in JavaScript. A similar function in JavaScript would look like Figure 5-6.

Again, I don't expect you to understand what this means yet, but you should at least recognize that this will be much easier than writing out numbers for machine instructions!

Hopefully this exercise has helped you understand the precision with which computers perform their processing and the exactness required from the programmer. If even one of the instructions for the computer programs were written incorrectly, the whole program would fail. While you probably won't ever need to do this again, the goal was to get your brain in line with the way that computers think. This will make thinking about programming much easier in the future.

If you enjoyed this process, a few other machine language programs are available in Appendix E.

5.5 Machine Opcode Tables

This section lists out the different machine opcodes used by the simulated machine in this chapter. The opcodes are ordered by category, not by number, but this shouldn't be too much of a hindrance as there are fewer than 20 of them. While we will not be using all of the listed opcodes, they are included for completeness and also for the examples in Appendix E.

Each opcode is listed along with what types of operands it uses. The operands are the list of values that will be used for processing the instruction. For instance, for an add instruction, the operands would be the locations which hold the values to be added together and where the result should end up. This simulated machine has four types of operands:

- Immediate operands: An immediate operand means that the number represents itself. That is, if we want to load the value 1 somewhere, we would use an immediate-mode operand.

- Register operand: Registers are temporary storage locations within the ALU. Therefore, if an opcode takes a register operand, this operand will refer to the register number.

- Memory operand: A memory operand is a number, called a **memory address**, that refers to a storage location in the computer memory from which to load or store values.

- Indirect operand: An indirect operand uses the value in a register as the memory location that is to be used for this operand. For instance, let's say that an indirect operand had the value 1. That would mean to look at register 1 and use the value in that register as the memory address that the instruction needs to operate on. So, if register 1 has the value 35, then we would read or write to memory address 35.

The first set of instructions we will look at are the load/store instructions (Figure 5-7). These instructions simply move data around between storage locations. They also make the most use of the different operand types discussed above.

Opcode	Name	Operand 1	Operand 2	Description
20	Load Immediate	Register	Immediate	Loads the value specified in operand 2 into the register specified in operand 1.
21	Load Register	Register	Register	Loads the value contained in the register specified in operand 2 into the register specified in operand 1.
22	Load Memory	Register	Memory	Loads the value contained in the memory location specified in operand 2 into the register specified in operand 1.
23	Load Indirect	Register	Indirect	Takes the value in the register specified in operand 2, and use that as a memory address to load a value from. The value in the memory address is loaded into the register specified in operand 1.
25	Store Memory	Memory	Register	Takes the value in the register specified in operand 2, and stores that in the memory location specified by operand 1.
29	Store Indirect	Indirect	Register	Takes the value in the register specified in operand 2, and stores that in the memory location specified by the register specified by operand 1.

Figure 5-7. *Load/Store Instructions*

The next set of opcodes are the arithmetic opcodes (Figure 5-8). These are opcodes that modify values by adding, subtracting, etc. In our simulated machine, there are very few arithmetic opcodes, but most real computers have a fairly large set of them. Nonetheless, even with our limited opcode list, a lot can be done with them using a little creativity. Note that the comparison opcode is included in this list.

Opcode	Name	Operand 1	Operand 2	Description
133	Add	Register	Register	Takes the value in the register specified by operand 2 and adds it to the value in the register specified by operand 1, storing the resulting value in the register specified by operand 1.
149	Subtract	Register	Register	Takes the value in the register specified by operand 2 and subtracts it from the value in the register specified by operand 1, storing the resulting value in the register specified by operand 1.
37	Compare	Register	Register	Takes the value in the register specified by operand 2 and compares it to the value in the register specified by operand 1. If the value in the register specified by operand 2 is greater than the value in the register specified by operand 1, it stores the number 2 in the register specified by operand 1. If the value in the register specified by operand 2 is less than the value in the register specified by operand 1, it stores the number 1 in the register specified by operand 1. If the value in the two registers are equal, it stores the number 0 in the register specified by operand 1.

Figure 5-8. *Arithmetic Instructions*

The last list of opcodes are the jump instructions (Figure 5-9). These instructions cause the instruction pointer to change, usually based on a certain condition. The conditions are made to match the results of the Compare opcode above (i.e., 37). A common pattern is for a Compare instruction to be followed by a conditional Jump instruction based on the result of the Compare. We don't use the indirect versions of the jump instructions in this book, but they are listed here because they are very powerful and important features available in all general-purpose processors.

Opcode	Name	Operand 1	Operand 2	Description
64	Jump Always	Immediate	0	Changes the instruction pointer to the value in operand 1, causing the next instruction executed to be the one listed at that location. Note that the second operand is *always* 0.
76	Jump Always Indirect	Register	0	Changes the instruction pointer to the value in the register specified in operand 1.
65	Jump if Zero	Immediate	Register	Changes the instruction pointer to the value in operand 1 if the value in the register specified by operand 2 is zero.
77	Jump if Zero Indirect	Register	Register	Same as the previous instruction, but operand 1 specifies a register to use to find the next instruction pointer.
81	Jump if One	Immediate	Register	Change the instruction pointer to the value in operand 1 if the value in the register specified by operand 2 is one.
93	Jump if One Indirect	Register	Register	Same as the previous instruction, but operand 1 specifies a register to use to find the next instruction pointer.
97	Jump if Two	Immediate	Register	Change the instruction pointer to the value in operand 1 if the value in the register specified by operand 2 is two.
109	Jump if Two Indirect	Register	Register	Same as the previous instruction, but operand 1 specifies a register to use to find the next instruction pointer.
0	Halt	Unused	Unused	This instruction ends the computer program.

Figure 5-9. *Jump Instructions*

That's it! That is all that computers are. Even though it may seem confusing, the fact that you can write out all of the rules in a few pages is pretty amazing. Computers really are simple at heart. The confusion most people make is thinking that they are complicated. But really, they just do exactly what you tell them. Exactly.

While performing these minute calculations may seem overwhelming to you, to the computer they are rather simple. In fact, it is their simplicity that makes it possible for computers to run quickly. Modern computers can perform around 5,000,000,000 of these types of instructions *every second.* They have to be that fast in order to keep up with the latest software. Every time you move your mouse, the computer has to do very similar operations as the above in order to recalculate the new mouse position and redraw your cursor on the screen. You might have noticed that even with 5,000,000,000 instructions per second, sometimes it is still not enough!

☞ OPCODE NUMBERING

You might be thinking that the numbering system for the opcodes is kind of strange. However, the numbering system actually has a very logical ordering, but this plan is only evident if you write out the numbers in binary. Each opcode is a combination of a general instruction type (load, add, jump, etc.) and the types of operands that it takes, with 2 bits dedicated to each operand. This is often true of computers—what may seem arbitrary or strange oftentimes makes a lot more sense with a little more knowledge.

Don't worry, I don't expect you to go through and convert the opcodes into binary—after all, this is just a toy system to help you understand how these things work. But nonetheless, keep in mind that not only computers but all of life is filled with things whose logic may not be directly visible but is knowable if you are willing to dig a little deeper and look beneath the surface.

5.5.1 Review

In this chapter, we covered how machines really work. We have learned the following:

- The main parts of the computer are the CPU, the computer memory, the input/output system, and the data bus.

- The CPU works by taking instructions one at a time, decoding them, and then running the processes they specify.

- Each instruction on a CPU performs a single, very small task.

- The computer can only do exactly what you tell it to do.

- All steps of a program must be specified exactly in order for the computer to perform it correctly.

5.5.2 Apply What You Have Learned

1. Think about what would happen if one instruction in the program was changed. How would a missing or faulty instruction affect the result?

2. Did you notice that the code and the data were both in the same memory? By storing everything as numbers, both code and data can be stored using the same system. What problems might you run into if you accidentally overwrote an instruction with a data value?

3. Choose one of the programs from Appendix E and see if you can run it successfully.

4. How would you modify the first program in this chapter to multiply by 3 instead of 2?

PART II

Basic Ingredients for Web Programming

JavaScript is primarily a language for making websites more interactive. This part introduces the basics of the technologies that make web pages work—HTML, CSS, and JavaScript. This part does not go into any depth for any of these topics but should give enough background to help you understand how they work together to make a web page.

CHAPTER 6

The HTML File Format

In Chapter 4, we took a look at how computers format data. In this chapter, we are going to look at the data format used on the Internet for displaying web pages. That format is HTML—the HyperText Markup Language. This book is not a book on HTML, but it is needed to really understand how JavaScript works. The introduction to HTML in this chapter will not go into great depth but should give you a functional understanding of how HTML works.

6.1 A Quick Introduction to HTML

HTML has many features that have made it popular, and it has become the official format of the web. First of all, it is a hypertext format. That means that each file contains **hyperlinks** (or just **links** for short) to other files on the Internet. This is what enables the weblike structure on the Internet. Each document (i.e., web page) contains a number of links to other web pages, which themselves have more links to more web pages. Thus, the file format follows the basic idea of the web—that information is connected to each other, and if we want to know more about something, we can just click the link.

Another great feature of HTML is that it is a **markup language**. The term "markup language" comes from the way manuscripts were edited and laid out before computers. Writing by hand is a little different than making a print book. When you make a book, you need to know what font you want to use for the text, how big you want the letters, and whether you want some of them bold, etc. Typewriters and handwritten material don't convey any of this information for a printer. Therefore, when an author wrote a book, they would "mark it up" with annotations telling the printer how he should make the final text look.

© Jonathan Bartlett 2023
J. Bartlett, *Programming for Absolute Beginners*, https://doi.org/10.1007/978-1-4842-8751-4_6

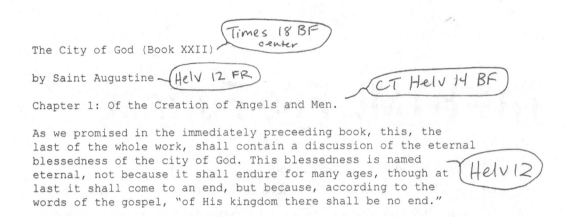

Figure 6-1. *An Example of How Authors Marked Up Documents for a Printer*

Figure 6-1 shows what a marked up document looks like. Since manuscripts were written by hand or using a typewriter, authors couldn't type the document in the font that they wanted, so they put in these markup annotations to tell the printer what to do. "Helv 12" tells the printer to make the font 12-point Helvetica; "BF" means to use a bold-faced font; and "FR" means to flush the text right. These types of instructions tell the printer exactly how to typeset each piece of text. Sometimes that can get tiresome, and, instead, the instructions to the printer tell them what *function* the text serves, and then a separate sheet tells how to typeset that function. In this example, "CT" tells the printer that the marked text is the chapter title, so the printer also knows to put that title into the page header at the top of each page. Sometimes the markup would tell the printer exactly what to do (e.g., "Helv 12" says to use 12-point Helvetica font), and sometimes the markup would tell the printer the function of the text in the document (e.g., "CT" tells the printer that the text is a chapter title). If the author specified the function of the text, they would also supply a separate sheet telling the printer how each type of text piece should be handled. This idea of separating the structure and function of the document from the way that it is displayed is something we will return to in Chapter 7.

```
<!DOCTYPE html>
<html>
<head>
<title>This is the title of this document</title>
</head>

<body>

<h1>This is a large heading</h1>
<p>This is a paragraph.</p>

<h2>This is a smaller heading</h2>
<p>This is another paragraph.</p>

</body>
</html>
```

Figure 6-2. *A Simple HTML Document*

HTML is a very similar concept. It is a markup language, meaning that it consists of text and then additional text telling the computer how that text is to be interpreted. Figure 6-2 shows a short bit of HTML to give you the feel of the language.

As you can see, an HTML document consists mostly of text with additional codes written around the text to tell the computer what function the text is to play. In HTML lingo, these codes are called **tags**. <p> is a **start tag** that tells the computer to treat that text as a paragraph, and </p> is an **end tag** that tells the computer that this is the end of the paragraph. Similarly, <h1> tells the computer to treat the text as a large heading (i.e., heading level 1), and </h1> tells the computer that this is the end of the large heading. HTML has a predefined set of tags that you can use to make your document. By arranging text and tags in a text file, you can easily build your own web pages!

☞   PRACTICE ACTIVITY

1. Open your text editor, and type in the HTML document shown in Figure 6-2 into a new file.

2. Save the file so that it has a `.html` extension.

3. Open up your browser. Rather than typing in a URL, go to the "File" menu and choose "Open." Open up the file you just saved.

4. Observe how the browser displays each piece of tagged text.

5. Also observe the location bar of your browser. If it tells you the protocol, notice that it is *not* an HTTP URL but rather a `file:` URL. This is because it is getting the file from your hard drive and not from a web server.

6. Go back to your text editor and add a new heading and a new paragraph of text and save it.

7. Click the refresh button on your browser to see your changes.

8. Add extra spaces between words and before and after tags. Save the file and reload the browser. Did anything change? Other than separating text into words, blank space (termed **whitespace**) is not used in HTML. If you need to alter spacing, you have to use tags to tell the computer what you want to do.

6.2 The Parts of an HTML Document

Now that you've seen what an HTML document looks like, it is time to dig deeper into the format. The first thing to know are the basic rules of tagging. These are important, so pay special attention.

1. All tags are enclosed in angled brackets (i.e., < and >).

2. For nearly every tag, there is a start tag and an end tag. For the paragraph tag, the start tag is <p> and the end tag is </p>. The only difference between them is that the end tag has a forward slash (/) before the tag name. If you forget the end tag, many browsers won't complain, but you may get strange results.

3. Pairs of start and end tags must be fully within other pairs of start and end tags. For instance `<p>hello <i>there</p></i>` is not allowed, but `<p>hello <i>there</i></p>` is allowed. In the first example (which is incorrect), the `<p>` tag starts *before* the `<i>` tag, but the end tag `</p>` occurs before the end tag `</i>`. Therefore, the `<i> </i>` pair is not fully within the `<p> </p>` pair.

4. For the few tags that do not have an end tag, you combine the start and end tag together. `<br>` does not have an end tag, so it is written `<br />`. This is called a self-closing tag.

5. The combination of a start tag, end tag, and their enclosed content and tags is called an **element**. `<p>` is a tag but `<p>hello</p>` is an element.

6. Blank space (called whitespace) is used to separate words, but is not used for anything else. HTML ignores all extra spacing before, between, and after words. This includes line breaks and spaces for alignment. All of these things are controlled by tags, not by trying to do the spacing yourself.

From here on out, I will only refer to a tag by its start tag. You should always assume that the start tag requires an end tag unless we explicitly say otherwise.

Now, you may have noticed that in our original HTML example, there were several tags that didn't seem to do anything—namely `<html>`, `<head>`, and `<body>`. The `<html>` tag is known as the document root tag. It is the tag that contains all other tags and is required to be there. In this book, if you see an example that doesn't have an `<html>` tag, then it is only showing you a fragment of the document—the rest is assumed to be there, but we are only showing the important parts to make the example clearer. The first tag of every document should be an `<html>` tag, and every document should end with an `</html>` end tag. The `<head>` tag includes tags that tell the browser *about* the document, but which are not displayed within the document itself. In the example given, the `<head>` tag contained a `<title>` tag, which told the browser what the title of the document was. The browser probably displayed this title in the top of the window and would also use it if you bookmarked the page. The `<body>` tag tells the browser that we are starting the portion of the document which should be displayed.

Some basic tags that you will encounter in most HTML documents include the following:

> `<html>` This is the main container of all other tags within a document.
>
> `<head>` This tag contains tags which give information to the browser *about* the page instead of the page content itself.
>
> `<title>` This tag tells the browser the title of your page.
>
> `<body>` This tag contains the actual page content.
>
> `<h1>` This tag is used for the largest heading on the page.
>
> `<h2>` This tag is for a subheading in the page. HTML has additional subheading sizes down to `<h6>`.
>
> `<p>` This is the paragraph tag. Browsers usually give a blank line between any two paragraphs.
>
> `<br>` This is a line break. This tag self-closes and is used to force a line break anywhere in the document.
>
> `<b>` This tag tells the browser to use a bold font.
>
> `<i>` This tag tells the browser to use an italic font.
>
> `<u>` This tag tells the browser to underline its contents.
>
> `<div>` This is a general-purpose tag used for grouping blocks of content together.
>
> `<span>` This is a general-purpose tag used for grouping letters or words together within a paragraph or other block of text.

Also notice that we began our file with `<!DOCTYPE html>`. This is called the **doctype declaration** and tells the browser that, yes, this really is an HTML document.

☞ **PRACTICE QUESTIONS**

1. If <h4> is a start tag, what is its end tag?

2. Which of the following HTML fragments use tags in an invalid way? Why?

   (a) `<h1>My Heading</h1>`

   `<p>This is a <i>great</i> section.`

   `<b>Don't you think?</b></p>`

   (b) `<h1>My Heading</h1>`

   `<p>This is a <i>great</i> section.`

   `<b>Don't you think?</p></b>`

   (c) `<h1>My Heading</h1>`

   `<p>This is a <i>great</i> section.</p>`
   `<p><b>Don't you think?</b></p>`

3. Open up any web page on the Internet. View the HTML source of the web page (see Appendix B.4 for instructions on doing this). Try to identify tags from the list above.

4. In a previous practice activity, you created an HTML file. Modify your HTML file using some of the tags in the list above.

```
<div width="100">
   This block is only 100 pixels wide,
   no matter how much text I put into it.
</div>
```

Figure 6-3. *Tag Attributes Example*

6.3 Adding Attributes to Tags

HTML tags can also have what are called **attributes**. An attribute modifies or specializes an HTML tag. For instance, most tags take a width attribute, which tells the browser how wide to make the tag's content. An attribute example is shown in Figure 6-3.

As you can see, the attribute is placed *inside* the start tag. It has the format attribute-name="value". The value should always be surrounded by quotes, though you may choose either single quotes or double quotes.[1] The allowable values inside the quotes depend on the particular tag you are using. You can also specify multiple attributes on the same tag. If you specify multiple attributes, just separate your attributes by a space (*not* a comma), and you can add as many attributes as you want.

I should note that setting a width in this manner is actually frowned upon in HTML (you will see a better approach in Chapter 7). I only present it here because it illustrates the concept of attributes in a simple manner.

6.4 Tags That Refer to Other Documents

As mentioned previously, one of the things that makes HyperText valuable is its ability to refer to other documents. HTML pages refer to other documents either to include them into the current page or to link to them for when a user performs an action. The tags that you will run into most often are as follows:

---

[1] Note that in computer programming, you should never use the curvy quotes that your word processor uses. It is actually fairly problematic to type something into a word processor and then copy and paste it into a document. The reason is that word processors often auto-convert straight quotes (") into curvy quotes ("). This is an error in most programming and markup languages.

<img /> This tag is used to include an image into the page at the location where the tag is placed. The src attribute tells the browser where to find the image. Note that <img /> is a self-closing tag. Using the tag <img src="https://placekitten. com/200/300" /> will place a cat image into your web page.

<a> This tag is used to link to another document when the text inside the tag is clicked. The href attribute (i.e., hypertext reference) tells the browser what URL to go to next. Using the tag <a href="https://mindmatters.ai/">Click Me</a> will make a link to the MindMatters News website.

<link /> This tag is used to connect style sheets to your HTML page. We will cover more about style sheets in Chapter 7. Note that <link /> is a self-closing tag.

<script> This tag is used to connect JavaScript programs to your HTML page. We will start covering JavaScript in Chapter 8.

An example of a few of these tags in a document is shown in Figure 6-4.

```
<!DOCTYPE html>
<html>
<body>
<h1>This document refers to other documents</h1>
<p>
   Click on
   <a href="https://www.mindmatters.ai/">this link</a>
   to access the MindMatters website.
</p>
<p>
   Below is an image of a cat:
</p>

<img src="https://placekitten.com/200/300" />

</body>
</html>
```

Figure 6-4. *Example Document Showing Tags Referencing Other Documents*

As you can see in this example, the `<a>` tag creates a link to another document. The document to link to goes in the `href` attribute, and the text to link to goes between the start and end tags. Then, at the end, the `<img />` tag refers to an image file at a specified URL and includes that within the page.

☞ PRACTICE QUESTIONS

- Create a new HTML file using the example document in this section. View it in your browser to make sure you entered everything correctly.

- Modify this HTML file. Add links for all of your favorite places to go on the Web.

- Find an image on the web that you like. Find out its URL (see Appendix B.5). Add that image to your web page.

When a document refers to another document, it is not always necessary to refer to the full URL of the destination document. In addition, if you ever have to move a set of documents, it is difficult to modify the links in all of the web pages to point to the new URL. For instance, let's say that you owned the website `www.example.com.` But then, someone offered you a large sum of money so that they could own the domain name. So now you have to move your stuff to be under a different domain. However, if all of your links refer to `www.example.com/whatever`, you now have to modify each one to point to the new domain! In a more practical scenario, think about if you were building a new version of your website. While you are still building it, the current website needs to stay where it is, so you put your test version on another site. Wouldn't it be great if all of the links just worked when you moved it over? That doesn't work with complete URLs because they refer to the exact location on the Internet. Once we move locations, the URL is now wrong.

In order to solve this, URLs can be rewritten to be *relative* to the location of the current document. Let's say that I have one file at `www.example.com/fruit/oranges.html` and another at `www.example.com/fruit/apples.html` but they each link to the other. Under the scheme demonstrated so far, we would have the first file have a link that looks like this:

```
<a href="http://www.example.com/fruit/apples.html">See the Apples</a>
```

The second file will have a link back to the first file that looks something like this:

```
<a href="http://www.example.com/fruit/oranges.html">I prefer oranges</a>
```

This is rather tedious, especially since they are in the same directory (i.e., `www.example.com/fruit`).

The HTML standard gives us three choices of what to do. The regular URL, also called the **fully qualified URL** or **absolute URL**, that we have been using contains all of the data necessary to connect. The **relative URL** takes most of its connection information from the *current* URL, which, for linking purposes, is also called the **base URL**. So, in the previous example, if we were already looking at `www.example.com/fruit/apples.html`, we could link to the other file just by referring to `oranges.html` like this:

```
<a href="oranges.html">See the Oranges Page</a>
```

This is a relative URL and it tells the browser to look in the same folder that we are currently in, but just change out the last part of the URL so that it points to this new file. Using relative URLs not only gives us less typing, but it also makes it easier to move groups of documents. As long as `apples.html` and `oranges.html` stayed in the same directory together, you could move them around to be under a different site or to a different directory on your site, and their links would still work. In short, relative URLs use the current URL, up to and including the current directory, as the starting point. The relative URL just tells how to get to the document *from where you already are*. You can tell a relative URL from a fully qualified URL by the fact that it doesn't include a protocol and it doesn't start with a slash.

There are two other kinds of URLs which are hybrids between absolute and relative URLs. The first is the **absolute path**. The absolute path tells the browser to use the current protocol and server but replace the path entirely with the one specified. In our example, the absolute path to `apples.html` is `/fruit/apples.html`. Note that absolute paths *always* begin with a slash. If it does not begin with a slash, it is considered a relative URL.

The final type of URL is the **network path**. This URL uses the protocol of the current page, but you specify everything else. So, the network path of `oranges.html` is `//www.example.com/fruit/oranges.html`. Network paths are rarely necessary, but it is good to know what they mean in case you see them.

☞ **PRACTICE QUESTIONS**

---

1. Create another simple web page in the same directory as your other web pages.

2. Create a link from your new page to one of your other pages. Remember to use relative links!

3. Create another link to some other page on the Internet.

4. Save the page, and open it up in your browser.

5. Test out your links. Did they work? If not, check the URL in your browser to see where the browser thought you were asking it to go.

6.5 Relative URLs

Relative URLs have a lot of features that make them helpful both when building a website and when using a book like this. For instance, since the files we create will be on your hard drive instead of a web server, it is much easier to use relative URLs rather than the extremely long `file:` URLs that specify where on your hard drive another document is. In addition, by using relative URLs, it means that the web pages you create will still work if you hand them in to a teacher or parent. If you use `file:` URLs, then all of the URLs would be wrong when your parent or teacher loads them on their computer, because they would be in a different location on their computer than they were on yours. If, instead, you use relative URLs, then, as long as you deliver all of the files together, the URLs will still work in their new destination. For the purposes of this book, every time you reference a file that you create or that you store on your hard drive, you should use a relative URL, but when you reference a file stored somewhere else on the web, you should use absolute URLs.

Another feature of relative URLs is that you can use them to refer to subdirectories. Let's say that you want the page at `www.example.com/fruit/apples.html` to link to the file `www.example.com/fruit/exotic/rambutan.html`. You will notice that they share a lot of their URLs between them. The relative URL tells you how to get to the document from the current directory. From `www.example.com/fruit/` I only have to say that I want to go to `exotic/rambutan.html`. Therefore, I can link to this page like this:

```
<a href="exotic/rambutan.html">the rambutan fruit</a>
```

Now, let's say that I am writing the page on rambutans, and I want to see my page on apples. How does that work with relative URLs? There is a special directory name that refers to the enclosing directory (also called the **parent directory**). This is referred to with two periods (i.e., ..). If you are writing the page www.example.com/fruit/exotic/rambutan.html and you want to link to www.example.com/fruit/oranges.html, you can write the link like this:

```
<a href="../oranges.html">oranges</a>
```

You can include as many directories as necessary in your URL. For example, if you were writing the page www.example.com/fruit/exotic/rambutan.html and wanted to link to the page www.example.com/fruit/poisonous/snowberry.html, you would write the following:

```
<a href="../poisonous/snowberry.html">snowberry fruit</a>
```

One other important special directory name is the . directory. While the two periods (..) refer to the parent directory, the single period (.) refers to the current directory. This is rarely used in HTML, but you will see it on occasion.

6.6 Other HTML Features

HTML has many other great features. The goal of this book is to get you just enough HTML to get started and to understand what you read about HTML on the Internet. There are many tags which do many different things. In this section we will cover a few of the more popular tags and simple features, but this is not meant to be exhaustive.

6.6.1 Entities

Because HTML uses the < and > characters to signify that the given text is a tag, how would you then actually write those characters? HTML provides **entities** to refer to characters that either have a special use by the HTML format or are hard to type (e.g., characters from other languages). An HTML entity starts with an ampersand (&) and ends with a semicolon (;). Common entities include:

> >

< <

& &

" "

' '

  a "non-breaking" space—a space that doesn't allow a line break at that point

© ©

6.6.2 Lists

Lists are great ways of organizing things in HTML. A list can either be unordered (i.e., a bulleted list) or ordered (i.e., a numbered list). The tag that encloses the whole list is <ul> for an unordered list or <ol> for an ordered list. Then, each list item is enclosed in an <li> tag for both kinds.

Figure 6-5 shows a short HTML fragment that illustrates how these lists are used. The first list will display as a bulleted list, while the second list will be numbered.

6.6.3 Table Tags

In addition to paragraphs, headings, and lists, people often need to represent tables of data on web pages. HTML has a set of tags specialized for displaying tables of data. Let's say we wanted to make a list of our friends, with their name, their email, and their phone number. We would want the first row to be the headings (such as "Name," "Email," and "Phone") and the other rows to be the data. For that, we will need several tags:

```
<h1>An Unordered List of Plants in my Garden</h1>
<ul>
   <li> Tomatoes </li>
   <li> Peas </li>
   <li> Beans </li>
</ul>

<h1>An Ordered List of my Favorite Books by G. K. Chesterton</h1>
<ol>
   <li> <i>The Everlasting Man</i> </li>
   <li> <i>Manalive</i> </li>
   <li> <i>Heretics</i> </li>
</ol>
```

Figure 6-5. *Simple Lists*

`<table>` This tag wraps around the whole table.

`<tr>` This tag wraps around a row of data.

`<td>` This tag wraps around the contents of a single data cell.

`<th>` This is just like the `<td>` tag, but it is used for headings (it usually makes the content bold).

`<thead>` This tag is not strictly necessary, but it is often used to wrap around the row(s) of your table heading.

`<tbody>` This tag is also not strictly necessary, but it is often used to wrap around rows of data in your table.

`<tfoot>` Just like the `<thead>` tag, but used for footers of tables.

Figure 6-6 is a fragment that shows how we can put these tags together to make a table.

This will display something like this:

Name	Email	Phone
Jeff	jeff@example.com	555-555-1234
Melissa	melissa@example.com	555-555-6789

```
<table>
   <thead>
      <tr>
         <th>Name</th>
         <th>Email</th>
         <th>Phone</th>
      </tr>
   </thead>
   <tbody>
      <tr>
         <td>Jeff</td>
         <td>jeff@example.com</td>
         <td>555-555-1234</td>
      </tr>
      <tr>
         <td>Melissa</td>
         <td>melissa@example.com</td>
         <td>555-555-6789</td>
      </tr>
   </tbody>
</table>
```

Figure 6-6. *An Example Use of Table Tags*

6.6.4 Form Tags

A lot of web pages allow you to enter data. Data entry web pages are commonly referred to as "forms." These tags allow the user to enter in their own values. They won't be useful until we know how to process them, but we will list some of those tags for future use. Notice that the <input /> tag can actually be several different input elements. The element that is displayed on the page is chosen based on the type attribute. The <input /> tag should also be written as a self-closing tag.

<form> This tag normally encloses other form tags. If the form is supposed to submit data to a server, that destination is usually put in the action attribute.

<input type="text" /> This is a basic, single-line data entry field.

<input type="checkbox" /> This is a single box that can be checked on or off.

<textarea> This is a multiline data entry field.

<select> This is a drop-down list. Each option is specified inside this tag using the <option> tag.

<button> This is a basic pushbutton. The enclosed text is the text of the button.

Most of these tags also have a name attribute that you can use to specify what the field is for (this will be important later) and a value attribute to give the field an initial value or, in the case of check boxes, to give the value that this box represents.

Figure 6-7 shows an example HTML fragment for a form (note that this doesn't actually *do* anything; it just lets the user interact with it).

6.6.5 Standard Attributes

There are a few attributes which are standard for every HTML element. There are three that are important to this book: id, class, and style. The id attribute essentially gives a name to your HTML element that is unique within the document. We can use this attribute to locate the element for processing by JavaScript or for styling. Note that the browser won't complain if there are two elements with the same id attribute on the same page, but it could cause subtle errors.

```
<form>
   Here is an input field: <input type="text" /> <br />
   Here is a checkbox: <input type="checkbox" /> <br />
   Here is a multi-line input field:
      <textarea></textarea> <br />
   Here is a drop-down list:
      <select>
         <option>Option 1</option>
         <option>Option 2</option>
      </select>
      <br />
   Here is a button: <button>Click Me</button>
</form>
```

Figure 6-7. *Form Element Demonstration*

The `class` attribute is more of an ad hoc attribute—you can basically use it for whatever you want. Usually, it is used to group certain items together that should be given a similar style or where an entire group of elements should be processed by JavaScript.

Finally, the `style` attribute can be used to explicitly set styling information (see Chapter 7) on an element.

6.6.6 Comments, Declarations, Processing Instructions, and CDATA Blocks

When we talk about the structure of a language, we are talking about its **syntax**. The syntax includes what sorts of letters, symbols, and features are allowed in what places. For instance, the tag is an integral part of HTML's syntax. To get a good example of what syntax is, perhaps an example of a violation of that syntax will help. We have seen tags like this: `<p><i>This is an italicized paragraph</i></p>`. This is perfectly legitimate. Imagine, however, that instead of starting with `<p><i>` we accidentally typed `<p <i>>`. That would be a *syntax error*, meaning that we didn't properly follow the structure of HTML.

Syntaxes are important because that is how the computer knows what we are attempting to do.

The two primary units of HTML syntax we have discussed so far are tags and entities. There are several other syntactical units that are important to know, but they will rarely be used in this book.

A popular syntactical unit is the HTML **comment**. For writing any kind of code, most programming and markup languages allow for developers to add comments to their code. Comments are notes that the programmer writes to himself or any other developer looking at the code. It basically says something like "I did it this way because I had trouble getting some other way to work" or "here are the reasons the code looks this way." It holds important information that is not immediately obvious to someone looking at the code, but which is ignored by the browser.

In HTML, like most other computer languages, comments are essentially ignored by the browser. This feature allows for another use of comments—temporarily disabling parts of your code. Let's say that you have built a large web page and you want to see what it looks like without a big chunk of your code. Rather than deleting that code and having to retype it later, you can just wrap it in a comment, and the browser will ignore it.

This is called *commenting out* code, because you are taking the code out of the document or program using comments.

So what does a comment look like? Comments are simple. They start with <!-- and they end with -->. Here is a short HTML fragment with a few comments:

```
<h1>Web Page with Comments</h1>
<!-- Here is an unordered list -->
<ul>
    <li>Here is a list item</li>
    <!--
        <li>This list item is not visible because it has been commented
            out</li>
    -->
    <li>Another list item</li>
</ul>
```

Another feature of HTML is the declaration. Declarations are used to identify, and possibly extend, the list of valid tags, attributes, and entities. Usually, the only declaration you will see is the HTML *doctype* declaration, which tells the computer the basic type of document you are working with so it knows what tags are valid and what they mean. HTML doctype declaration tells the computer that, yes, you are really looking at an HTML document. In its basic form, it looks like this: <!DOCTYPE html>. It is always placed *before* the first <html> tag. There are other, fancier ways of writing it, but the meaning is basically the same—yes, computer, you are looking at an HTML document.

Another feature is the processing instruction. These are used to give document processors (such as browsers) special information on how to handle your document. However, with the exception of a single processing instruction, this feature is almost entirely unused. The processing instruction looks like a start tag and can include attributes, but it has a question mark before the processing instruction name and before the right-angled bracket, like this:

```
<?processing-instruction-name attribute1="value1" attribute2="value2" ?>
```

The only processing instruction you are likely to see is this one, known as the XML declaration:

```
<?xml version="1.0" encoding="UTF-8" ?>
```

If used, this goes at the beginning of the document, before the doctype declaration, and even before any blank lines or whitespace. It tells the browser to use special, more strict rules when processing the HTML document. For instance, if you don't use this tag, the browser is much more forgiving for small violations of the HTML standard.

One last feature that is sometimes seen is CDATA sections. A CDATA section is most often used when you have a lot of angled brackets to write in the document itself, but don't want to have to write entities for each one. A CDATA section tells the browser to just treat the text as literal text and don't try to find tags, comments, or entities. CDATA sections start with <![CDATA[and end with]]>.

Figure 6-8 shows a short example.

Many browsers don't fully support CDATA sections in all circumstances, so it is best not to use them, but it is good to know what they are in case you see one.

```
<h1>A CDATA Example</h1>
<p>
    This is me writing a tag name that I want displayed without CDATA:
        &lt;p&gt;
</p>
<p>
    <![CDATA[
        This is me writing a tag name to display with CDATA: <p>
    ]]>
</p>
```

Figure 6-8. *A CDATA Example*

6.6.7 Review

In this chapter we covered the basics of HTML, what it is, and how to write it. We have learned the following:

- A markup language is a text document that uses tags (which are also text) to specify the structure and function of the different pieces of the document.

- HTML is the markup language that is used on the Internet for web pages.

- In HTML, spacing is essentially ignored—tags are used instead to mark locations of paragraphs and line breaks.

- URLs specify the location of documents on the Internet.

- An HTML document can reference another document on the Internet using URLs.

- A relative URL can be used to reference other related files on the same website.

- Relative URLs make it easy to keep document links working even when the files are moved, as long as they are moved together.

- HTML has a number of tags for many different situations.

- Tags can have attributes which further specialize their function.

- The id, class, and style attributes can be applied to any tag.

6.6.8 Apply What You Have Learned

1. Create a new HTML file. Place an image in the same directory (one with a .jpg or .png extension). Can you figure out how to write an <img /> tag to include the image into your web page using a relative URL?

2. Create a sequence of three web pages that relate to each other on the same subject. At the top of the web page, put links to each of the other pages in the group. Test it out and make sure that you can navigate between them on your browser.

3. Go through the list of tags in this chapter. Modify your pages so that each page has one or more headings and your sequence of pages has at least one table, one list, and one entity.

4. Go to several of your favorite websites, and view the HTML of several of the pages on that site (see Appendix B.4). Identify which tags you know and which tags you don't know. Look up on the Internet at least two tags that you aren't familiar with. The official list of tags in the current version of HTML is available at www. w3.org/TR/html-markup/elements.html.

5. As you go through different websites, make note of how their sites
    are organized and laid out. What types of content are common
    to all of the websites? Are there common ways of laying out the
    website? The basic structure of the web pages themselves and
    their organization on the site are known as the site's **information
    architecture**, also known as IA. Can you sketch the basic layout of
    the web page—where they put their menus, where they put their
    images, where they put their content, etc.? Can you draw a map of
    how you move from page to page on the site?

CHAPTER 7

Introduction to Cascading Style Sheets

7.1 The Origin of Cascading Style Sheets

When HTML was first developed, it was entirely used for communicating information. HTML was originally built as an easy way to browse and view documents. Therefore, HTML documents were never pretty but were very functional. In addition, there was a direct match between the tag used and the purpose that the tagged text served in the document. For instance, <h1> tags meant that the given text was a main heading. If you were looking at the HTML code itself, you would know precisely what it meant if you found text with that tag. In fact, if you knew the tags, you could almost just as easily read the document source with the tags as you could read it rendered in the browser.

However, as more and more people started using the Web, HTML started serving more purposes than purely informational ones. The modern web is much more user-focused and incorporates many other types of media and functionality, including navigation, entertainment, advertising, and branding. In the early days, in order to accommodate for these new uses, HTML's tag and attribute set expanded and expanded. The problem was, however, that the initial beauty and simplicity of HTML was lost. Web pages became complicated messes of undecipherable tags. In addition, different browsers rendered the tags slightly differently. Therefore, in order to write a web page, you had to know not only what each tag *did* but how the tag would *look* in every browser and how to get them all to work together to produce a good-looking web page.

The organizations that control the standards for the Web recognized this problem and decided to move HTML back closer to its roots. In order to achieve this, they attempted to separate **content** from **presentation**. Content refers to the data that the web page is intended to communicate. Presentation refers to how that page will look to

© Jonathan Bartlett 2023
J. Bartlett, *Programming for Absolute Beginners*, https://doi.org/10.1007/978-1-4842-8751-4_7

the user. Headings, paragraphs, figures, etc. are all part of the content. The background, formatting, layout, colors, fonts, and decorations are all part of the presentation.

In order to do this, they removed styling from HTML and created a new language, called **Cascading Style Sheets** (CSS for short), to tell browsers how the HTML should look. In this new paradigm, the structure and content of the document is written in HTML. How that content should be laid out, formatted, and presented is written in CSS. The advanced interaction between the user and the content is written in JavaScript. This separation is not perfect, but it is a huge improvement.

☞ THE PROGRESSION OF TECHNOLOGY

It is interesting to note the way that technology progresses. The way HTML progressed is very similar to many other technologies. The first version was very simple and direct. It accomplished the needs of its users very well.

However, its success led to many problems. Because everyone was using it, new people, with different needs than the original users, were also using it. In order to accommodate this, they simply added a bunch of features to HTML. However, it quickly became apparent that simply adding features was making a mess of things. It did expand the capabilities of HTML but at the cost of making all HTML work more complicated (and expensive).

The next step in the progress of HTML was to reevaluate the different aspects of how HTML worked and the different needs they served. As it turned out, there were several needs that were plainly distinct. There was the need to handle content, the need to display content in a visually pleasing manner, and the need to make the content interactive.

Because these needs were distinguishable, they were then **refactored** into entirely separate pieces. HTML would handle the content, CSS would handle the presentation, and JavaScript would handle the interactivity. HTML was a great content language, but a bad styling language. So this new setup allowed HTML to do what it did best and left styling and interaction to other technologies which were better suited for the task.

Refactoring is a common occurrence in the progress of technology. The word "refactoring" is based on the idea of factoring in mathematics. In math, factoring refers to taking a number and separating it out into its prime components. The number 15 has the prime factors 5 and 3. In technology, refactoring is similar. It is reevaluating the technology you have and looking for components which are more basic that the technology can be divided into. This usually happens when the growth of a technology causes it to become overly complex. At that point, it needs to be reevaluated to find if there are *simpler* components that the technology can be divided into.

Refactoring is not a panacea and must be used judiciously. If refactoring is done prematurely, all of the different components may not be clearly seen, and it may be refactored in ways that make progress more difficult rather than less. However, for the most part, refactoring tends to give new life to old technology as it increases both flexibility and understandability.

7.2 The Structure of a CSS Document

The best way to understand the basic operation of CSS is to see it in action. To start with, create a file called `basic.css` with the content shown in Figure 7-1 (as usual, be sure to enter it *exactly* as shown).

What this document says is that

- All text inside `<h1>` tags should be shown as blue text in a 20-point font (a **point** is a unit of measurement in typography—1 point is $\frac{1}{72}$ of an inch).

- All text inside `<p>` tags should be shown as black text in a 12-point font.

Now, create a document called `basic.html` in the same directory as `basic.css` with the contents as shown in Figure 7-2.

The part of the file that links together these two files is the `<link>` tag. The `<link>` tag can be used to specify all sorts of related documents (what it is linking is specified by the `rel` attribute), but its most important usage is to specify the style sheet to use for a web page. The document that the `<link>` tag refers to is listed in the `href` attribute. So, in short, the `<link>` tag in the document above says to use the file `basic.css` as its style sheet.

```
h1 {
    font-size: 20pt;
    color: blue;
}

p {
    font-size: 12pt;
    color: black;
}
```

Figure 7-1. *A Simple CSS Document*

```
<!DOCTYPE html>
<html>
<head>
<title>Stylesheet Test</title>
<link rel="stylesheet" href="basic.css" />
</head>
<body>
<h1>This is a Heading</h1>
<p>This is a paragraph.</p>
</body>
</html>
```

Figure 7-2. *A Web Page Using CSS*

If you open this file with your browser, you will find that, indeed, it renders the document as we specified. If it doesn't, go back through and try to find your mistake (to start with, be sure they are both in the same directory).

The CSS file format is fairly simple and straightforward. It consists of two major parts: selectors and properties. CSS properties list out the styles to be used, and CSS selectors tell which pieces of HTML those styles are to be used on. So, in the file we were looking at, h1 and p were the selectors. The selector was followed by a property list wrapped in curly braces ({ and }). The property list tells what styles to use on the text.

The two properties we use in Figure 7-1 are color, which defines the color to make the text, and font-size, which tells what size font to use for the text. CSS2 defines 98 different properties available to use, and CSS3 defines even more. However, there aren't that many properties that you need to know to get started. This chapter will only cover the most important ones, but you can see a fairly comprehensive list of CSS properties at www.w3schools.com/cssref/.

7.3 Understanding Selectors

The CSS selectors used in the previous section listed the tag name that was to be styled. However, such a selector has limited use and will not give us the kind of flexibility needed to produce really nice documents.

Let's say, for instance, that you have different types of paragraphs that you wanted to lay out in different ways. You want one paragraph to be red text on a blue background and another paragraph to be green text on a black background. In order to do this, the CSS file will have to be able to distinguish between these two different types of paragraphs, but HTML only provides one paragraph (<p>) tag. To accomplish this, CSS can also use attributes to choose which tags that a set of properties applies to. In order to facilitate this process, HTML defines a class property available on *all* HTML tags, which can be used for whatever purpose the writer wants. Usually, they are used to make distinctions between tags for CSS to process.

```
<!DOCTYPE html>
<html>
<head>
<title>Testing HTML Classes</title>
<link rel="stylesheet" href="classes.css" />
</head>
<body>

<div class="section1">
<h1>A Title</h1>
<p class="style1">My paragraph 1.</p>
<p class="style2">My paragraph 2.</p>

</div>

<div class="section2">
<h1>Another Title</h1>
<p>Another paragraph.</p>
</div>

</body>
</html>
```

Figure 7-3. *An HTML File Using Classes*

Let's look at how this works.

Create the HTML file shown in Figure 7-3, and name the file `classes.html`:

This document uses `<div>` tags to group the document into two sections, where each section has a title and one or more paragraphs. The sections are differentiated from each other by the `class` attribute. In the first section, the paragraphs are differentiated from each other by the same way.

CSS allows us to use HTML attributes to supply specific styles for different uses of the same tag.

To see this in action, create a file called `classes.css` in the same directory as the previous file with the contents shown in Figure 7-4. After typing both the HTML and CSS files, open the `classes.html` file and see what the results look like.

```
p {
    font-size: 10pt;
}

p[class=style1] {
    color: red;
    background-color: blue;
}

p[class=style2] {
    font-size: 12pt;
    color: green;
    background-color: black;
}
```

Figure 7-4. *A CSS File Styling Classes*

Now let's take a look at how the styles specified in Figure 7-4 work on the HTML. The first selector is just like before—it is a tag name followed by styling properties. It says that paragraph tags should have a font size of ten points.

The next selector, however, is different. This selector says `p[class=style1]`, which means that it applies *only* to `<p>` tags that have the `class` attribute set to the value `style1`. The properties for this say that paragraphs with the `style1` class should be red text on a blue background. Note that a `<p>` tag with the `style1` class would *also* match the first selector, since the first selector applies to *all* `<p>` tags. Therefore, any attribute set in the original selector would still be applied, so it uses a ten-point font as well.

The final selector is just like the previous one, except that it is set to match paragraphs with a class of style2. It displays the paragraph with green text on a black background. It also sets the size of the font to 12 points. This is in conflict with the setting that was set in the first group of CSS properties, which set all <p> tag sizes to ten points. However, *because the selector for these properties is more specific*, its properties supersede the ones from the more general selector.

```
p {
    font-size: 10pt;
}

p.style1 {
    color: red;
    background-color: blue;
}

p.style2 {
    font-size: 12pt;
    color: green;
    background-color: black;
}
```

Figure 7-5. *A CSS File Using Simplified Notation for Classes*

You can select HTML elements by any attribute you want. However, selecting by the class attribute is very common. In fact, it is so common that there is a special simplified notation for selecting by class. Instead of writing p[class=style1] for a selector, I can just write p.style1 as a shorthand.

Therefore, if I were to rewrite my classes.css file using this simplified notation, it would look like Figure 7-5. Not only is that easier to write, but it is easier to read!

CSS has a rich supply of selectors that allow you to style documents in a very dynamic way. You can have selectors that indicate tags that are within other tags, tags that are preceded by some other tag, and a number of other ways of selecting HTML elements for styling. This book, however, only covers the very basic elements of CSS that you will need on your way to understanding how to program web pages, so we won't go into any more depth on CSS selectors.

7.4 The CSS Box Model

In order to dive deeper into how CSS styling works, it is important to understand how CSS looks at the content on a web page. This is known as the CSS "box model," because CSS thinks about web pages in terms of boxes. There are several ways that CSS looks at content, but there are two primary ones—either as lines of text (known as *inline* style) or as a rectangular box (known as *block* style). There are other, more specialized structures, such as table, list, and flex structures, but this chapter will just concentrate on inline and block styles. The other styles have a lot of complexities that are outside the scope of this book.

Most tags we have dealt with, such as <div>, <p>, <h1>, <h2>, etc., are all block style tags by default. This means that when the content is generated, the browser will put the given element into a rectangular box. Unless otherwise specified, this box will be as wide as possible (i.e. the size of its container) and as tall as required to hold all of the content. Inline tags, such as the <a> and <span> tags, are primarily for text *within* a paragraph. Therefore, these are not strictly rectangular boxes, since you could have text that started in the middle of one line and wrapped onto the next line, producing an irregular shape.

So, block tags are for styling paragraphs, groups of paragraphs, and other blocky content, and inline tags are used for styling text *within* a paragraph (or other block). You can also change an HTML element from inline to block and vice-versa using the display property. By setting the property using display: block; or display: inline; you can force HTML elements to behave in a different way than their default.

The general box model is presented in Figure 7-6. Block elements make use of all of the elements of the box model in a straightforward way, while inline elements can sometimes act a little weird due to the irregular shape of their contents.

Every box that CSS makes for a block element is a rectangle of content surrounded by padding, a border, and a margin. These work together in the following way:

- The **content** is the HTML that you put inside of the element, whether just text or other tags (or even possibly nothing at all).

- The **padding** is the area immediately surrounding your content (the size of the padding can be set for each side).

- The **border** is a line (usually solid) that surrounds the padding.

- The **background**, if set, extends behind the content, the padding, and the border.

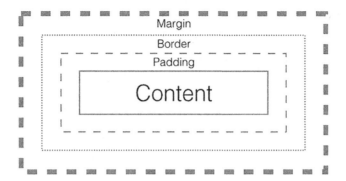

Figure 7-6. *The CSS Box Model*

- The **margin** is the area outside the border. The margin is a little different, however, as it is the *minimum* amount of space between one element and the next, so if two elements next to each other both have a margin set, it simply uses the larger of the two margins (it doesn't add them together).

The size of the content area can be set manually using the width and height properties. If the width is not set, then the width is automatically set so that the entirety of the box (including content, padding, border, and margin) fit the entire width of the containing box (or the screen if there is not another containing box). Then, given the determined (or manually set) width, the height is set to whatever is required to contain the content. Oftentimes you don't see all of these pieces (especially the border) because they are zero-width. However, you can, using CSS, set the size and other properties of each one of these aspects of any box.

Inline content, because of its irregular shape, can have padding and a border, but the margin works strangely. Essentially, for inline elements, the top and bottom margin are ignored, but the left and right margin are utilized at the beginning and ending of the elements. However, if the inline content spans multiple lines, the left margin is only used on the first line, and the right margin is only used on the last line.

If you go back to the HTML from Figure 7-3, we can modify the CSS style sheet (classes.css) to show how the box model works. The HTML is divided into two sections by <div> tags. We will set each <div> tag with a border, a background, a padding, and an internal width. Figure 7-7 shows the code to use.

This gives us two large boxes, one for each section, and several smaller boxes. Remember, unless otherwise constrained, the boxes take up as much width as they can. The top box takes up the width of the page (minus the margin around itself). The boxes within that box also take up as much width as they can, but they are constrained by the margin, border, and padding of the box around them.

```
div.section1 {
   border: 1px solid black;
   padding: 20px;
   margin: 10px;
}
div.section2 {
   border: 1px solid red;
   background-color: green;
   width: 50%;
   padding: 50px;
   margin: 10px;
}
p {
   border: 1px solid blue;
}
```

Figure 7-7. *CSS Example for the Box Model*

The second box does not go all the way across the screen because we set the width of that box to be 50%. Therefore, it only goes halfway across the page. Likewise, the boxes within that box are constrained to this new size.

While we have set the margin, padding, and border on all sides to be the same value, we can also set them to be different on different sides. Instead of just using padding, we can instead set padding-right, padding-left, padding-top, and padding-bottom to separate values.

So far, we have seen several different units for the sizes of things in CSS. CSS has several units of measure available, but the most common are pt for points, px for pixels, in for inches, mm for millimeters, and % for percentage of the containing size. Additionally, CSS also has a few units that are relative to the currently selected font size. The em is the size of the letter "m" in the current font, ex is the size of the letter "x" in the current font, and ch is the size of the "0" in the current font. The rem is the size of the letter "m" in the font size of the root element of the page. The rem unit is very popular because, if used everywhere, it allows auto-scaling the entire web page by simply changing the size of the font on the root element.

7.5 Other Capabilities of CSS

We have only scratched the surface of CSS in this chapter, but hopefully you have a taste for what it can do and how it works. In addition to the capabilities we have discussed so far, CSS also has the ability to move boxes around, put data into tables, put numbers on lists, generate small amounts of content, use images for backgrounds, show and hide elements, and even more. Also, CSS can adjust your layout based on the screen size. So, for instance, if you have a lot of content on your page but only want to show a small part of it if you are looking at it on a small screen (like a phone), CSS will let you hide or show different elements based on the screen size or use different styles for them. Designs which readily adapt to radically different screen sizes are often known as **responsive** layouts.

There are a number of different extensions to CSS that have been developed over the years which allow lots of additional features such as animations, some 3D manipulation, gradient backgrounds (where one color slowly transitions to another color), and more. These extensions are not all supported across every browser, but every year more features become available for developers to use.

To see the amazing flexibility of CSS, you should check out CSS Zen Garden, which is at `www.csszengarden.com`. This is a collection of styles which all display *the same web page*, with the only difference being the CSS used. It is almost unbelievable the amount of creativity that can be achieved in this fashion. It should also be noted that this is possible precisely because HTML was refactored into separate content and design components. Thus, you really can change the design of an entire website just by switching out the style sheet. Before the advent of CSS, such changes required rewriting the entire website. Now it only requires rewriting the style sheet.

7.5.1 Review

This chapter covered the basics of Cascading Style Sheets. We have learned the following:

- Technology often develops by refactoring old monolithic technologies into distinct concepts.

- Cascading Style Sheets (CSS) developed when HTML was refactored to separate out content, presentation, and interactivity on a web page.

- CSS files are meant to handle the presentation of content written in HTML.

- CSS allows HTML to hold the content of a web page without regard to how it will be displayed.

- CSS works by having a list of style properties applied to HTML elements designated by selectors.

- CSS selectors are often based on the names of tags and the values of attributes.

- CSS lays out a page on the basis of the CSS box model, in which each HTML element is assigned a rectangular box on the page and has its own padding, border, and margin.

- The variety of layouts possible for HTML content simply by changing style sheets is quite dramatic.

- Because the styling for a page or set of pages lives in an external file, CSS allows the look of an entire website to be changed by updating only the shared CSS file.

7.5.2 Apply What You Have Learned

1. Take the HTML file from Figure 7-3 and write a new style sheet for it. Put the headings in a 16-point font and the paragraph text in a 12-point font. Put a 12-point gap between the paragraphs.

2. Create a new HTML file with a new CSS file. Create four rectangles on the screen with different widths, heights, and background colors.

3. Come up with your own design for the content in Figure 7-3. First, draw on a sheet of paper how you might want to lay it out—be creative! Then, try to see what parts of that design you can replicate with your current knowledge of CSS. Don't worry if

your imagination is more than what you know how to do. Just do what you can! Feel free to also look on the web for additional CSS properties you can use to make your design come to life. Sites like w3schools.com have a wealth of information on CSS creation.

4. Find your favorite design on CSS Zen Garden (csszengarden.com). Somewhere on the page is a link that says "View This Design's CSS." Click on it and see if you can decipher what the CSS file is doing. Don't worry if there are a lot of things you don't understand. Focus on the things that you *do* understand.

CHAPTER 8

Your First JavaScript Program

So far, we have covered the basics of web page content (using HTML) and presentation (using CSS). As we noted, HTML is a *markup language*, which is used to tell the computer about the structure of text. CSS is HTML's counterpart, acting as a *styling language* to tell the computer how you want the HTML to look. These are both limited, special-purpose document languages. They tell the computer about the static structure of a document, or set of documents, but not how to perform any function or computation. Neither HTML nor CSS is truly a general-purpose **programming language**. Therefore, in order to add interaction and computation to our web pages, we will need to use the JavaScript programming language.

This chapter covers one, short, simple program. However, it is important to read it in detail because we cover a lot of the terminology that we will use when talking about how programs and programming languages work.

8.1 A Short History of JavaScript

JavaScript was created by Brendan Eich in 1995, while he was working for Netscape (Netscape is now known as Mozilla). JavaScript was a revolution in the way that the Web worked because it moved the Web from being primarily a group of interlinked documents to being a truly immersive and interactive environment. Many developers (including myself) were initially skeptical of the usefulness of JavaScript when it first came out. Over the years, however, it has proved its usefulness. When it was first released, several other vendors tried to compete with JavaScript by having their own scripting language. The biggest of these was VBScript, implemented by Microsoft starting in version 3 of Internet Explorer (1996). However, by 2019, VBScript support has been officially removed from all browsers.

© Jonathan Bartlett 2023
J. Bartlett, *Programming for Absolute Beginners*, https://doi.org/10.1007/978-1-4842-8751-4_8

There have been other technologies that also make web pages more dynamic, such as Java, Flash, Silverlight, ActiveX, and other plug-ins, but these have not been nearly as integrated into HTML documents as JavaScript. These other technologies usually work by taking a specific area of your web page away from the browser and handling it itself. JavaScript, on the other hand, works as an integrated part of the web page itself. These other technologies were developed to augment areas where JavaScript fell short, such as animation, video, and integration with other parts of your computer (such as your camera) which are not normally part of the browsing process. JavaScript, however, has been slowly taking over these tasks as well, and today there is hardly any aspect of your browsing experience that isn't available through JavaScript. JavaScript has withstood the test of time and continues to prove its usefulness.

One confusing thing about JavaScript is the name. As mentioned in the previous paragraph, there is another, *different* web programming language called Java. These are not the same thing, nor are they even very similar. It is important to always refer to JavaScript by its full name, because it works and acts significantly different from Java.[1]

Over the years, support and standardization of JavaScript has increased dramatically. In the early days of JavaScript, each browser handled JavaScript very differently, and it was difficult to write JavaScript that worked everywhere. Now, 30 years later, the situation is much improved. JavaScript was standardized by the ECMA under the name ECMAScript. Though it is standardized under a different name, this is the same language as JavaScript.

JavaScript is now by far the most standard way of developing interactive web pages. It is installed on every major browser, and almost all of the inconsistencies between the versions have been worked out. It is also supported by numerous third-party developers who write programming **libraries** (add-in functional modules) that provide JavaScript programmers with the ability to do just about anything imaginable.

---

[1] While Java was originally built as a language which runs in the browser like JavaScript, Java today is primarily used on the server. JavaScript can also be used on the server, but that isn't the focus of this book.

```
<html>
<body>
<h1>Simple JavaScript program</h1>

<script type="text/javascript">

// This is a program in JavaScript

var person_age_string;
var person_age_number;
var age_in_twenty_years;

person_age_string = prompt("What is your age?");
person_age_number = parseInt(person_age_string);
age_in_twenty_years = person_age_number + 20;

alert("In 20 years you will be " + age_in_twenty_years +
   " years old");

</script>
</body>
</html>
```

Figure 8-1. *A Simple Web Page with a JavaScript Program*

8.2 A Simple JavaScript Program

Instead of describing what JavaScript looks like and how it works, we will begin our study of JavaScript by just entering in an example program and *afterward* describing how it works.

Type the program shown in Figure 8-1 into your text editor, and save it as an HTML file.

After entering this program, load it in your browser. It will open up a dialog box asking you what your age is. It will then open up another dialog box telling you what your age will be in 20 years. Pretty simple, right? If your browser did not do these things, double-check to make sure you entered the code in *exactly* the same way it is listed. If it still doesn't work, see Appendix B.6.

So let's look at what this code does.

The first thing to notice is the `<script>` tag. This tag tells the browser that what occurs between the `<script>` start and end tags is JavaScript code. The browser will start running this code as soon as it comes across the end tag, even before it finishes loading the page. There are two possible attributes to the `<script>` tag. The one used here is the `type` attribute, which tells the browser what language the script will be in. This should always be `text/javascript`. The `<script>` tag can take another attribute, `src`, which tells the browser to look in another file (designated by the value of `src`) for the JavaScript code instead of it being in the web page itself.

After the `<script>` tag, there is a JavaScript single-line comment.

```
// This is a program in JavaScript
```

Whenever JavaScript code has two slashes together, from that point to the end of the line is considered a comment and ignored by the browser (see Section 6.6.6 for more information about comments). Another type of comment you will see in JavaScript starts with `/*` and ends with `*/` and is intended for comments which span multiple lines.

The first set of programming statements start with the word `var`:

```
var person_age_string;
var person_age_number;
var age_in_twenty_years;
```

`var` tells JavaScript that we need a temporary storage space, called a **variable**, to hold some data and gives that temporary storage space a name. Therefore, `var person_age_string` says that `person_age_string` is going to be the name of a temporary storage space which we will use to hold data. The way programmers state this is that `var person_age_string` creates a variable called `person_age_string`. This is also referred to as *defining* or **declaring** a variable. When we refer to `person_age_string` later, it will refer to this variable.

After this is a semicolon (`;`). In JavaScript, semicolons are used to separate statements from each other. So when we see a semicolon, we know we have come to the end of a statement.

The next two statements are just like the first, defining the variables `person_age_number` and `age_in_twenty_years`. Notice that we are using underscores (`_`) within the names of our variables. This allows us as programmers to see the words spelled out, but it makes sure that the computer knows that they are all one word. For instance, if I said "I am going to the bus stop," you know that "bus stop" is really one word. However, computers are not that smart. Therefore, if you were talking to a computer, you would need to say, "I am going to the bus_stop" (notice the underscore), so that the computer knows that bus_stop should be treated as one word.

The next statement has a lot more action in it. Here is the code:

```
person_age_string = prompt("What is your age?");
```

There are several important things going on in this line of code. First of all, notice the equal sign (=). In most programming languages (including JavaScript), the equal sign is a *command* that says to put whatever value is on the right side of the equal sign into the variable on the left hand side. It *does not* say that these two things are equal already; it says to *assign* the right-hand value to the left-hand variable. This is known as an **assignment statement**. The left-hand side of this statement is one of the variables we just defined. This statement says that we should put a new value into that variable. The right-hand side of this statement tells what the value should be.

The right-hand side is where things get interesting. `prompt("What is your age?")` tells the computer to put up a dialog box, ask the given question, and then give back the value the user entered. This is called a **function** because it accesses *function*ality that is defined somewhere else. Functions in JavaScript start with the name of the function (`prompt` in this case), then an opening parenthesis (`(`), then the function **parameters**, and then a closing parenthesis (`)`). A *parameter* (also referred to as an **argument**) is a value that is sent to a function that the function uses to carry out its functionality. In this case, the function has one parameter, `"What is your age?"`. This is a character string—a sequence of characters that are all combined together into a single unit (like we discussed in Section 4.4). In JavaScript, a string is enclosed in either double quotes (`"`), single quotes (`'`), or backticks (`` ` ``) and is treated as a single value, although you can also access the characters individually if you need to.[2]

We say that the parameter is *passed to the function* because the function will receive whatever value we put here. The `prompt` function can take either one or two parameters. The first parameter is the text you want to display to the user in front of the input box. The second parameter (which we are not using here) gives a default value to the user. If a function takes more than one parameter, each parameter is separated by a comma (`,`). So, if we wanted to give the user a default age, we would write it like this:

---

[2] The backticks have some additional functionality, but most of that isn't important for the present moment, except that if you want a string to span multiple lines, you will need to use backticks. Strings using single or double quotes should start and end on the same line.

```
prompt("What is your age?", "25")
```

Remember that `prompt` is working with character strings, not numbers, which is why we put our default value in quotes. The code does not continue until the function is finished, which, in this case, means that the user has typed in a value and clicked "OK." When the user does type something, that value is then used as the resulting value of the function. We say that the function *returns* that value.

Therefore, to use the terminology we have discussed so far, we say that the code `prompt("What is your age?")` calls the function `prompt` with a parameter "What is your age?" and returns whatever the user types as the value of that function.

Then, since the `prompt` function returns whatever the user types, the value that the user types gets stored into the variable `person_age_string`. Now, why did we call the variable `person_age_string`? Since we have no control over what the user types, we are getting what he types back as a string. We want the user to type in a number, but in reality he can type anything he wants—there is nothing to prevent him typing nonnumeric characters. Therefore, the `prompt` function always returns a string. Hopefully, the user did what we asked and typed in a number. But no matter what, `prompt` returned a string. We named the variable `person_age_string` so we remember that it is holding a string, not a number.

Now the program needs to add 20 years to whatever age the user typed. That isn't currently possible, because we are holding the *string* that the user typed in, but we need a *number* in order to perform addition. The next line, `person_age_number = parseInt(person_age_string)`, does the conversion we need. `parseInt` is a built-in function that takes a string and **parses** it into a number. *Parsing* is the process of taking a string and converting it into a more computerized representation that is easier for computer programs to manipulate. In this case, we are taking a string and converting (parsing) it into a number. `parseInt` is short for "parse integer," where an **integer** is a whole number (i.e., 1, 2, 3, 4, etc.). If you wanted a number with decimals in it, you would use `parseFloat`, which is short for "parse a floating-point number," with a **floating-point number** being a number with a decimal point in it (i.e., 31.25, 0.002, 23.12, etc.).

We then take the value from the `parseInt` function and store it into the `person_age_number` variable. Now we have the value we need in a variable as a number. Since it is a number, we can perform computations with it!

`age_in_twenty_years = person_age_number + 20` tells the computer to add 20 to the value in the variable `person_age_number` and then store the result in `age_in_twenty_years`. In JavaScript, + and = are considered **operators**, and the values that they operate on are called **operands**. Operators are special built-in operations in the language. They differ from functions because, as we will learn, you can write your own functions, but the operators of a language are essentially fixed. Operators are used to do special tasks (such as assignment) or in places where making a function call would look funny. For math operations, for instance, it is more natural to write 2 + 3 than it is to write something like add(2, 3).

Now we now have the value we are looking for; all we need is to display it. The next line of code displays the value.

```
alert("In 20 years you will be " + age_in_twenty_years + " years old");
```

This piece of code has several strange features. First of all, it uses the plus sign (+) with strings. How would you add strings? Well, in JavaScript, when the plus sign is used with strings, it no longer means addition, but rather **concatenation**. Concatenation means joining two things together. In this case, we are joining strings end-to-end. There is one problem—age_in_twenty_years is not a string but a number! JavaScript handles this automatically by converting anything that is added to a string into a string before the addition takes place. So, the plus sign indicates addition if it has numbers on both sides but concatenation if there is a string on either side of it. In addition, concatenation will convert the other value into a string if it isn't one already.

Another interesting feature of this code is that it combines several operations. It concatenates three items together and then passes the resulting string to the alert function. In most programming languages (including JavaScript), you can combine as many operations and functions as you want together to give you the final value. The innermost operations are performed first, and their results are then passed as inputs to the more outer operations.

Finally, this code introduces the alert function, which displays a popup to the user. The alert function returns when the user clicks on the "OK" button.

☞ PRACTICE QUESTIONS

1. What is a variable and how do you declare it in JavaScript?

2. What are the two different uses of the plus sign in JavaScript?

3. What do the prompt and alert functions do?

☞ **PRACTICE ACTIVITY**

In this activity we will try to modify the program in this section. Be sure that you have the original program working correctly before you begin the activity. Test your program after each step to make sure it is still working. If you wait until the end, and it doesn't work, you won't know where you made the mistake.

1. Add an alert before your prompt that simply says "hello."

2. Change the number of years added to 25. Be sure to change the final alert as well so it says the right thing!

3. Can you figure out how to combine the lines with the `prompt` and `parseInt` into one another so that the output of `prompt` becomes the input of `parseInt`? What variable is no longer needed in this case?

8.3 Moving the JavaScript to Its Own File

Just like CSS, JavaScript can either be embedded within your HTML file or stored in a separate file. My recommendation is to always keep your JavaScript in a separate file unless you have a specific reason to include it in your page. Sometimes the interaction between JavaScript and HTML can lead to unexpected results, such as the browser confusing some parts of your JavaScript with HTML tags. By keeping your JavaScript code in a separate file, these issues are avoided.

```
<!DOCTYPE html>
<html>
<body>
<h1>Simple JavaScript program</h1>

<script type="text/javascript" src="application.js"></script>

</body>
</html>
```

Figure 8-2. *HTML File Referencing External JavaScript*

In order to put your JavaScript into a separate file, all you need to do is copy the code between the `<script>` start and end tags and paste them in a new text document with the extension `.js`. Then, modify your `<script>` tag to have a `src` attribute (keep the `type` attribute the way it is) with the relative URL of your new JavaScript file. If we named our JavaScript file `application.js` and put it in the same folder as our HTML file, the HTML would look like Figure 8-2, and the JavaScript would look like Figure 8-3.

Keeping your JavaScript in a separate file has other advantages as well. First of all, it makes your HTML pages easier to read because they only have one language in them—HTML. By keeping your languages separated in their own files, you keep more of your sanity intact. Another reason is that it allows you to share JavaScript programs and pieces of JavaScript programs between multiple web pages so you don't have to write or copy the same code over and over again. This also means that if you change your code in one place, you don't have to search for and make the same change on every other page, a process which is both tedious and error-prone. If you have a large JavaScript application, separating your JavaScript can actually make your pages load faster because your browser only has to load your JavaScript once rather than have it take up space implanted in the middle of each file.

```javascript
// This is a program in JavaScript

var person_age_string;
var person_age_number;
var age_in_twenty_years;

person_age_string = prompt("What is your age?");
person_age_number = parseInt(person_age_string);
age_in_twenty_years = person_age_number + 20;

alert("In 20 years you will be " + age_in_twenty_years +
    " years old");
```

Figure 8-3. *Short JavaScript File Referenced from HTML*

8.3.1 Review

In this chapter, we covered the absolute basics of how to write a JavaScript program. We have learned the following:

- JavaScript is a general-purpose programming language that allows us to create dynamic web pages.

- ECMAScript is the name for the language used by the group which standardized it, but it is usually still referred to by most people as JavaScript.

- JavaScript can either be included on a page or stored in a separate file.

- JavaScript is designated in web pages using the `<script>` tag.

- Variables are storage locations for values and are declared using the `var` keyword.

- The = operator is used for assigning a value to a variable.

- Functions are named processes that are defined elsewhere.

- Functions can be given values, called parameters (or arguments), which are used by the function when it runs.

- Multiple function parameters are separated by commas.

- When functions complete, the value they give back is called the *return value*.

- JavaScript uses quotes (', ", or ') to signify character strings.

- `prompt` is a function that brings up a dialog box for the user type in a character string and returns that character string.

- `parseInt` is a function that converts a string to a number.

- `alert` is a function that brings up a dialog box with a message.

- The + operator either adds (in the case of numbers) or concatenates (in the case of strings).

8.3.2 **Apply What You Have Learned**

1. Create a new JavaScript program that asks the user for *two* values. Convert these values to integers, and then add these values together and display the result.

2. Try to rewrite the program you just created so that it doesn't use variables. Hint: Make the return value of your functions be the parameter to other functions. It also might help to combine code a piece at a time, eliminating a single variable each time.

3. What happens on these functions if you type in something that isn't a number? What does it display? Why do you think it does that?

PART III

JavaScript Fundamentals

This part covers many of the basic principles of programming needed to start programming in JavaScript.

CHAPTER 9

Basic JavaScript Syntax

All languages, whether human or computer, have what is called a **syntax**. The syntax of a language are the ways in which words and symbols are allowed to go together. For instance, consider the English sentence "I ate the the apple." That sentence has a *syntax error*—I put two "the"s in a row. That's simply not allowed (and nonsensical) in English.

But syntax has a larger role than simply telling you how not to form sentences. It also tells you what a sentence *means*. For instance, if I say, "I have a yellow banana and a red apple," you know that the word "yellow" describes my banana and the word "red" describes my apple. You know that because English syntax tells you what it means for an adjective to be in front of a word—it means that the adjective describes the word.

The syntax of a programming language is very similar. As usual, what makes programming languages different from human ones is that the syntax is stricter and more exact. The computer will never understand what you *mean*, only what you tell it. If I tell you, "I have a banana yellow," you might figure out what I mean. The computer, in most cases, will not.

Note that in order to run the programs in this chapter, you must create an HTML wrapper for them just like you created in Section 8.3. It is recommended that you keep the JavaScript in a separate file and merely reference it through the src attribute of the `<script>` tag.

9.1 Elements of Syntax

While every programming language has its own syntax, there are certain types of syntactical units (i.e., pieces of syntax) which are common to nearly all programming languages. For instance, nearly every programming language has a statement separator—a symbol which tells the programming language that you have ended a statement. In JavaScript (and many other languages), the semicolon (`;`) performs this function. Because programming languages need to know where statements begin and end, most of them include a syntactical unit in the language which says that we are done with a statement.

© Jonathan Bartlett 2023
J. Bartlett, *Programming for Absolute Beginners*, https://doi.org/10.1007/978-1-4842-8751-4_9

119

Standard elements of syntax which are included in JavaScript include:

Literals: A **literal** is how you write a specific value in the language. For instance, in JavaScript, 2 is a literal meaning the number 2, and "2" is a literal meaning the string that has one character, which is the "2" digit. We will discuss how to write different types of literals as we learn what they are. For now, numbers and character strings are the main types of literals we are concerned with.

Identifiers: An **identifier** is a programmer-defined name. The names of variables, for instance, are identifiers. Each programming language has rules as to how identifiers should be named, usually restricting you to only using certain characters for names. In most programming languages, identifiers should not contain spaces, dashes, or other symbolic characters but can contain underscores and should start with a letter. `my identifier` is not a valid identifier, but `my_identifier` is.

Keywords: A **keyword** looks like an identifier, but is defined by the programming language itself. `var` is a keyword that we have seen so far, which indicates that the next identifier will be the name of a new variable. Many syntactical units are indicated by certain keywords. In JavaScript, keywords are also **reserved words**, which means that you are *not allowed* to have an identifier with the same name as a keyword.

Operators: An **operator** is something (usually a symbol like + or -) that performs a task that would be inconvenient or unnatural to write as a function. The values that an operator uses to perform a function are called **operands**. So, for 2 + 3, + is the operator, and 2 and 3 are the operands.

Functions: A **function** is a way of grouping code together to perform as a unit which can be used over and over again. Most languages have both built-in functions provided by the language and a way to define your own functions to perform the tasks that are specific to your project. We will discuss creating functions in more detail in Chapter 10.

Expressions: An **expression** is a combination of functions, keywords, operators, identifiers, and literals which work together to produce a value. For example, 5 + 2 + 3 is an expression that produces the value 10.

Control Structures: A **control structure** (also called a **flow control statement**) is used to modify the flow of a computer program from its normal, sequential nature. For instance, if you wanted to only perform a task if someone checked a certain checkbox, you would need to use a control structure to make sure that it only ran when it was supposed to.

Keep in mind that the goal of this book is to provide you with a practical introduction, not a comprehensive list. There will be aspects of the syntax that we skip over, briefly mention, or oversimplify. In fact, I can guarantee you that if I gave you all of the details, you would put the book down and find something else to do! This is not a hindrance, however. It is actually very rare for a programmer to know all of the details of the syntax for the language they program in. Some of the details cover situations that the programmer would never think to do but are included by the person who created the language for the sake of completeness. So, in any language, you are almost always a student and rarely a master. The few who are masters are usually the ones writing the languages themselves. What is in this book should serve you well for a long time, but keep in mind that there is always more to learn.

9.2 Assignment Statements

In Chapter 8, we covered assignment statements quite a bit. Assignment statements are the foundation of most programming languages.

An example assignment statement is as follows:

```
x = 2 + 3;
```

Assignment statements have two sides—the left-hand side and the right-hand side. The left-hand side is either a variable or, as we will see in Chapter 11, some other reference to a location that can hold a value. For this chapter, the left-hand side of an assignment will be a variable.

The right-hand side of an assignment statement is an *expression*. As already mentioned, an expression is a combination of operators, functions, literals, and identifiers that yield a value. In this case, 2 + 3 yields the value 5. Therefore, the value of the right-hand side is 5. The value that is generated on the right-hand side then gets stored in the left-hand side.

Expressions can be simple—you can just have a literal value (i.e., 2). You can use variables in expressions, too. In fact, you can use the same variable in the expression that receives the assignment. Take a look at the following code:

```
var x;
x = 10; // x currently has the value 10
x = x + 13; // x now has the value 23
```

If you look at the last statement, the expression is x + 13. Since the value of x is currently 10 (the value that was assigned in the previous line), then the value of the expression is 10 + 13, or 23. Since this is an assignment statement, the value of the expression on the right-hand side (23) is now assigned to the variable on the left-hand side (x). Now, the value of x is 23.

Expressions can also be grouped together using parentheses in order to tell the programming language which operations you want to have happen first. For instance, look at the following code:

```
var x;
x = (2 + 10) * 3;
```

Here, 2 + 10 is evaluated first, which gives the value 12, and then 12 * 3 gets evaluated, giving 36. This number (36) is then stored in the variable x.

You can also include functions in your expressions. For instance, we can do the following:

```
var x;
x = "123"; // This is the string "123", not the number 123
var y;
y = parseInt(x) + 12;
```

The last line of this code combines a function call with the + operator. The function call takes the value in x and returns its integer value, and then that value is added to 12, yielding 135.

Expressions can also be contained within a function's arguments. Take a look at the following code:

```
var x;
x = parseInt("12" + "3");
```

Here we have "12" + "3" as an expression which yields the value "123" (because "12" and "3" are both strings). This then gets passed into the parseInt function, which then yields the *number* 123, which is then stored in x.

9.3 Control Structures

Control structures modify the flow of your program. Normally, you think of your program as going step-by-step, one statement to the next. Control structures are syntactical units which cause the flow of your program to be altered in some way. The two basic control structures that every programming language has to modify that flow are *conditional branching*, which causes the computer to perform either one section of code or another based on a condition, and *looping*, which causes the computer to perform a section of code repeatedly (the number of repetitions will depend on specified conditions).

9.3.1 The if Statement

The if statement is the primary way that JavaScript programmers do conditional branching.

The if statement has the following basic form:

```
if (some_condition) {
    // Put the code to perform if some_condition is true here
} else {
    // Put the code to perform if some_condition is not true here
}
```

First notice the use of curly braces ({ and }). In JavaScript, curly braces are used to group statements together into **blocks**. The if statement potentially has two blocks—one to perform if the condition is true and one to perform if the condition is false (preceded with the else keyword). You can put any number of statements inside the blocks.

```
var my_age;

// Prompt for an age and convert it into an integer
my_age = parseInt(prompt("What is your age?"));

if(my_age > 17) {
    alert("You are old enough to vote!");
} else {
    var years_to_vote;
    years_to_vote = 18 - my_age;
    alert("You have " + years_to_vote +
        " years left before you can vote.");
}
```

Figure 9-1. *An Example* if *Statement*

The second thing to notice is the some_condition after the if statement. if statements use **conditional expressions** to decide which block to perform. A conditional expression is just like any other expression, except, rather than the value of the expression being a number or a string, it is a **boolean** value. A boolean value is simply a value that is either true or false. Boolean expressions usually compare two values to determine if they are equal or if one is greater than the other or some similar operation that can be true or false.

To make it more clear, Figure 9-1 shows a program that uses an if statement. In this example, the conditional expression is my_age > 17. What this does is look at the variable my_age, and if the value of my_age is greater than 17, then the value of the expression is true. If the value of my_age is not greater than 17, then the value of the expression is false. The > operator works just like the math operators, except that the value it gives is a boolean (true/false) value rather than a number value.

Notice what happens in the code. If you your age is over 17, then it just gives an alert. However, if your age is 17 or under, it then performs multiple tasks—first, it performs a calculation to see how many years you have left before you can vote, and after that it displays the answer. The programming language knows which statements to execute together based on the condition because they are combined into blocks.

Common boolean operators (operators which yield true or false) include the following:

Operator	Meaning	Examples
==	Equality	2 == 2 yields true; 2 == 3 yields false
!=	Inequality	2 != 2 yields false; 2 != 3 yields true
<	Less than	2 < 2 yields false; 1 < 2 yields true
>	Greater than	2 > 2 yields false; 3 > 2 yields true
>=	Greater than or equal to	2 >= 2 yields true; 1 >= 2 yields false
<=	Less than or equal to	2 <= 2 yields true; 3 <= 2 yields false
===	Strict equality	2 == "2" yields true but 2 === "2" yields false.

Oftentimes, conditions need to be combined. Let's say that we want to know if *both* of these are true—you are exactly 18 years old and your name is Fred. You could do this in one of two ways. The first way is to embed one if statement inside another one, like this:

```
var my_age;
var my_name;

my_name = prompt("What is your name?");
my_age = parseInt(prompt("What is your age?"));

if(my_age == 18) {
   if(my_name == "Fred") {
      alert("Your name is Fred and you are 18!");
   }
}
```

Note that, first, I don't have an else branch on these if statements. The else branch is actually optional. If the condition is false, and there is no else branch, it will just skip it and go on to the next statement. The other thing to note is that we can have an if statement within a code block on a condition. In JavaScript, *any* code can go within these blocks.

However, this takes a lot of typing. It would be nicer if we could combine the two `if` statements into a single statement. We can do this by combining the boolean expressions. Boolean expressions can be combined with two operators, && (which is pronounced "and") and || (which is pronounced as "or"). && yields a true value if *both* of its operands are true, and || yields a true value if *either* of its operands are true. We can therefore combine these statements into a single `if` statement using &&:

```
var my_age;
var my_name;

my_name = prompt("What is your name?");
my_age = parseInt(prompt("What is your age?"));

if(my_age == 18 && my_name == "Fred") {
    alert("Your name is Fred and you are 18!");
}
```

The one other boolean operator that we need to cover is the ! (pronounced "not") operator. The ! operator, instead of having two operands, only has one, which appears on the right side of the operator. This operator returns the *opposite* of whatever boolean value is on its right. It is also best to use the ! operator with parentheses so it is obvious to you, to the computer, and to other people reading your code what expression you are applying it to.

So, for instance, if I wanted to find out if the variable `my_value` is not between 3 and 10, I can write `!(my_value >= 3 && my_value <= 10)`. The expression in parentheses will yield true if the value is within range, and then the ! operator will cause it to return the opposite.

9.3.2 The `while` Statement

Now that we've looked at conditional statements with the `if` statement, it is now time to look at looping statements. Loops are used to repeat a section of code a certain number of times or until a certain condition is reached. Let's say you have a quiz game, and you want someone to keep trying answers until they got the right one. You would use a loop because you would want the code to keep asking them the question and reading answers until they reach the right answer. In other words, you would want them to *repeat* the code that asks the question and checks the answer.

The most basic looping structure in JavaScript is the while statement. The while statement's overall structure looks like this:

```
while(some_condition) {
    // Perform tasks here
}
```

The while statement tells JavaScript to repeat the code in the given block until some_condition is false. It checks some_condition before each time it runs the block of code, and, if the condition is true, it runs the loop. If the condition is false, then it considers the loop completed and moves on to the next part of the code.

Here is an example program with a while loop that will repeat until the user enters the right value:

```
var answer;

while(answer != "Genesis") {
    answer = prompt("What is the first book in the Bible?");
}
alert("You got the answer right!");
```

What this will do is start out by creating a variable called answer. Unless otherwise specified, variables in JavaScript when they are created are given a special empty value that is called undefined. After creating the variable, the code starts the while loop. When it first starts, it evaluates its condition, known as the **loop condition**. The condition is answer != "Genesis". This checks to see if the variable answer is different from the character string "Genesis". Indeed, undefined is different from "Genesis", so the condition is true. This means that we can proceed with the loop.

After the loop condition comes a block of statements wrapped in curly braces known as the **loop body**. These statements are executed if the loop condition is true. Within this loop, there is only one statement, which asks the user to answer a question and stores the result in the answer variable. When the computer is done executing the body of the loop, it reevaluates the loop condition again to see if we should run the loop again or if we are done.

Let's say that the user had erroneously answered the question by typing in "Exodus." What would happen? answer would have the value "Exodus". When it evaluates the loop condition, answer != "Genesis" would still returns true. Therefore, it would run the loop body again.

Now let's say that this time they type in "Genesis" as they should. What happens now? Well, `"Genesis"` gets put into `answer`. Now the loop body is complete again, so it reevaluates the loop condition. This time, the condition `answer != "Genesis"` is false! When the loop condition is false, it transfers control to the first instruction after the loop body. In this case, that instruction tells the user that they entered the right value.

One thing to be careful of when writing loops is to make sure that the loop condition can, eventually, evaluate to false. Otherwise, what will happen? It will loop forever! In computer terms, this is known as an **infinite loop**. You should always double-check to make sure that your loops will eventually terminate. We will cover infinite loops more in the next section.

```
var num = 1; // This holds the next number to add
var sum = 0; // This holds the sum total so far

while(num <= 6) { // Check if we are done
   // Add the next number to the sum
   sum = sum + num;

   // Go to the next number
   num = num + 1;
}

alert("The sum of the numbers 1 through 6 is " + sum);
```

Figure 9-2. *Adding Up the Numbers 1 Through 6 with a* while *Loop*

9.3.3 The for Statement

One common reason for a loop is to perform a computation a specified number of times. Let's say that we wanted to write a program that added up all of the numbers between 1 and 6. This can be easily accomplished through a loop. Figure 9-2 shows how we would accomplish that with a while loop.

The way that this works is that it begins by putting starting values in each variable. This is known as **initializing** the variables. Oftentimes a program succeeds or fails based on whether or not the variables were initialized to the right values. In this case, num is set to the first number we want to add in our sum. The variable sum is set to zero. It is set to zero because that is the state of a sum before anything gets added to it—a sum of nothing is zero.

Next the loop condition is evaluated. Yes, num is less than or equal to 6 since its value is 1. Next, that number is added to sum and assigned back into sum, which is now 1. The next part is the most important part—you add 1 to num and store it back into num to move it to the next number. The value of num is now 2. Notice that even though it is still less than or equal to 6, it is a step closer to terminating the loop. Now we repeat the loop condition and loop body again. At the end of the next iteration through the loop, the value of num is, again, a step closer to terminating the loop.

After running the loop body six times, the value of num is 7, which will terminate the loop and give the answer.

Now take a minute to think—what would happen if we accidentally left off the code which added 1 to num at the end of the loop? num would never increase, and so it would *always* be 1, and therefore num <= 6 would *always* be true and the loop would never, ever finish. A loop that never finishes is known as an **infinite loop**. An infinite loop could lock up your browser or, even worse, your whole computer.

When you have a simple loop like this, where there is a single variable which is used to manage whether or not the loop repeats, that variable is called the **loop control variable**. In a while loop, the loop termination condition is separated from the location where we increment the loop control variable. In yet another location is the place where the loop control variable gets initialized. Having these important parts of the loop in different places can be dangerous as we can easily forget to include one or more parts of the loop control.

However, another flow control statement is available which, for simple loops, keeps all of the steps for managing the control variable in one spot. This statement is the for statement.

The structure of the for statement is like this:

```
for(loop_control_variable_initialization; loop_condition;
    loop_control_variable_modification) {
    // Loop Body
}
```

The three places where we used the control variable are now all packaged together in one location in the for statement. This makes the process of writing simple loops much less error-prone. So, if we rewrite our previous program using a for statement, it looks like Figure 9-3.

As you can see, everything we do with our loop control variable is contained. This syntax allows you to better manage your loop control variables by keeping all of the management code in one place. It also makes the code easier to read. while statements are still very important, especially for more complicated loops with more complicated conditions and controls. However, most of the time you can get away with using a for loop.

```
var sum = 0;
for(var num = 1; num <= 6; num = num + 1) {
    sum = sum + num;
}
alert("The sum of the numbers 1 through 6 is " + sum);
```

Figure 9-3. *Add Numbers 1 Through 6 Using a* for *Statement*

9.3.4 Review

In this chapter, we covered the basics of JavaScript syntax. We have learned the following:

- Syntax is the way that the structure of a program or sentence indicates its meaning.

- Every language has its own unique syntax.

- Types of syntactical units which are common to many programming languages include literals, identifiers, keywords, operators, functions, expressions, and control structures.

- An expression is a sequence of literals, identifiers, operators, and functions which combine to yield a value.

- JavaScript assignment statements have a right-hand side, which contains an expression which gives the value to be assigned, and a left-hand side that says where (in what variable) the value should be placed.

- Control structures are statements which modify the flow of your program.

- The two most common ways for a control structure to modify the flow of your program are by conditional branching and looping.

- The `if` statement is the primary method of conditional branching in JavaScript.

- Most looping in JavaScript is accomplished through either `while` statements or `for` statements.

- The basic structures of a loop are the loop initializers, the loop condition, and the loop body.

- Simple loops are focused around a single loop control variable, which is used in all three parts of the loop's structure.

- The `for` loop allows the programmer to collect all of the manipulation of the loop control variable into a single location, which is easier for the programmer to do correctly and easier for others to read and understand.

- Multiple statements can be placed in the body of a conditional branching statement or a looping statement. The curly braces denote which statements belong in the body of the control structure, which is known as a block.

- Conditional branching statements and loop statements can be placed inside of other branching and looping statements as well for more complex processing.

- The `var` statement can also be combined with an assignment statement to provide an initial value for the variable.

9.3.5 Apply What You Have Learned

1. Enter the code for the quiz game in Section 9.3.2. Be sure to create an HTML file that loads the JavaScript code. Verify that the game works.

2. Create your own quiz game with at least three questions.

3. Add additional code to this game to give someone hints if they answer a question incorrectly. If this is your first time programming, this may be harder than you think. Think through exactly how the program is running and what you would need to do to get it to give hints in the right place. Depending on how you decide to do it, you may need to embed an `if` statement within the body of your loop.

4. Enter the code for adding up the numbers 1 through 6 in Section 9.3.3. Be sure to create an HTML file that loads the JavaScript code. Verify that it works.

5. Modify the code so that you ask the user what number range they want to use for the additions. Don't forget to use `parseInt`!

6. In the previous example, it might be possible for someone to enter an invalid range (i.e., the start of the number range is greater than the end of the number range). Add `if` statements to account for this, either by alerting the user or just fixing the problem.

CHAPTER 10

Introducing Functions and Scope

In the previous chapter, we learned about the nuts and bolts of how programming works, with assignment statements, conditional branching, and loops. For small programs, this is all you need. In fact, you can do any possible computation you might need to do with only these features. However, as your programs get larger—even just a little bit larger— you will need tools that will enable you to get more work done with each line of code and to organize your code into logical blocks. Imagine, for instance, if your program was 10,000 lines long. If you needed to change a line, it might be hard to find!

Likewise, let's say there was a task that you had to do over and over again. If you had to type out the code for it each time, that would be a lot of wasted effort! In addition, let's say that you found an error (known as a **bug**) in your code that you had been copying. If you had 20 copies of the code, you would have to find each copy and fix it. This is tedious, wasteful, and error-prone.

What we need to do is to take sections of code and package them up into a unit. Doing this will make our code both better organized and reusable. Most programming languages use **functions** to organize and reuse sections of code.

```
var square_a_number = function(num) {
   var value = num * num;
   return value;
};

alert("The square of 3 is " + square_a_number(3));
alert("The square of 4 is " + square_a_number(4));
```

Figure 10-1. *An Example of Using Functions*

© Jonathan Bartlett 2023
J. Bartlett, *Programming for Absolute Beginners*, https://doi.org/10.1007/978-1-4842-8751-4_10

10.1 Your First Function

You already have some experience with functions. Remember parseInt, prompt, and alert? These are known as **built-in** functions because they are part of JavaScript itself. However, you can define your own functions that you can call in the same way.

To begin our discussion of functions, let me show you a simple program that illustrates how functions work. Remember to wrap this and the other programs in this chapter in an HTML file like we described in Section 8.3. Figure 10-1 shows the code. What this program does is define a function which takes a single value and returns that value squared (i.e., multiplied by itself). It then uses that function twice, giving it different numbers to square.

The function in this code is defined using the function keyword. After the function keyword comes a parameter list—a list in parentheses of all of the parameters that the function can take. The function we are defining takes a single parameter, which we have named num. This means that the value that is sent to the function gets stored into num for the duration of the function, so we have a name to call it by. Since it is in the parameter list, we do not use the var keyword to define it.

In short, function(num) tells JavaScript to define a function that takes a single parameter and name that parameter num. When we use num within the function, we will be working with whatever value was sent when the program was called. We could have used any valid name instead of num, but num seemed like an appropriate name for a number.

Inside the curly braces is the block of code that defines what the function will do. In this case, we are creating a new variable called value, multiplying num by itself, and then storing it into value. Then, the return statement tells JavaScript what to give back to the code that called our function. In this program, the return statement says that the result currently in value should be given as the result for the function.

The function operator defines a function. However, we need to be able to call the function from our code. It therefore needs a name. How do we name something in JavaScript? We store it in a variable. As you can see in the code, we are storing the function in a variable we created named square_a_number. As usual, don't forget the semicolon (;) at the end of the assignment statement, or JavaScript might get confused.

Now that we have the variable square_a_number which contains our function, we can call it exactly like we called other functions like parseInt. square_a_number(5) will yield 25, and square_a_number(6) will yield 36.

☞ **PRACTICE QUESTIONS**

---

1. In the same file as the `square_a_number` function, define another function called `cube_a_number` that returns the cube of a number (i.e., the number times itself and times itself again).

2. Call the `alert` function a few times giving it the results of the `cube_a_number` function, like we did for `square_a_number`.

3. The body of the `square_a_number` function creates a variable called `value` to store the temporary result of the calculation. However, because the calculation is so simple, we don't really need this variable. Can you rewrite `square_a_number` so that it doesn't use a variable?

4. Change the program so that it asks the user to type in a number, then call `square_a_number` to calculate the square, and then show the result to the user.

5. Take the program you've just written and put the interactions with the user in a `for` loop that runs three times so that it will ask the user for a number and give the result three times.

6. Change the loop from a `for` loop to a `while` loop, and perform the operation until the user enters a zero for the number to square.

```
var sum_range = function(range_start, range_end) {
  var sum = 0;
  for(var num = range_start; num <= range_end; num = num + 1) {
    sum = sum + num;
  }
  return sum;
};

var start_val = parseInt(prompt("Enter the first number"));
var end_val = parseInt(prompt("Enter the last number"));
var result = sum_range(start_val, end_val);
alert("The sum of all of the numbers between " + start_val + " and " +
  end_val + " is " + result);
```

Figure 10-2. *A Function with an Embedded* `while` *Loop*

10.2 More Function Examples

To make sure that you grasp the concept of a function, let's do another example. Let's say that we wanted to have a function that summed up a range of numbers, like all of the numbers between 2 and 12. This would be similar to the code we wrote in Section 9.3.3, but it would take the start and end values as parameters. How would we write that? Well, we would need a function, but that function would also need to have a loop inside of it to loop through all of the numbers from the start to the finish. The code would look like Figure 10-2.

This function has a few differences from our previous function. First of all, it has two parameters instead of one—range_start and range_end. Functions can have as many parameters as you want. It can even have zero, which would be indicated by writing function(). In this case, we need two values because we need both a start and an end value for the range. In JavaScript, parameters are *positional*, which means that the order that you define them with the function keyword is the same order as the values that you have to give when the function is called. In other words, since range_start is the first parameter, the first value in the function call gets placed here. Since range_end is the second parameter, the second value that is sent to the function call gets placed here. So, calling sum_range(start_val, end_val) tells JavaScript to run the function sum_range, put the value of start_val into range_start, and put the value of end_val into range_end. It then runs the function and returns the value, which, in this case, is placed in the variable result. Next, we have a for loop embedded in the function. Just like any block of code in JavaScript, we can embed any type of statement or operator within a function.

For this small program, since we only use the sum_range program once, it doesn't save us a lot of typing. But can you see how, if we needed it in several different parts of the program and used it over and over again, putting that code into a function will save a lot of typing and headaches in the future?

Even though this example doesn't save us any typing, using functions still has a distinct advantage—it separates out different components of our application. In this program, we have both user interaction (prompting, receiving input, and displaying output) and computation (summing all of the numbers in a range). By putting the computation in a function, we have made both parts clearer.

Imagine if we had simply stuck all of the code together without a function. It might be difficult to even understand what the program was trying to do. Instead, by separating out a piece into a function with an easy-to-understand name (i.e., sum_range), then we make it clearer what the whole program is doing. You can look at it and say, "Oh yes, this piece of code with the name sum_rage sums up numbers within a range. And look! Over here we use the function with the two inputs from the user."

Again, this is not as big of an issue with small programs, but when you write programs with many thousands of lines of code, having the code broken up into manageable, understandable components, each with a small, well-defined task makes the code much easier to understand and modify.

In general, separating out the user interface from the computation is a good idea in computer programming. This leads to a number of long-term benefits for the program itself. Many times in computer programming, user interfaces will change regularly even when the underlying logic stays the same. Therefore, having the core logic separated from its interface makes it easier for the program to grow and change without causing undue headaches. Oftentimes programs will have more than one user interface into the logic or perhaps a user interface and an interface that is used by outside programs. Here, separating out the core logic makes it so that this logic will not have to be repeated in each interface. Additionally, it is a good practice to write tests to make sure your code works. Testing core logic is usually more straightforward than testing user interfaces, so writing the core logic separately allows it to be more easily tested.

👉 PRACTICE QUESTIONS

1. Create a function that takes three parameters and returns the largest of the three parameters. You will have to use several if statements to accomplish this.

2. Create a function called multiply which will take two parameters and perform the same function as the * (multiplication) operator. However, don't use the * operator in your code. Instead, perform the task by repeated adding of the first parameter. Be sure to include code to run the function and display the result so that you know whether you did it correctly!

10.3 Functions Calling Functions

Functions can also call other functions. For instance, we can create a new function called sum_squares_for_range that is similar to the sum_range function, but, instead of summing up the numbers in the range, it calls square_a_number on each number to sum up the squares of the numbers in the range. Before looking at the code (Figure 10-3), think about how you might implement such a function.

As you can see, just as we can call a function from anywhere else in our program, we can call a function from within a function as well. Using this feature, we can make functions that are more and more complex. We can take several small functions that we often use together and write a larger function that combines them in an interesting and useful way. Likewise, if we have a large function that is difficult to understand, we can try to break the function up into well-defined pieces and create individual functions for those pieces.

10.4 Variable Scopes

Now that we know how functions work in JavaScript, we need to talk about **variable scope**. The scope of a variable refers to the locations within a program where the variable is created, is active and available for use, and is destroyed. In some of the earliest programming languages, all variables had **global** scope—meaning that the variable always existed throughout the whole program and was accessible everywhere within the program. However, this can quickly lead to problems. We have created temporary variables several times already to hold intermediate values, such as the sum variable in the sum_range function. If all of your variables have global scope, when you call one function from another function, if both of them use the same name for a temporary variable, then your temporary result will be overwritten by the other function!

```
var square_a_number = function(num) {
  var value = num * num;
  return value;
};

var sum_squares_for_range = function(range_start, range_end) {
  var sum = 0;
  for(var num = range_start; num <= range_end; num = num + 1) {
    sum = sum + square_a_number(num);
  }
  return sum;
};
alert("The sum of squares between 2 and 5 is " + sum_squares_for_range(2,
  5));
```

Figure 10-3. *A Function Calling Another Function*

If all variables had global scope, the only way to avoid this situation is to make sure that each variable had a unique name. This would be tedious and time-consuming, both to keep track of the variable names and to write the inevitably excessively long names that would result. Programming languages quickly adopted new scoping policies that allowed programmers more freedom.

The type of scoping that JavaScript does for variables declared using var inside a function is called **function scope**. This means that in addition to the global scope, each function has a unique, separate scope. If we declare a variable var myvar outside of a function, that variable exists within the global scope and is called a **global variable**. Since it is global, I can access myvar from *anywhere in my program*. If we instead declared var myvar from *inside* a function, then myvar would only be available *within that function*. Such variables are often called **local variables**. Parameters to functions also act as if they were local variables in the function's scope.

```
var myvar = 3; // Global variable

var my_function = function() {
    myvar = 5; // Writing to a global variable
};

alert("myvar = " + myvar);
my_function();
alert("After calling my_function, myvar = " + myvar);
```

Figure 10-4. *Modifying Global Variables*

```
var myvar = 3; // Global variable

var my_function = function() {
    var myvar = 5; // This version of myvar is now *local*
};

alert("myvar = " + myvar);
my_function();
alert("After calling my_function, myvar = " + myvar);
```

Figure 10-5. *Global and Local Variables*

To illustrate this, Figure 10-4 shows a program in which we modify a global variable inside the function. In this code, when it starts, it creates myvar as a global variable (it is defined outside of any function) and sets it to 3. Then, it calls my_function(). This function sets myvar to 5 and then returns. Now, when we show the variable again, it has the value 5.

Contrast that to what happens in the program in Figure 10-5. In this example, because myvar has the var keyword in front of it in the function, it creates a local variable that is specific to that function. It exists nowhere else. Even though there is a myvar that exists in the global scope, during the function myvar will refer to the local variable with the same name. Therefore, setting the local variable myvar from inside the function has no effect on the global scope. Both alerts will give the same value because the modification happened to a local variable.

Additionally, if there was another function that also had a locally scoped `myvar`, it would be a different variable than either the globally scoped `myvar` or the `myvar` that is locally scoped to this function. Each function's local variables belong to that function and cannot even be referenced outside of that function.

Having local scopes allows functions to work as "black boxes," meaning that the person who writes the code that calls a function doesn't have to care about the details of how that function is implemented. If we only had the global scope, then, before I called a function, I would need to go and look up all of the variables it was using to make sure I wasn't also using the same variable. However, if a function writer only uses local variables, then if I used that function in my program, I wouldn't have to worry that it might accidentally overwrite a variable I am using. This is true in larger programs even if there is only one programmer. You will not remember the names of every variable you use in your functions. But, if you make sure that you only use local variables and parameters within your functions, you won't need to remember all of the variable names since they will all be within the scope of the given function.

Occasionally, you will need to use the global scope. In fact, this is what we are doing on the names of the functions themselves—we are storing them in global variables. In JavaScript, functions are stored in variables just like any other value. Therefore, in order for functions to call each other, they must exist in the global scope. You can also define a function inside of another function, but we will save that discussion for Chapter 14.

10.4.1 Review

In this chapter we discussed what a function is and how we can use functions in our code. We have learned the following:

- The `function` operator creates a function.

- A function takes parameters, which are variables that refer to values passed to the function.

- Function parameters are positional, which means that the order that they are defined using the `function` operator is the same order that the function call must use.

- A function has a function body, which is the code that tells the computer what to do when the function is called.

- Functions are stored in named variables so that they can be easily called. Programmers usually store functions in global variables so that the function is accessible from anywhere in the program.

- Functions can call other functions.

- Functions can be used to organize your code into well-defined, understandable units.

- Functions can be used to minimize the amount of code that needs to be written by moving repeated sections of code into a function.

- When repeated code sections are moved into a function, this also makes it easier to fix bugs as they only need to be fixed in one place.

- A variable's scope refers to the period when a variable becomes active and the places from which it can be accessed.

- Variables in the global scope can be accessed from anywhere in your code.

- Variables in a function's local scope can only be accessed from within that function.

- If a function has a local variable with the same name as a global variable, the global variable is hidden from view during that function.

- If two functions have a local variable with the same name, these refer to two *different* variables because they each exist in different scopes.

10.4.2 Apply What You Have Learned

With the knowledge you have learned so far, you can now start making real programs. Remember your tools—`if`, `while`, `for`, and `function`—and you will be able to make all of the following programs.

1. Create a Celsius-to-Fahrenheit converter. It should ask the user for a Celsius temperature and return a Fahrenheit temperature. The conversion from Celsius to Fahrenheit is to multiply the Celsius temperature by 9, divide the result by 5, and add 32. Be sure that the actual conversion is contained within a function.

2. Create a fuel efficiency calculator. It should ask for the number
    of miles you drove, how many gallons you used, and the price
    per gallon of fuel. It should then tell you the number of dollars
    per mile that it cost you to drive. The formula for this is to take
    the price per gallon, multiply by the gallons, and divide by the
    number of miles. Be sure that the formula is handled in a function.

3. Implement the factorial function. The factorial function takes a
    number and multiplies together every number from 1 to the given
    number. For instance, the factorial of 6 is 6 * 5 * 4 * 3 * 2 * 1.
    The factorial of 3 is 3 * 2 * 1. Note that since you are repeating
    an operation, you will need a loop. Be sure that your factorial
    calculation is written in a function. Write a user interface that
    allows the user to enter the number they want the factorial of.

4. Take any one of these calculators and make it so that the user can
    enter as many values as they want. You can do this by either asking
    the user afterward if they want to keep going or have a special
    value that the user types to signal that they are done. In any case,
    make it so that the user can keep using the application until they
    are ready to be finished.

CHAPTER 11

Grouping Values Together with Objects and Arrays

So far, while programming, we have basically been dealing with simple values, such as individual numbers and strings. However, when writing computer programs, you usually have to deal with multiple values grouped together. For instance, think about a bank transaction—what values would you need to store? You would need to know when the transaction happened, how much the transaction was for, who sent the money, and who received the money. Therefore, you would need, at minimum, four values—the timestamp of the transaction, the amount, the account number it was coming from, and the account number that it was going to.

Now we could represent this with four separate variables. We could have something like this:

```
var transaction_timestamp;
var transaction_amount;
var transaction_from_account;
var transaction_to_account;
```

Writing it in this way, if we had to pass these variables into a function, we would have to pass them as four separate parameters. Imagine if we then added additional data that went with the transaction, such as a transfer fee and the currency that the transfer is in. The number of variables we need to move around has now gone up to 6! Not only that, every function that touches the data would have to be rewritten to take the extra parameters!

This is not an unusual situation. In many programs, there may be several dozen values that all relate to each other. Passing them around as individual values can quickly get out-of-control.

© Jonathan Bartlett 2023
J. Bartlett, *Programming for Absolute Beginners*, https://doi.org/10.1007/978-1-4842-8751-4_11

11.1 A Basic Introduction to Objects

In order to package pieces of data together, JavaScript uses **objects**. An object is simply a collection of named values. It's like packaging up several variables into a single unit.

Going back to our bank transaction example, I could package all of those variables up into a single variable which has named values for each component. Unlike some programming languages, JavaScript does not care how many values you pack into an object, and you don't even have to tell JavaScript what they will be ahead of time. You usually start with an empty object and simply stash whatever values you want in there using whatever names you want. That doesn't mean that the names don't matter—it matters a great deal since that is how you will be keeping track of them, but JavaScript itself does not care.

Objects in JavaScript can be generated in a variety of ways. The first way we will look at is using the new keyword. To get a blank object, you simply type in `new Object()`.

```
var my_transaction = new Object();
```

Objects themselves are values and can be stored in variables and used in expressions just like any other value.

Now, let's look at how we assign values to objects:

```
var my_transaction = new Object();
my_transaction.timestamp = "2014-02-05";
my_transaction.amount = 1000;
my_transaction.from_account = "12345";
my_transaction.to_account = "54321";
```

JavaScript stores values in objects based on their name. These values are often called **attributes** or **properties** of the object. So, when you type `mytransaction.amount`, that tells JavaScript to look up the `amount` property of the `mytransaction` object.

This is the information we would need for a bank transaction. However, a transaction needs information about the accounts, too. What would a bank *account* object look like? Such an object would need the account number, the name of the person on the account, and their current balance. Therefore, we might have an object that looks like this:

```
var my_account = new Object();
my_account.account_number = "12345";
my_account.owner = "Fred Fredston";
my_account.current_balance = 1200;
```

Now let's say that I want to define a function that processes a transaction against an account. What I want it to do is to take my_transaction and apply it to my_account (i.e., give the money in my_transaction to the balance in my_account). To do this, I can create a function, which takes the two objects, picks out the values it needs, and processes the transaction. If the account number matches the from_account of the transaction, it removes the money from the account, and if it matches the to_account of the transaction, it gives the money to the account. Figure 11-1 shows what this looks like.

Now I can call this function by typing process_transaction(my_account, my_transaction);. Notice that we didn't have to pass in every value; we only had to pass in the objects which *contained* the values we needed.

Another important point is that when we passed in objects, we could actually *modify* the object that we were receiving. Note that this function doesn't return a value. Instead, the function modifies the account object itself. The result is the modification of the object, not the return value. This is known as a **mutating function** because it modifies (i.e., mutates) the objects passed as parameters rather than return a value. Mutating, however, only works with objects. Basic values (i.e., numbers, strings, etc.) passed directly as parameters cannot be modified like this.

Note that if a function doesn't have a return value, it returns the special value undefined, which means "no value."

In any case, objects allow functions to manipulate values, not just process them. When we were just passing in numbers and strings, even if we modified the parameter variable, it wouldn't modify the value in the sending function. Now that we are using objects, we can modify the *properties* of any object passed in. However, we cannot replace the whole object with a new one, though we can modify all of its properties.

```
var process_transaction = function(account, transaction) {
   if(account.account_number == transaction.from_account) {
      account.current_balance = account.current_balance -
         transaction.amount;
   } else {
      if(account.account_number == transaction.to_account) {
         account.current_balance = account.current_balance +
            transaction.amount;
      } else {
         // Do nothing
      }
   }
};
```

Figure 11-1. *A Function Taking Two Objects*

👉 PRACTICE QUESTIONS

1. Find a product catalog (of any kind). Look through the catalog. List out the data fields that it has for each catalog item. Pick out two catalog items to use for the rest of this practice.

2. Create a program that builds two objects—one for each item you picked out. It should use the fields you listed in the previous step (feel free to skip fields if they are complex fields, such as an image). Use an alert function to show some of the pieces of data you have put in your objects.

3. Create a function that displays all of the information about a single item that takes one parameter—the item to display. It should display each property defined on that object. Then call that function for each item.

4. Create a function that asks the user for the values to be placed in that object and then returns a new object with those values assigned to properties on that object.

11.2 Simplifying Object Creation

Now, because JavaScript programmers create objects using new Object() all of the time, JavaScript has a special syntax that allows you to create a new object more quickly and easily: {}. This, just like new Object(), creates a new, blank object. Therefore, we could have started our code with this instead:

```
var my_transaction = {};
my_transaction.timestamp = "2014-02-05";
my_transaction.amount = 1000;
```

However, {} has a few more tricks available as well. You can actually use it to specify a set of starting attributes at the beginning, so you don't have to assign them one-by-one. The syntax looks like this:

```
var my_transaction = {
    timestamp: "2014-02-05",
    amount: 1000,
    from_account: "12345",
    to_account: "54321"
};
```

As you can see, with this syntax, in between the { and }, there are sets of named values that will be our object properties. Each property name is followed by a colon and the value of the property we are trying to set. This makes initializing objects much faster and cleaner than the long way. Keep in mind that the names of properties should generally be limited to the same types of names that are allowed for variables (i.e., don't put spaces, dashes, or special characters in the property names).

☞ PRACTICE QUESTIONS

Modify the practice work of the previous section to use the shorter object creation syntax.

11.3 Storing Sequences of Values Using Arrays

So far we have dealt with objects, which are collections of named values. In this section, we are going to talk about **arrays**, which are *ordered sequences* of values.

In Section 4.3, we talked about how computers stored sequences of values. In short, it stores the number of things in the sequence, and then it stores the values themselves. Such a structure in JavaScript is called an array. Arrays in JavaScript aren't quite stored the way that we talked about in Section 4.3, but that is nonetheless a helpful way to think about them.

Why would we need a sequence of values? Let's say I wanted to store the ages of my children. I *could* do that with an object, but it would be rather awkward. With an object, I could do this:

```
var children_ages = {
    first_child: 11,
    second_child: 8,
    third_child: 7
};
```

That somewhat works, but it would be hard to use such a structure. For instance, if I wanted to write out each of their ages, it would be hard to write a loop to go through each child and write out their ages, especially if I didn't know how many children there were ahead of time.

An array, on the other hand, allows us to define ordered sequences of values. So, instead of our awkward object, we could write something more elegant like this:

```
var children_ages = new Array();
children_ages[0] = 11;
children_ages[1] = 8;
children_ages[2] = 7;
```

In this code, children_ages is first assigned a blank array—that's what new Array() does. The first line tells JavaScript to make an empty sequence of values and store it in the variable children_ages. In the next line, we tell JavaScript that the first value in the sequence should be 11. The [ ] notation says that we need to use the number inside the brackets to tell us which element of the array we are referring to and, if it doesn't exist yet, to create it.[1] Elements in an array are referred to by their **index** number. Index numbers *start at zero* (not one) and go up from there.[2] Therefore, [0] says to refer to the first member of the array.

The code `children_ages[0] = 11;` tells JavaScript to look in the `children_ages` array and try to find the first value, and it will create one if it doesn't already exist. Next, it will look at the right-hand side of the equal sign and see what the value of the expression is. In this case, the value is 11 so it stores the number 11 at index 0 of `children_ages`.

The same thing happens with index 1 and 2. At the end of the code, there are three values in `children_ages`—11, 8, and 7.

11.4 Using Arrays in Programs

Now that we have the values in an array, they are much easier to manipulate. When we tried to store the values in an object, we had to know the name of each value (i.e., `first_child`, `second_child`, etc.). If we don't know ahead of time how many children we have, we won't know what to name the variable. By storing them in an array, each value gets a numbered index rather than a property name. These are much easier for a computer to go through sequentially.

Let's say we wanted to go through an array of children's ages and find the age of the oldest child. How might we do that? Well, when we say we want to "go through an array," that means we want to repeat some code for each element in an array. What sort of programming structure do we use when we want to repeat code? A loop, of course!

The problem is that we have to know when we are finished. That is, we need to know how many values there are in the array so we know when we don't want another value. Arrays, in addition to being able to access its values by index, also work in some ways like an object.

---

[1] Note that, in many programming languages, it is an error to assign to an array index without the variable being set up to hold at least that many values ahead-of-time. JavaScript handles it just fine, however. JavaScript knows that if the array member doesn't exist, it should create it.

[2] In ordinary life, we are used to labeling sequences of values starting with a 1, but computers usually label sequences of values starting with a 0. This is known as **zero-based indexing**. The reason for this is that, at least historically, the index was actually the *offset* from the start of the array. Since the first element *is* the start of the array, the first element isn't offset at all from the start of the array, so its index/offset is zero.

```
var largest_age = function(age_array) {
   var the_largest = 0;
   for(var i = 0; i < age_array.length; i++) {
      if(age_array[i] > the_largest) {
         the_largest = age_array[i];
      }
   }

   return the_largest;
};
```

Figure 11-2. *Finding the Largest Value in an Array*

An array has a few special properties that can be used to find out information about the array. The most important property that an array has is the length property. The length property returns the number of values that the array holds. So, in our code, children_ages.length would yield 3 since it holds three values. Notice that, since JavaScript arrays use zero-based indexing, this is one more than the largest *index*, which is 2. The fact that the size of an array is one larger than the largest index is a quirk of computer programming that you will frequently have to keep in mind.

Figure 11-2 shows a function that takes an array of ages and returns the largest one. In this code, the for loop repeated using i as the loop counter. i starts at zero since the array indexes start at zero. At the end of every loop, i increases by 1 (i++ is just a short way of writing i = i + 1). Incrementing the index by 1 basically means "go to the next value in the list." The middle part of the for statement is the condition. Here, the condition is i < age_array.length. Since the array length is *one greater* than the last index of the array, this condition says to keep going as long as we have a valid index for the array. When i finally makes it to age_array.length, it will no longer point to a valid value, so we should stop looping.

What do we do inside the loop? We are simply testing each value (age_array[i]) to see if it is greater than the previous value (the_largest). If it is greater, we write the current value into the_largest. Otherwise, we ignore it. Then, after the loop has completed, we return the value of the_largest for the result of the function.

Figure 11-3 shows how this function can be incorporated into a larger program.

```
var children_ages = new Array();
children_ages[0] = 11;
children_ages[1] = 8;
children_ages[2] = 7;

var largest = largest_age(children_ages);
alert("The oldest child is " + largest + " years old");
```

Figure 11-3. *Using the* largest_age *Function*

Just like we were able to simplify object creation with the {} syntax, arrays have a special syntax, too, which makes them easy to create. In JavaScript, you can create an array just by putting in a list of numbers in square brackets ([ ]). Here are some examples:

```
// Create an empty array
var empty_array = [];
```

```
// Creates the array we had before
var children_ages = [11, 8, 7];
```

```
// Gets the largest value in children_ages
var largest = largest_age(children_ages);
```

```
// Skip the variable, pass in the array directly
var largest_inline = largest_age([11, 8, 7]);
```

Using this syntax saves us a lot of effort in programming.

One other trick to note is how to add a value to the end of an array no matter how long the array is. While there are several methods for this, the one that best matches your current learning right now is to simply use the length of the array as the index. Remember, the length is always one more than the last index, so it is also the *next* index that would be added.

The following code shows how to add three numbers to an array:

```
var my_array = [];
my_array[my_array.length] = 23;
my_array[my_array.length] = 99;
my_array[my_array.length] = 10;
```

If you need to access the last element of the my_array array, you can do it with my_array[my_array.length - 1]. The first element is always my_array[0]. Also, if you want to get rid of elements at the end of the array, you can also set the length property. To get rid of all elements of the array my_array, just do my_array.length = 0;.

🖝 PRACTICE QUESTIONS

1. Type out the entire largest_age function. Test it by sending it different arrays and making sure it always returns the largest age.

2. Instead of creating the array values yourself, have the user type the values. For the first time around, have the user type in exactly three values. Make sure these values get converted to numbers before storing them in the array!

3. Extend your program so that the user can type in as many values as they want. Remember to include a way that the user can indicate that they are finished either by asking them if they are done after each one or asking the user to type a special sentinel value that indicates that they are done.

11.5 Mixing Objects and Arrays

While objects and arrays are pretty powerful in their own right, you can increase the power of both of them by mixing them together. The values held in object properties don't have to be just numbers and strings—they can be any JavaScript value including other objects or arrays! Likewise, array values don't have to just be numbers; they can be any value that JavaScript supports, including objects and other arrays. Mixing and matching objects and arrays gives you the flexibility to represent just about any real-world data set.

For instance, let's say that I wanted to put more information about my children than just their age. I also wanted to include their name and favorite color. In addition, let's say that I really want the list of children to be on a larger record about me, not just sitting by itself in a variable. How would I write that? Figure 11-4 shows how you would write it the long way.

```
var my_record = {};
my_record.name = "Jon";
my_record.children = [];
my_record.children[0] = {};
my_record.children[0].name = "Jim";
my_record.children[0].age = 11;
my_record.children[0].favorite_color = "blue";
my_record.children[1] = {};
my_record.children[1].name = "Jack";
my_record.children[1].age = 8;
my_record.children[1].favorite_color = "black";
my_record.children[2] = {};
my_record.children[2].name = "Joel";
my_record.children[2].age = 7;
my_record.children[2].favorite_color = "orange";
```

Figure 11-4. *Building a Complex Object*

As you can see, we start out with a blank object in the variable my_record. We then add a name to the object. Next, we add an empty array to the object, and we name the property children. Now, to access this array, we have to use my_record.children. Since my_record.children is an array, we can use indexes on it. Therefore, my_record.children[0] refers to the first value in the my_record.children array. Since that index doesn't exist yet, it gets created. But what is stored there? It's a new, blank object! Therefore, my_record.children[0] now refers to an empty object. What can we do with objects? We can add properties. We can create a name property on this new, empty object by doing my_record.children[0].name = "Jim";. We then set the age in the same way. At the end of this process, we have an object that has an array of objects.

Now, if we wanted to use our largest_age function, we would have to rewrite it. Why? Because now the array is no longer an array of numbers but of objects. Therefore, for each object, we would have to look for the age property. Figure 11-5 shows the code.

What we did in this function is modify our loop so that it stores the object *temporarily* in a variable called child. We then use child.age to access the child's age. Note that instead of using this extra child variable, we could have just done it directly by typing in child_array[i].age, but creating the extra variable makes for much less typing and much easier reading in the long run.

```
var largest_age = function(child_array) {
   var the_largest = 0;
   for(var i = 0; i < child_array.length; i++) {
      var child = child_array[i];
      if(child.age > the_largest) {
         the_largest = child.age;
      }
   }

   return the_largest;
};
```

Figure 11-5. *The* largest_age *Function Using Objects*

To call this function on our list of children from my_record, we would simply write largest_age(my_record.children).

Figure 11-4 showed the long way to build a complex object. However, just as there is an easier way to write simple objects and arrays, complex objects and arrays can also be built using the simplified syntax. Figure 11-6 shows the exact same object that we built in Figure 11-4, written using the simplified notation.

As you can see, this takes much less typing and is much easier to read. It takes up more space because of how it is written, but you don't have to do it that way—JavaScript does not care how much or little space is used. You could write that whole complex object on one line if you wanted to, but I think the clarity that comes from having things separated out is worth the extra space it can take up.

11.6 Object Methods

A **method** is a function which is physically attached to an object. The functions we have seen so far (such as alert and prompt) are stored in global variables that are available anywhere. A method is a function that is stored as a property on the object itself. Remember, creating functions is actually a two-step process—the function keyword *creates* the function, but then we have to assign it to a variable in order to call it by a name. However, just as we can store a function in a variable, we can also store it in an object's property. Functions stored in this way are called methods.

```
var my_record = {
  name: "Jon",
  children: [
    {
      name: "Jim",
      age: 11,
      favorite_color: "blue"
    },
    {
      name: "Jack",
      age: 8,
      favorite_color: "black"
    },
    {
      name: "Joel",
      age: 7,
      favorite_color: "orange"
    }
  ]
};
```

Figure 11-6. *Complex Objects Using the Simplified Notation*

Since they are stored in object properties, they don't have a global name; they are only accessible *through* the object. Additionally, methods implicitly pass the object that they are a property of when they are called.

As an example, let's look at a built-in method of array objects, known as push. The push method simply adds an item to the end of an array. The following code creates the array [5, 6, 7]:

```
var my_array = [];
my_array.push(5);
my_array.push(6);
my_array.push(7);
```

What my_array.push(5) does is look at the push attribute on the my_array object and call the function that it finds there. Because it is called in this manner, it implicitly passes my_array to the function and explicitly passes the number 5 as the first parameter. The push method then accomplishes the equivalent feature of writing my_array[my_array.length] = 5;.

157

Object methods allow for a number of benefits. First of all, they reduce the number of globally defined methods. Just like we generally try to eliminate global variables because it takes mental space to remember which ones are already in use, packaging functions into methods on objects instead of into global variables reduces the number of globally defined methods we need to care about.

Similarly, because the methods are defined on the objects themselves, we can actually reuse the same method name on different objects. On arrays, push means "push the value onto the end." However, push may mean something entirely different for other types of objects (like a lawnmower). Therefore, on a different object, there may be a push method that means something else entirely. If all of these different functions had to exist on the global scope, they would all need different names, such as array_push and lawnmower_push. This takes more typing and winds up actually being more confusing.

Finally, the method syntax makes it clear who the primary player is in the method. The object that the method is defined on is usually the most important parameter in the method and provides the context for the action. It makes code read somewhat similar to a sentence. You can read my_array.push(5) as saying, "tell my_array to push the number 5." At least to me, this is clearer (or at least cleaner) than if the syntax would be array_push(my_array, 5).

The mirror image of the push method on arrays is the pop method. The pop method removes the last element of the array (decreasing its length by 1) and returns the value that was removed.

We will dive deeper into methods (and how to create your own methods) in Chapter 15. However, for now, I just want you to be familiar with how they operate, as we will be using them more in Chapter 12.

☞ PRACTICE QUESTIONS

1. Write a program so that a user can continually add items to an array until they are done. Add them using the push method. Then, when finished, add up all the values in the array and show the result.

2. See if you can create an object and assign a function to one of its properties. You won't know how to receive the implicitly passed object until Chapter 15, but you can at least practice assigning and using functions as object properties.

11.6.1 Review

In this chapter, we covered the basics of composite values—objects and arrays. We have learned the following:

- Objects hold related pieces of data together in a single, cohesive unit.

- Each value in an object is placed into a property, which is a name that is used to access the value.

- Sequences of data are called arrays.

- Each array holds a sequence of related values.

- Values in an array are accessed through their index.

- Array indexes are zero-based, which means that the first index is always 0 and the last index is always 1 less than the length of the array.

- If you assign a property to an object or a value to an array index which does not yet exist, the property or index will be created for you automatically.

- Each array has a `length` property which tells you how large the array is.

- The `length` property can be used in loops to control the number of times the loop occurs.

- Objects and arrays can be embedded within each other—a property can have an array value, and the value at a particular array index can be a full object (which might also have an array).

- Objects and arrays both have special syntax (`{}` and `[]`) to make typing them easier.

- Functions can be stored as object properties as well and are known as methods.

- When methods are called using the syntax `objectname.methodname()`, the object is implicitly passed as a parameter to the method.

11.6.2 Apply What You Have Learned

1. Create an array of products so that each product is an object that contains a name, a code, a description, and a price.

2. Now create a function that takes two parameters—a product array and a single product code. The function should loop looking for the object that matches the code. When it finds the object, it should return the full object that has a matching code.

3. Now add user interaction. The user should be able to type the product code, and the program will look up information about that product and display it using alerts.

4. Extend the program so that the user can look up any number of codes that they want.

CHAPTER 12

Interacting with Web Pages

In previous chapters, we have learned how objects work and how to build our own objects. However, JavaScript also comes with several existing, built-in objects for you to use. These standard objects are the gateway between your program and the rest of the system, including the HTML document, the screen, computer storage, communication facilities, and other important system features. In this chapter, we are going to use the standard document object to interact with the web page.

Note that for the first part of the chapter, we will *only* be interacting with the JavaScript console. Extra steps are needed to make this work with a script that is loaded from a web page, which will be covered in Section 12.6.

12.1 Using the JavaScript Console

In order to see the document object in action, we are going to use the **JavaScript console**. The JavaScript console allows you to type JavaScript code one line at a time and see the results immediately. For information on how to access the JavaScript console on your system, see Appendix B.4.1.

Before we begin using the console, type the web page shown in Figure 12-1 into a file and load it into your browser.

© Jonathan Bartlett 2023
J. Bartlett, *Programming for Absolute Beginners*, https://doi.org/10.1007/978-1-4842-8751-4_12

```
<!DOCTYPE html>
<html>
   <head>
      <title>My Document</title>
   </head>
   <body id="mainbody">
      <h1 id="console_heading">Using the JavaScript Console</h1>

      <h2 id="subheading">A Heading</h2>

      <p id="first_paragraph">
         This is my first paragraph.
      </p>
   </body>
</html>
```

Figure 12-1. *Basic HTML File for Manipulation*

Now that you have your web page loaded, open up the JavaScript console as described in Appendix B.4.1. Now, just to get used to how the console works, enter 2 + 5 into the console and hit enter. What happened? It should have given 7 as the result. After each command, when you hit the enter key, the console gives you the value of what you typed.

Now type in var a = 2 + 5; and hit enter. What happened this time? It should give back undefined. Why is this? The value 7 got loaded into the variable a, but the result of the variable declaration is nothing. So, don't be surprised if, after declaring a variable, the result is undefined. That is normal.

To make sure that a received our value, just type a into a line by itself. It should return the value 7, which means it knows the value of a. Now we are going to intentionally make a mistake. Type into your console a = 7 +; and hit enter. It should give you back some sort of error, such as "syntax error" or a similar error message. This is important to pay attention to. If you are using the console, and you get an error message, *pay attention to it* because you probably entered something wrong somewhere. Recheck what you typed to make sure it is valid. Programming languages tend to be very picky. A miscapitalized word, an accidental space, or a misplaced semicolon will prevent your code from working.

☞ **PRACTICE QUESTIONS**

Before moving on to manipulating the web page, you should practice with the JavaScript console.

1. Use the `alert` function to display a popup message.

2. Use the `prompt` function to get a value from the user.

3. Enter the `square_a_number` function from Chapter 10. Because the console processes each line as you type it, you will need to put the whole function on one line.

4. Now use `square_a_number` to find the squares of 3 and 6 in the JavaScript console.

12.2 Finding and Modifying Web Page Elements

Now that we have some familiarity with how the JavaScript console works, it is time to interact with our web page. JavaScript provides a special object stored in the global variable document that provides the gateway to interacting with the web page. In JavaScript, every tag on the web page is represented by its own object with its own properties and methods. The list of standard object types for HTML pages, with their properties and methods, is called the **Document Object Model**, often known just as the **DOM**. We will cover some of the more common methods for these objects in this chapter.

The first thing we are going to do is to look up one of our HTML elements. Remember, an *element* is the combination of a start/end tag and all of the content in-between. Note that in the file, we added id attributes to several of our tags. This makes them easy to look up in JavaScript. The document object has a method that looks up HTML elements by their id attribute, called getElementById. It takes one parameter, which is the HTML id value to look up, and returns the given HTML element as a JavaScript object. If the element is not found, it returns the special JavaScript value null, which is considered an "empty" value. In your console, type in the following:

```
document.getElementById("first_paragraph");
```

This will yield an object that represents the HTML element of the first paragraph. Once we have this object, we can make modifications to it that will be reflected in the web page itself. Each browser will display this value differently in the console, but the underlying result is the same—it is a JavaScript object that represents the HTML element we see on the screen. In any case, we don't just want to display the value, we want to manipulate it. A good first step is to store the object in a variable. Therefore, do the following:

```
var x = document.getElementById("first_paragraph");
```

Now the object representing the HTML element is stored in our variable x. What can we do with it? One simple thing you can do is to change out the text. HTML elements that only have text in them (i.e., they have no child elements) can have that text accessed or changed through their textContent property. Type out the following:

```
x.textContent
```

It should give back the value "This is my first paragraph", though possibly with some extra spaces. So, now that we can access the textContent property, we can also change it. Type the following to put new text on your paragraph:

```
x.textContent = "This is a changed paragraph.";
```

You should see your web page instantly change with the new paragraph text.

As you can see, if we attach the id attribute to our HTML elements, we can easily find them and manipulate them in our JavaScript programs.

👉 PRACTICE QUESTIONS

Use the JavaScript console to accomplish the following tasks:

1. Look up and modify the text for our <h1> element.

2. Look up and modify the text for our <h2> element.

3. Use the prompt function to ask the user for a string and store that in a variable. Now set the text of the paragraph to that value.

12.3 Creating New HTML Elements

Now that we have looked up and modified an HTML element, it is time to learn how to create a new element. The document object has a method called createElement that does just this.

Enter the following code into the console:

```
var new_element = document.createElement("p");
new_element.textContent = "This is a new paragraph";
```

This creates a new element but doesn't add it to the page. It is merely floating in memory, only existing in the variable. We haven't told the document where we want it to go. We now want to put our new element as the last thing in the <body> element. So, first, we need to look up the body element:

```
var body_element = document.getElementById("mainbody");
```

Now we need to tell the body element to append our new element to the end of its child elements. This is done using the appendChild method of our body element. Type the following:

```
body_element.appendChild(new_element);
```

As soon as you type this, the new paragraph should appear!

☞ PRACTICE ACTIVITY

To practice adding HTML content to web pages, we are going to create an <ul> tag and then, through the JavaScript console, add additional <li> tags to it. If you get confused on any step in here, go back through the previous sections to find out how to do each step.

1. Start out by altering the HTML file used in this section to add a <ul> tag in it with at least one <li> tag in it.

2. Give the <ul> tag an id attribute so you can find it with JavaScript in the next step.

3. Open up the JavaScript console. Use the getElementById method from document to find the <ul> element and put it in a variable.

4. Now use the `createElement` method from document to create a new `<li>` tag to put in it.

5. Now use the `textContent` property on the new tag to set it to whatever text you want.

6. Now use the `appendChild` method on your `<ul>` element to add the new `<li>` tag to the end of your list.

7. Practice by adding yet another `<li>` tag to the list.

8. See if you can create a brand new `<ul>` tag with JavaScript and add it to the bottom of the page. Then add additional `<li>` tags to your JavaScript-created `<ul>` tag.

12.4 Communicating with Input Fields

Up to now, all interaction with users has been through the `alert` and `prompt` functions. However, you might have noticed that, on the Web, most interaction occurs directly within the web page itself. This is done almost exactly like the web page manipulation that we did in the previous sections. The difference is that we are going to be working with `<input />` tags. The `<input />` element object works just like the objects for other elements that we have seen but has a special attribute called `value` that represents the text in the field.

To get a feel for how these input fields work, enter the HTML from Figure 12-2 into a file and load it into your browser.

One thing to notice—*be sure to include* the `type="button"` attribute on your button. Otherwise, clicking on the button can cause the page to reload which will cause you to lose all of your variables that you have created.

```
<!DOCTYPE html>
<html>
   <head>
      <title>Input Fields Example</title>
   </head>
   <body>
      <h1>Input Fields Example</h1>
      <form>
         <p>
            Input Field 1:
            <input type="text" id="field1" />
         </p>

         <p>
            Input Field 2:
            <input type="text" id="field2" />
         </p>
         <button type="button" id="my_button">Click Me</button>
         <p>
            Results:
            <span id="results"></span>
         </p>
         <p id="another_paragraph">
            Another paragraph
         </p>
      </form>
   </body>
</html>
```

Figure 12-2. *HTML File with Input Fields*

Now, open the JavaScript console. The first thing we need to do is look up the two
<input /> elements and store them into variables. To do this, enter in the following:

```
var fld1 = document.getElementById("field1");
var fld2 = document.getElementById("field2");
```

Now type fld1 on a line by itself to make sure that it gives back an HTML element as
a value. If it doesn't, you mistyped something. Do the same to check fld2.

Now type in the following:

```
fld1.value = "Hello";
```

167

As soon as you type this, the text "Hello" should appear in the first field. Go into the second field and type in the text "Goodbye" into the web page. Now type this into the JavaScript console:

```
fld2.value
```

It should now print onto the console the value that you typed ("Goodbye" if you followed directions). Now we know how to set and read values from <input /> elements!

Now look up the <span> tag. Remember, the <span> tag is used for specifying a region of text. In our case, we are specifying the location where we want to write the result. In any case, do the following to look up the <span> tag, so we are ready to write to that location in the page:

```
var results_span = document.getElementById("results");
```

Now type in results_span on a line by itself so that you can see if you correctly retrieved the <span> element.

What we are going to do is read a number from each input field, multiply them together, and write the result into the <span> element.

Start out by typing in two numbers, one in each input field. For this example, let's assume that you type in "5" in the first field and "7" in the second field. Now, remember, since this is typed from the keyboard, it is treated as a string, not a number. Therefore, fld1.value will be the string "5" not the number 5 and fld2.value will be the string "7" and not the number 7. What we need to do, then, is use our parseInt function to convert these strings into numbers.

Type the following in the JavaScript console to read the values of the fields and store them into variables:

```
var val1 = parseInt(fld1.value);
var val2 = parseInt(fld2.value);
```

Now, val1 and val2 should have the numbers that you entered in them. You can verify this by typing the variable name in the console on a line by itself and making sure it gives you back the correct value.

Now, we need to multiply the two numbers together. Type in the following to accomplish this:

```
var result = val1 * val2;
```

`result` now has the result in it.

Now we just need to write the value in `result` back into the page. We will use the `textContent` property of `results_span` to do this. JavaScript will automatically convert the number to a string before it displays it. Here is the code to do this:

```
results_span.textContent = result;
```

☞   PRACTICE ACTIVITY

Practice your skills by using the JavaScript console to change the text of the final paragraph in the HTML file to the value typed into one of the `<input />` elements.

12.5 Adding Functionality to Buttons

So far, we have been able to manually perform some JavaScript processing on input fields within a document. But this is not how web pages usually work. Usually, the user tells the computer to complete a function by clicking a button. Therefore, we have to attach the functionality we want to the button.

```
var multiply_fields = function() {
   var fld1 = document.getElementById("field1");
   var fld2 = document.getElementById("field2");
   var val1 = parseInt(fld1.value);
   var val2 = parseInt(fld2.value);
   var result = val1 * val2;
   var results_span = document.getElementById("results");
   results_span.textContent = result;
};
```

Figure 12-3. *A Function to Multiply Two Text Fields*

So, to start with, we are going to create a function that performs the tasks that we did in the previous section. For readability, I am going to write it out in several lines. However, because the JavaScript console interprets one line at a time, you *must* type out the whole function on a single line. Don't worry, the JavaScript language works exactly the same whether it is one line or many—that is why it uses the semicolon to separate statements. So, as long as you type everything correctly, it will work just fine on one line. Figure 12-3 shows the function.

Notice that it uses the document object. This works because document is a global variable. Also note that the function takes no parameters. It simply works by using the document global variable.

Once you have typed the function (all in one line) into the console, calling the function should perform all of the tasks. To test it out, put two different numbers in the input fields, and then, in the JavaScript console, write the following:

```
multiply_fields();
```

This should multiply the two numbers and write the result in the results <span> tag. If it did not work, recheck your function.

Now, we want this function to run whenever a user clicks on our button. This is actually very easy to do. <button> tags have a property called onclick. If you set onclick to a function, it will call that function whenever it is clicked! For right now, you should only use functions that take no parameters.

So, to get this set, we need to look up the <button> on the page and then set its onclick property. Here is the code:

```
var btn = document.getElementById("my_button");
btn.onclick = multiply_fields;
```

Note that we are not *calling* the function multiply_fields here. We are *storing* the function itself in the onclick property for later use. Remember, JavaScript functions are themselves values and are stored in variables and properties just like any other value. Therefore, we are storing the function in the btn object, and the btn object will call the function when it is time.

To try it out, put in two values and click the button. If everything was set up right, it should display the results in the proper place.

12.6 Putting It All Together

Now, what we really want is to have all of this functionality load with the web page. To do that, we are going to need to put all of our code into a JavaScript file. Create a text file called multiply.js in the same directory as your HTML file.

Enter the code from Figure 12-4 into `multiply.js`.

Now we need to attach it to the HTML file. To do this, add the following tag to the HTML file within the `<head>` element:

```
<script type="text/javascript" src="multiply.js" defer="defer">
</script>
```

Notice the new attribute we added—`defer="defer"`. This attribute changes *when* the JavaScript is loaded and run. Normally, JavaScript is loaded and run at precisely the point where the tag is included. In our case, that would mean that only the `<head>` element was present, since the tag occurs before the rest of the page. This would not work, because `document.getElementById("my_button")` would return `null` (i.e., no value), because it is not yet part of the page. The attribute `defer="defer"` tells your browser to wait until after the whole page is loaded before running the JavaScript code.

```
var multiply_fields = function() {
    var fld1 = document.getElementById("field1");
    var fld2 = document.getElementById("field2");
    var val1 = parseInt(fld1.value);
    var val2 = parseInt(fld2.value);
    var result = val1 * val2;
    var results_span = document.getElementById("results");
    results_span.textContent = result;
};
var btn = document.getElementById("my_button");
btn.onclick = multiply_fields;
```

Figure 12-4. *Full Code for Multiplying Two Fields*

Now, after you have added your `<script>` tag to the HTML file and have saved everything, reload your page. After you type in two numbers and hit the button, it should give you your answer.

```
┌──────────────────────────────────────────────────────────────┐
│                  ☞   PRACTICE ACTIVITY                        │
└──────────────────────────────────────────────────────────────┘
```

Now that you know how to add functionality to a web page, this activity will have you add a second function to the same page.

1. Start with the completed file from this section.

2. Next, create a new function in your JavaScript file that will add the two numbers rather than multiply them. Call the function add_fields. *Do not* remove the existing multiply_fields code. Just add a new function.

3. Now add a second button to the page. Be sure to give it a distinct id attribute so you can find it. Do not remove the existing button.

4. Now add code to your JavaScript file so that it will find the new button and attach your add_fields function to the button.

5. Test out your new page. Be sure that both buttons do the appropriate operations.

12.7 Logging to the Console

If your program has actual errors, those are generally reported in the JavaScript console. Therefore, when doing development, I almost always have the console open so I can see where I screwed up.

However, you can also write values to the console yourself. This is often helpful if you have complicated code or calculations and want to keep track of the status of the computations as you go along. JavaScript helpfully has a global variable called console which allows you write to your console. The console object has a log method which allows you to write whatever you want to the console.

Modify your previous program to add in the following line somewhere in you multiply_fields function:

```
console.log("I am here");
```

Now, when you click the button, it should write "I am here" to your console.

Most browsers have additional tools for debugging your JavaScript programs. The details of how to use these are beyond the scope of the book, but I'll at least mention the most common and most powerful one—breakpoints. A breakpoint tells the JavaScript interpreter to stop at a certain line of code. Then, you, the programmer, can look at the values of all the variables at that point and step JavaScript through your code one line at a time to see how each line affects what is happening.

Console logging and breakpoints are often used as substitutes for each other, but they each have areas where they are more suited to the problem than the other. Console logs are useful for monitoring running programs in real time. By having console logs report important status information, you can watch your program as it goes through computations. Breakpoints are good when you have a specific location in your code that is failing and need to see how every step in the process affects the results. Why is this variable being set to that value? Which condition is causing this to take the wrong branch? Which value is unexpectedly null or undefined? These questions are quickly answered by setting appropriate breakpoints and walking through your program.

☞ A BROADER VIEW OF PROGRAMMING INTERFACES

This chapter introduced you to the Document Object Model (DOM). You may wonder how you know what objects, properties, and functions are available to you. It might seem mysterious or even arbitrary that if you stick a function in the onclick property, it magically calls that function when a button is clicked. When programmers create systems such as JavaScript and the DOM, they have to make choices about how things are represented and interacted with— what the objects and properties are called and how they are used. The names of these objects, functions, and properties are essentially arbitrary—they are whatever the programmer decided to name them. Hopefully the names make sense and can help you learn how to use them, but sometimes, either through sloppiness or history, things wind up with weird names that don't make sense. This is fairly normal in programming.

The list of standard objects, properties, and functions that a system supports is called its **Application Programming Interface** or, more commonly, its **API**. How do you know what objects, properties, and functions are available in an API? Usually, this is done by programmers writing them down and sharing them through **documentation**. Most programming systems have a reference which lists all of the available functions. However, these are usually pretty lengthy since system developers try to think of all of the things that you might want to do and provide functions for each of them. Usually, though, most APIs are focused around just a few concepts, and once you learn those, the rest are details that you can look up later.

12.7.1 Review

In this chapter, we practiced interacting with web pages using JavaScript. We have learned the following:

- JavaScript comes with built-in objects that allow us to interact with the rest of the system and the network.

- The document object is the gateway that allows us to interact with the current web page.

- The DOM is the list of objects and properties that can be used when interacting with an HTML page and its elements.

- The id attribute of an HTML tag can be used to find the element from JavaScript for manipulation.

- The getElementById method of the document object allows us to use the id attribute to get objects which represent HTML elements in our page and store them in variables to inspect them and manipulate them.

- The textContent property of an HTML element's object allows us to retrieve and set the text content of an HTML element.

- Elements can be created using document's createElement method.

- Newly created elements can be added into a page using an element's appendChild method. This adds the element as the last child, or sub-element, of the given element object.

- The <input /> tag can be used to allow a user to enter in data for processing.

- The value property of the <input /> tag's object can be used for reading or setting the value of the text field.

- The <button> tag can be used to initiate processing. Be sure to set the type="button" property so it will work correctly.

- Setting a <button> element object's onclick value to a function will cause that function to run when the button is clicked.

- Setting the `defer="defer"` attribute on `<script>` tags will cause it to wait for the document to be fully loaded before executing the JavaScript. This should be added to all `<script>` tags from here on out.

- The `console` object is a built-in JavaScript object that has a `log` method which writes any value to the console.

- An API is the list of standard objects, properties, and functions available to a programmer from the system.

- An API's documentation is the description of what objects, properties, and functions are available and the details of how they work.

12.7.2 Apply What You Have Learned

1. Now that you know how to get input from a user from an HTML page and how to write output to the HTML page, pick a program from the previous chapters and rewrite it to use `<input />` tags instead of the `prompt` function.

2. Create an HTML page that just has an empty `<body>` tag with just an `id` attribute. Write JavaScript to build a page with a heading, a paragraph, and a `<ul>` list with two items in it using only JavaScript code.

3. Create an HTML page that has an empty `<ul>` tag with just an `id` attribute. Write JavaScript that uses an array and a `for` loop to populate the `<ul>` element with `<li>` elements. Use the array `["One", "Two", "Three"]` and have your code loop through each element of the array to add a new `<li>` element for each member of the array.

PART IV

Intermediate JavaScript

This part dives deeper into the mechanics of the JavaScript language. This will require you to think deeper about the internals of how JavaScript interprets what you write and what is actually happening on the computer when you write code.

CHAPTER 13

Recursive Functions and the Stack

In Chapter 10, you learned that functions can be used to package together pieces of code into well-defined units that can be reused over and over again. In this chapter, we are going to go into more detail about how JavaScript keeps track of these functions.

13.1 The Program Stack

Previously, we talked about local variables (variables defined within functions) and global variables (variables defined outside of functions). We mentioned that local variables are specific to the function that they are defined in. That is, if we have a global variable called x, and a function has a local variable also called x, these refer to *different* variables. Therefore, the function is able to modify their local x without modifying the global x. One of the many benefits to this is that our functions can be developed without worrying about what someone else working on another part of the program has called their variables.

Imagine if you were working with a partner developing a program together. If you both had to agree on every single variable name (to prevent one person from accidentally clobbering the other person's variables), that would get tedious and make the process very slow. With local variables, as long as the variable is defined within a function, it doesn't matter what its name is. You may still have to agree on the names of global variables, but those should be much more rare, especially in large projects.

So, how does JavaScript keep track of local variables? It turns out that nearly every programming language keeps track of local variables in roughly the same way—through a mechanism known as the **program stack**, or just the stack. The stack is the way that

© Jonathan Bartlett 2023
J. Bartlett, *Programming for Absolute Beginners*, https://doi.org/10.1007/978-1-4842-8751-4_13

the programming language keeps track of what is currently going on in the program. It is, quite literally, a stack of information that the programming language is keeping about what is happening in the program.

For instance, when a program calls a function, it has to remember where to return to after the function completes. Therefore, it pushes the return location onto the stack, so it remembers where to go after the function is finished. If that function calls another function, then it pushes another return location onto the top of the stack. When the second function finishes, it looks at the top of the stack to see where it should return to, pops (removes) the value, and resumes operation at the point indicated. When the original function finishes, its return location is now back at the top of the stack, so it knows where it should return to.

Figure 13-1 shows some functions that call each other. It includes comments showing different locations that the program will be executing (marked as "position 1," "position 2," etc.) so that we can discuss the flow of the program through the functions. If you skip the declaration of the variables for the functions, the actual code starts at position 8. For our purposes, we can conceive of the stack being empty when the program starts running.

The first thing the program does is call the function `function_one`. When `function_one` ends, where should the program continue? It should continue running at position 9. The stack looks like Figure 13-2.

Now, look at `function_one`. The code starts running at position 1, and there is an immediate function call to `function_two`. Think about where the code should continue running after `function_two` finishes—it should continue running at position 2. Therefore, that position is pushed to the top of the stack. The stack now looks like Figure 13-3.

Now, what does `function_two` do? It calls yet another function, `function_three`. Since the next place it should start executing after `function_three` finishes is position 5, that is now pushed onto the stack. The stack now looks like Figure 13-4.

Now, `function_three` makes its own function call, but this time to a built-in function. Function calls to built-in functions work exactly like other function calls. So, where should `function_three` resume after `alert` finishes? It should go back to position 7, and the stack will look like Figure 13-5.

Now things get interesting. What happens when `alert` finishes? How does it know where to go? It just looks at the top of the stack! The top of the stack says, "When you are done, return to position 7 in the code." JavaScript then removes the top of the stack and continues operation at position 7. Now the stack looks like it did in Figure 13-4. But then, the only thing left to do at position 7 is to return from the function. Therefore, it performs the procedure again—it looks at the top of the stack to see where it should return to. Now it says to return to position 5, and the stack is back the way it looked in Figure 13-3. Again, the only thing to do in position 5 is to return, and the stack says to return to position 2. We therefore return to position 2 and remove it from the top of the stack. The stack is then back to looking how it did in Figure 13-2.

```
var function_one = function() {
  // Position 1
  function_two();
  // Position 2
  function_three();
  // Position 3
};

var function_two = function() {
  // Position 4
  function_three();
  // Position 5
};

var function_three = function() {
  // Position 6
  alert("Hello");
  // Position 7
};

// Position 8
function_one();
// Position 9
```

Figure 13-1. *Example of Functions Calling Each Other*

```
Return Location: Position 9
Bottom of Stack
```

Figure 13-2. *Stack After First Function Call*

```
Return Location: Position 2
Return Location: Position 9
Bottom of Stack
```

Figure 13-3. *Stack After Second Function Call*

```
Return Location: Position 5
Return Location: Position 2
Return Location: Position 9
Bottom of Stack
```

Figure 13-4. *Stack After Third Function Call*

```
Return Location: Position 7
Return Location: Position 5
Return Location: Position 2
Return Location: Position 9
Bottom of Stack
```

Figure 13-5. *Stack After Built-in Function Call*

Now it gets really interesting. What happens at position 2? It calls function_three again, but this time with a *different* return location than the previous occasion—position 3. The stack now looks like Figure 13-6.

Now when function_three runs, it knows to go back to position 3 instead of position 5 like it did when it was called from function_two. So, as you can see, the stack keeps track of what is happening in the program and helps the computer know how and where to return from function calls.

```
Return Location: Position 3
Return Location: Position 9
Bottom of Stack
```

Figure 13-6. *Stack After Second Call to function_three*

Oftentimes, what happens in code is more complicated than this. Since many of our functions have return values, and the functions are actually only part of the statement, the return must send the program to the correct place in the middle of the line of code.

This is the same idea as before, only that the positions that the computer keeps track of are more complicated than just line numbers like we had for the example. For instance, take the following code:

```
var square_a_number = function(x) {
    return x * x;
};

var y = square_a_number(square_a_number(2) * 4);
```

In this case, we are calling a function several times *in the same line*, and each one returns to a *different place in the line*. Don't worry. JavaScript knows exactly where to return to each time. Its positioning system is much more exact than our crude examples above.

Also, as we will see going forward, JavaScript stores much more information in the stack than just the return location.

13.2 Local Variables in the Stack

The other primary thing that JavaScript keeps in its stack is a list of the local variables used in the current function. To talk about this, let's look at a function that will sum all of the values in a range, which we will call sum_range. For instance, if you give it the numbers 3 and 7, sum_range(3, 7) will calculate 3 + 4 + 5 + 6 + 7 and give 25. Figure 13-7 shows what this looks like in code.

In this example, we have local variables—r_start, r_end, x, and total. Remember that local variables are not visible to the global scope. The way that JavaScript does this is by keeping the list of current variables on the stack.

Therefore, when the function is called, not only does the return location get put on the stack, but it also creates a "scope" (list of accessible variables) in memory and links the stack to that scope.

```
var sum_range = function(r_start, r_end) {
   var total = 0;
   for(var x = r_start; x <= r_end; x++) {
      total = total + x;
   }

   return total;
};

var result = sum_range(3, 7);
alert("The sum of the numbers 3 through 7 is " + result);
```

Figure 13-7. *Summing All the Values in a Range*

So, when we call sum_range, the stack looks a little more complicated. Figure 13-8 shows how the stack looks when the sum_range function is underway when it first begins its for loop.

Note that there is a big black line around the current scope and the current location. That is known as the **stack frame**. The stack frame is all of the data that is packaged together on the stack for a specific function call. The scope and the return location go together for each function call, and together they make up a stack frame.

The stack frame points JavaScript to the scope that is currently being used to process variables. The way that the scope works is that when you refer to a variable, say x, in your program, JavaScript first looks on the stack to see where your current scope is. It then looks for that variable in the current scope. If it finds it, that is what it uses for the variable. Do you see the box at the top of the local scope that says "Parent Scope"? Each scope links to a parent scope, which tells JavaScript where to look for variables if they are not in the current scope. In this case, the parent scope is the global scope. In Chapter 14, we will see how we can chain together even more scopes.

So, when a function is called, not only is the return location put onto the stack, but a *brand new* scope is created, and a link to this new scope is also placed on the stack.

Let's look at another, similar program which will declare a function called sum_squares_of_range. This works just like sum_range, except that it will square each of the numbers in the range. The code for this can be found in the following:

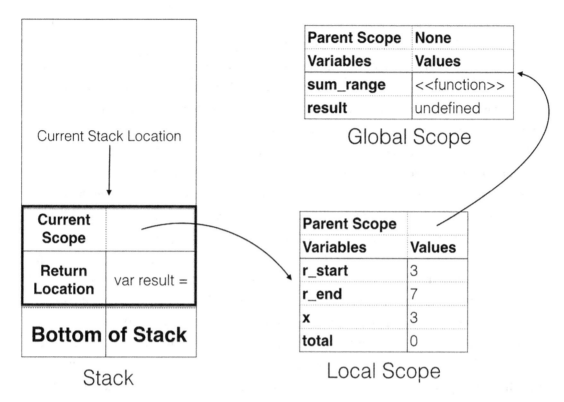

Figure 13-8. *Conceptual Layout of Computer Memory in a Function Call*

```
var square_number = function(num) {
   var x = num * num;
   return x;
};

var sum_squares_of_range = function(r_start, r_end) {
   var total = 0;
   for(var x = r_start; x <= r_end; x++) {
      total = total + square_number(x);
   }

   return total;
};

var result = sum_squares_of_range(3, 6);
alert("The sum of the squares of the values from 3 to 6: " + result);
```

Figure 13-9. *Summing the Squares of a Range of Numbers*

In this program, the stack gets two levels deep. First, it calls sum_squares_of_range. This leads to a situation similar to the previous example. Then, to calculate the square of each number, it calls square_number on each of them. Figure 13-10 shows the stack layout after the first call to square_number just before it returns. Notice that all of the local variables *exist* for both functions, but they are only *reachable* from within their own functions. When the square_number function is active, the "current scope" points to the local scope for square_number, which has its variables plus a link to the global scope.

Therefore, when square_number sets the value of x, it only affects its own value for x. The x from sum_squares_of_range is not even visible to this function. Therefore, even though we are assigning a value for x, it is only for the *local* copy of x that is specific to this function. When the function returns, it will remove *both* the link to the local scope and return location. When sum_squares_of_range starts executing again, its own scope will be at the top of the stack, and it won't see the scope of square_number at all.

One additional thing to note is that when a function first starts executing, the local scope *only* has entries for the parent scope and the parameters. JavaScript relies on the var keyword to create new variables in its scope. The var keyword causes JavaScript to look in the current scope (and *not* any parent scope) to see if the variable exists *in that scope*. If the variable does not exist, JavaScript creates the variable in the current scope. If the variable already exists, JavaScript *does not* create a new copy but keeps using the one that is already there.

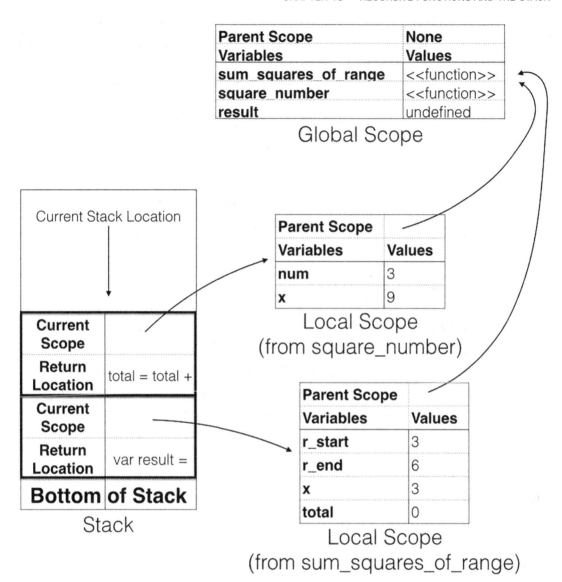

Figure 13-10. *Stack Frame with Two Functions Active*

☞ PRACTICE ACTIVITY

---

1. Look at the programs you wrote in Chapter 10 that use functions. Pick one of them.

2. Print out your function. Draw lines from any function call to the beginning of the function that is being called. Draw lines from the `return` statements to the place in your program where the program returns.

3. Create a diagram for this program of the stack, local scope(s), and global scope, similar to the one in Figure 13-10, for when at least one function is active.

13.3 Recursive Functions

Now that we know how stack frames and local variables work, it is time to learn about **recursive functions**. A recursive function is a function that is defined in terms of itself. Think about the program back in Figure 13-7 that summed all of the values between two numbers. In the program, we used a loop to go from one side of the range to the other. But is there another way to think about that problem? Another way to pursue it?

Think about summing all of the numbers from 4 to 10. Is there a smaller, similar problem that works the same way that we might be able to use? Indeed, summing all of the numbers from 4 to 10 is the same thing as adding 4 to the sum of the numbers from 5 to 10. So, `sum_range(4, 10)` gives us the same answer as `4 + sum_range(5, 10)`. Likewise, `sum_range(5, 10)` gives us the same answer as `5 + sum_range(6, 10)`.

Defining a function in terms of itself is called a recursion. How might we write a program that uses recursion? Figure 13-11 shows a partial implementation of what that might look like.

```
var sum_range = function(r_start, r_end) {
    var value = r_start + sum_range(r_start + 1, r_end);
    return value;
};
```

Figure 13-11. *Partial Recursive Definition of the* sum_range *Function*

As you can see, the function is defined in terms of itself. However, one problem you would realize if you tried this function is that it never stops! There is nothing in the function that makes it stop when it gets to the end of the range so it will just keep on going.

When writing recursive programs, there are two main situations to code for—the **base case** and the **inductive case**. The inductive case is the one we have already written—it is the case that uses recursion to solve the problem. The inductive case gets its name from inductive proofs in mathematics, which are very similar to recursive functions. The case we are missing is the base case—it is the case that stops the recursion to return an answer. In our program, the base case happens when r_start and r_end are equal. When this happens, we don't need to recurse anymore—we know what the answer is! When the start and end of the range are equal, we just return *that* number.

Therefore, the full definition of our sum_range function using recursion looks like Figure 13-12.

As you can see, there is now an if statement that checks for the base case and immediately computes the answer if it is found. Otherwise, it proceeds recursively.

However, you might have noticed something funny. Here we are using local variables, but we are using the same local variables over and over. Wouldn't these variables get clobbered each time we call the function? As a matter of fact, they don't. The reason for this is that JavaScript creates a *new* local variable scope *every time the function is called*. Therefore, each time that sum_range is called, there is a new local scope created. So, if you call sum_range(2, 5), it will create four local variable scopes, one for each time sum_range is called.

After the third call, the stack would look like Figure 13-13. Notice how, after the third call to sum_range, there are exactly three copies of the sum_range local scope in the drawing, each of them with the global scope as a parent scope and, with it, their own values for r_start and r_end. This is how the computer makes recursive function calls possible.

```
var sum_range = function(r_start, r_end) {
  // Check for the base case
  if(r_start == r_end) {
    // Base Case
    return r_start
  } else {
    // Inductive Case
    return r_start + sum_range(r_start + 1, r_end);
  }
};

var result = sum_range(3, 12);
alert("The sum of the numbers between 3 and 12 is " + result);
```

Figure 13-12. *Full Recursive Implementation of the sum_range Function*

In the example so far, there wasn't a reason to use recursion. In fact, with all of the function calls, stack frames, and local scopes generated, our code was actually much slower than when it used a simple loop. Nonetheless, there are many times when recursion is the way that makes the most sense or it is the easiest to write a program for. Programs today rarely need a lot of optimization. While the speed of the program itself shouldn't be discounted, what usually counts the most is the amount of time the programmer takes to write the program or the amount of time another programmer takes to read and understand a program. Those are usually more important than raw computing speed.

Knowing recursion will help you see the solutions to some problems more easily. When you become comfortable with recursion, you begin to see many complicated problems as merely simple problems in disguise. Additionally, knowing recursion will help you better understand other people's code when *they* use recursion. The best time to use recursion is when you can envision the problem as being the same problem over and over again, with each step just being a smaller version of the previous problem.

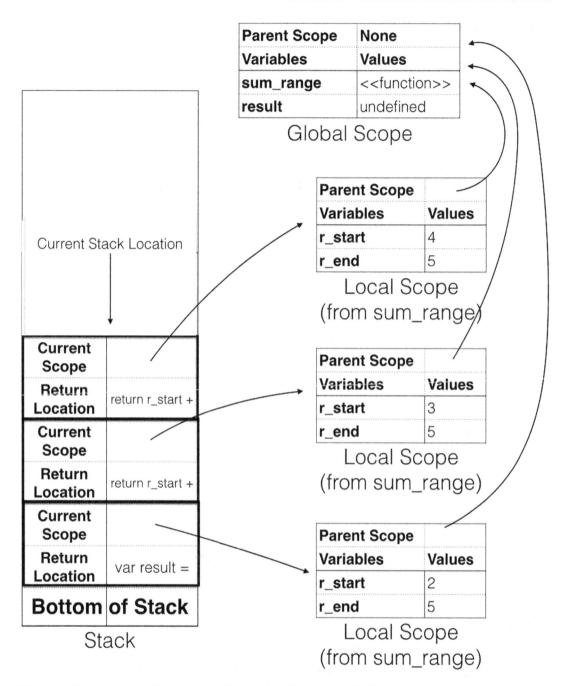

Figure 13-13. *Stack Frame for Recursive Function Call*

13.3.1 Review

In this chapter, we learned how the JavaScript stack worked and how it enables us to write recursive functions. We have learned the following:

- JavaScript uses the stack to keep track of what is going on in your program.

- Every time a function is called, JavaScript pushes a bookmark of the return location onto the stack telling it where to go when the function completes.

- Every time a function completes, JavaScript pops a bookmark off of the stack to find out where it should resume processing.

- This stack system allows JavaScript to return to the right spot in your code even if a function is called from more than one location.

- JavaScript keeps a separate list of local variables (the local scope) for every time a function is called even if it is the same function called more than once.

- Every time a function is called, JavaScript pushes a link to the new local scope onto the stack as well so it knows what scope is currently being used. This scope is popped at the end of the function along with the return location.

- When your program references a variable, JavaScript refers to the *current* local scope only and tries to look up your variable there.

- Each JavaScript scope has a link to a parent scope. If the variable you reference cannot be found in the local scope, it tries to look it up in the parent scope.

- Using the var keyword causes a new variable to be created in the current local scope. If there is not a current local scope (i.e., the program is not inside a function), it creates the variable in the global scope.

- Recursive functions are functions that are defined in terms of themselves.

- Each recursive function needs at least two cases—the inductive case and the base case.

- Recursive functions are best used when each step of a problem is just a reduced form of the larger problem.

- The JavaScript stack is what enables recursive programs to work since the stack keeps a separate local scope for every time the function is called, thus allowing the function a separate copy of each variable for every time the function is invoked.

13.3.2 Apply What You Have Learned

1. Figure 13-13 shows the stack frame for the code in Figure 13-12 at one particular point in its execution. Make similar drawings for what the stack and scopes look like after *every* function call. You should have four drawings at the end.

2. In Section 10.4, we discussed and implemented a factorial function. Try to implement the factorial function as a recursive function. If you get stuck, use the code in Figure 13-12 as a template to help you out.

3. Print out your factorial function. Circle the inductive case and the base case.

4. Expand the program in Figure 13-12 so that a user can enter the start and end of the range.

5. Expand your factorial program so that a user can enter the number that he wants to make a factorial of.

6. Expand either of the two previous programs so that, after the program produces an answer, it asks the user if they want to keep going. Put the program in a loop so that the user can run the calculation as many times as they want and only stop when they want to.

CHAPTER 14

Manipulating Functions and Scopes

In Chapter 10, we learned about functions and how they create local scopes. Chapter 13 went into further depth about how the JavaScript program stack helps JavaScript keep track of where it is in the program and what local scope to use. In this chapter, we are going to go deeper and show how functions can be passed as parameters and returned as values and how to generate new functions that inherit from a different scope than the global scope.

14.1 Functions as Parameters to Functions

Throughout this book, I have tried to emphasize the fact that, in JavaScript, functions are values just like any other value. We have seen that they can be created with the `function` operator and assigned to variables with the = operator. They can also be passed as parameters of functions and returned as the result of functions.

In Chapter 13 (Figure 13-9), we looked at a function called `sum_squares_of_range`, which took a range of numbers, squared each of them, and returned the sum of all of them.

The code is repeated in Figure 14-1 for your reference.

Let's say that instead of squaring each number, we wanted to cube the number (multiply the number by itself and then by itself again). The function would be identical, but instead of calling the `square_number` function, it would instead call a function called `cube_number`.

© Jonathan Bartlett 2023
J. Bartlett, *Programming for Absolute Beginners*, https://doi.org/10.1007/978-1-4842-8751-4_14

```
var square_number = function(num) {
   var x = num * num;
   return x;
};


var sum_squares_of_range = function(r_start, r_end) {
   var total = 0;
   for(var x = r_start; x <= r_end; x++) {
      total = total + square_number(x);
   }

   return total;
};


var result = sum_squares_of_range(3, 6);
alert("The sum of the squares of the values from 3 to 6: " + result);
```

Figure 14-1. *Summing the Squares of a Range of Numbers*

```
var cube_number = function(num) {
   return num * num * num;
};

var sum_cubes_of_range = function(r_start, r_end) {
   var total = 0;
   for(var x = r_start; x <= r_end; x++) {
      total = total + cube_number(x);
   }

   return total;
};

var result = sum_cubes_of_range(3, 6);
alert("The sum of the cubes of the values from 3 to 6: " + result);
```

Figure 14-2. *Summing the Cubes of a Range of Numbers*

```
var square_number = function(num) {
   return num * num;
};

var cube_number = function(num) {
   return num * num * num;
};

var sum_range_with_transformation = function(r_start, r_end,
   transformation) {
   var total = 0;
   for(var x = r_start; x <= r_end; x++) {
      total = total + transformation(x);
   }

   return total;
}

var result_squares = sum_range_with_transformation(3, 6, square_number);
var result_cubes = sum_range_with_transformation(3, 6, cube_number);
alert("The sum of the squares of the values from 3 to 6: " +
   result_squares);
alert("The sum of the cubes of the values from 3 to 6: " + result_cubes);
```

Figure 14-3. *Summing a Range of Numbers with a Transformation*

The code for that is shown in Figure 14-2. As you can see, the only difference between sum_squares_of_range and sum_cubes_of_range is that square_number is replaced by cube_number in the new code. Wouldn't it be nice if we could have just one function for both of them and then just send up whichever function (we'll call it the *transformation function*) that we want to apply to each number? Well, in fact, you can do just that. What we can do is create a parameter to be used for the transformation function.

The new code looks like Figure 14-3. As you can see, this is still the exact same code; the only difference is that square_number is replaced with transformation, which is passed in as a parameter! These types of functions, whose functions are modified by other functions passed in as parameters, are called **higher-order functions**.

☞ **PRACTICE QUESTIONS**

---

1. Modify the program in Figure 14-3 so that you add a function that raises the number to the fourth power and then pass it into `sum_range_with_transformation`.

2. Modify the program again so that it simply sums the numbers from 3 to 6 without any transformation. (Hint—create a function that just returns the number given.)

14.2 Functions That Return Functions

Now that we have seen functions as parameters, we will look at functions that return functions.

The first example (Figure 14-4) isn't useful at all but will illustrate the point. In this program, we have our traditional `square_a_number` function. However, rather than using it directly, we have another function, called `get_square_a_number_function`, which returns that function. Note that the return statement on `get_square_a_number_function` *does not call* `square_a_number`; there are no parentheses after the function name that would indicate a function call. Instead, the function itself is returned from this function.

Then, in the main program, the value returned by `get_square_a_number_function` is stored in `my_func`. What value is this? The `square_a_number` function! Therefore, `my_func` is actually holding the `square_a_number` function itself. Since `my_func` is holding a function, it can be called as a function. This is what is happening with `my_func(5)`—it is calling the function stored in `my_func`, which is the number-squaring function. This will, as expected, return the number 25.

14.3 Functions That Create Functions

Let's say that we wanted to have a function that operated as a counter. That is, every time we called the function, it would give us the next number. The first time we called the function, it would return 1, then 2, and so forth. How might we write that function?

```
var square_a_number = function(x) {
   return x * x;
};

var get_square_a_number_function = function() {
   return square_a_number;
};

var my_func = get_square_a_number_function();
var result = my_func(5);
alert("The result of calling my_func(5) is " + result);
```

Figure 14-4. *Function That Returns a Function*

Let's start by looking at a way that *does not* work. Take a moment to see if you can figure out what is wrong with the program shown in Figure 14-5. If you haven't figured it out yet, try putting it into a web page and running it. What happens?

The problem with the program is that the definition of counter is a local variable. Therefore, every time the function is run, it will create a brand new variable named counter and set it to zero. Because of this, this function will always return the value 1.

One way around this is to make the counter variable into a global variable instead of a local one. The code in Figure 14-6 will work a little better. This one actually behaves the way we want it to, but it has two very large drawbacks. The first drawback is that the counter variable is a global variable. This means that the person using the next_value function has to know about the counter variable so they don't use it themselves. It is bad programming practice for the user of a function to have to know so much about how a function is implemented. The second drawback is that this only allows for one counter function in the program. In order to get a second counter function, we would need to recode it. It seems very wasteful to write the exact same code twice, only changing the variable names.

In order to solve these problems, we need a way to make the scope of counter isolated from the global scope and to be able to create new instances of the counter function on the fly with each having their own independent counter variable. Both of these can be solved by making function-generating-functions.

```
var next_value = function() {
   var counter = 0;
   counter = counter + 1;
   return counter;
};

var first_value = next_value();
var second_value = next_value();
alert("First value: " + first_value);
alert("Second value: " + second_value);
```

Figure 14-5. *Incorrect Program for Creating a Counter*

```
var counter = 0;
var next_value = function() {
   counter = counter + 1;
   return counter;
}


var first_value = next_value();
var second_value = next_value();
alert("First value: " + first_value);
alert("Second value: " + second_value);
```

Figure 14-6. *Using a Global Variable for a Counter*

```
var create_function = function(x) {
  var new_function = function() {
    return x;
  };

  return new_function;
};

var my_func_a = create_function(12);
var my_func_b = create_function(20);

var my_val_a = my_func_a();
var my_val_b = my_func_b();

alert("The result of calling my_func_a is " + my_val_a);
alert("The result of calling my_func_b is " + my_val_b);
```

Figure 14-7. *Example of a Function with a Local Scope as a Parent Scope*

In Chapter 10, we learned that the `function` operator creates a new function with the given code. In Chapter 13, we learned that each time the function is called, a new local scope is created for that function. We also looked at how each new local scope has a link to a parent scope, which, so far, has been the global scope. (Go back and look at Figures 13-8, 13-10, and 13-13 for a refresher.) So how does that parent scope link get created, and can it point to anything other than the global scope?

It turns out that the parent scope points to *whatever scope is active* at the time that a function is created. So far, when our functions have been created, the active scope has been the global scope. That is why the parent scope on our functions has always been the global scope. If, instead, the function had been created while another function was active, its parent scope would have been the local scope that was active at the time it was created! When such a function is called, it still creates a brand-new local scope for its parameters and all variables declared with the `var` keyword. However, when referring to any variable not defined in its local scope, it will look to its parent scope, which will be the local scope that was active when the function was created. When a computer programming language stores the scope of an active function as the parent scope for functions created within that scope, this is known as having **lexical closure**.

Figure 14-7 shows this parent scope manipulation in action. This example was kept very short so you could more easily see all of the pieces moving. From a high level, the create_function function takes one parameter and creates a function that always returns that value. Note the line that says var my_func_a = create_function(12);. This causes create_function to build a new function that will always return the value 12 and stores this new function in my_func_a.

How does create_function do this? Well, let's walk through the code.

The first thing that the create_function function does is to create a function. The function operator can be used anywhere to create a new function. It then stores this function into new_function, which is a local variable for create_function. It then returns this newly created function.

What is so special about this newly created function? Since it was defined *within* create_function, its parent scope is the local scope that was created at the time that create_function was invoked. Therefore, each time that create_function is run, it will create a *new version* of the new_function function with a *different* parent scope (i.e., the one that was created when the create_function function was called). Now, when create_function returns, its local scope is no longer active, but it is not destroyed because the function that it returns still refers to it. It will just lie dormant until the created function is called, and then it will become the parent scope of the created function's new local scope.

Therefore, when you call create_function(12), that creates a new local scope with the variable x, and x is given the value 12 from the parameter list. When the function that will be stored in new_function is created, the current local scope (with x as a local variable) is linked to the function so that it will be the parent scope of each new local scope created from calling the function. This function is then returned and stored in my_func_a. When my_func_a is called later on, it creates a new local scope for the function call. However, the parent scope is set to the scope that was active when the function was created—the scope that has x set to 12. Therefore, when it runs the code return x;, it first looks in its newly created local scope for x and doesn't find it. It then goes to the parent scope and finds x defined there. If it did not find x in the parent scope, it would move up the chain to the global scope.

Note that my_func_b is created in the same way. However, as we've mentioned, every time a function is called, a new local scope is created. Therefore, when create_function(20) is called, there is a *new* local scope created, and this scope has x set to 20.

This scope gets attached as the parent scope for the function that is created and stored in my_func_b. When my_func_a gets called, the parent scope is the one that has x set to 12, but when my_func_b gets called, the parent scope is the one that has x set to 20.

```
var create_counter = function() {
   var current_val = 0;
   var counter_function = function() {
      current_val = current_val + 1;
      return current_val;
   };
   return counter_function;
};

var mycounter_a = create_counter();
var mycounter_b = create_counter();
var mycounter_c = mycounter_a;

alert(mycounter_a()); // 1
alert(mycounter_a()); // 2
alert(mycounter_a()); // 3
alert(mycounter_b()); // 1
alert(mycounter_a()); // 4
alert(mycounter_b()); // 2
alert(mycounter_c()); // 5
```

Figure 14-8. *A Function to Create Counter Functions*

We now have two different functions that come out of the same code. These functions both work differently because they have *different parent scopes* when they are invoked.

Now, let's return to the problem of the counter functions. We wanted a function that would create a new counter function for us. So, what we really want is a counter function that can be attached to different parent scopes that each has their own current count.

Figure 14-8 shows how this works in code. This code is very similar to the code that just spits out the value from the parent scope. The only difference is that we manipulate the value of current_val in the parent scope first (we add one to it) before returning it. This modification is kept because every time you call mycounter_a, it pulls that same scope in to be the parent scope. Since current_val is *not* declared with a var keyword within counter_function, it will always refer to current_val in its parent scope whether it is reading or writing the value.

Since mycounter_a and mycounter_b were created from different calls to create_ counter, they each maintain different parent scopes and therefore independent values for current_val. Note, however, that mycounter_c continues on just as if mycounter_a were called again. Why is that? It is because mycounter_c *is not a new function.* It is *the same* function as mycounter_a since it was simply assigned.

mycounter_a and mycounter_b were both created by a call to create_counter, but mycounter_c simply gets the same function that was in mycounter_a. Remember that functions are stored in variables just like any other value and can be assigned back and forth to different variables, and these assignments do not change the underlying values. Therefore, mycounter_a and mycounter_c both refer to the exact same function (using the exact same parent scope).

14.4 Currying Functions

In Section 14.1, we learned how to take multiple, specific functions and combine them into a single higher-order function that takes a function as a parameter. In this section, we will look at the reverse process—taking a generalized, or higher-order, function and creating new, more specific versions of it by specifying one or more parameters beforehand.

Go back and look at Figures 14-1, 14-2, and 14-3. You will notice that the functionality of both Figures 14-1 and 14-2 are both present in Figure 14-3. You might rightly conclude that the function sum_range_with_transformation that is defined in Figure 14-3 is, therefore, more powerful than the individual sum_cubes_of_range and sum_squares_of_range functions defined in the other programs. However, sometimes calling functions that take another function as a parameter can be confusing. If, for instance, a programmer usually has to sum the squares of a range, but only rarely has to sum another transformation, it might be useful to have sum_squares_of_range as its own function.

Now, we still want to make use of our sum_range_with_transformation function. The reason for this is that if you have code that performs a task, you don't want to have two copies of it lying around. If you find a bug in one copy of the function, you would have to remember to fix it in the other one. If you find a better way of implementing the function, you also have to remember (and take the time) to rewrite the other function to match.

```
var sum_squares_of_range = function(r_start, r_end) {
  return sum_range_with_transformation(r_start, r_end, square_number);
};
```

Figure 14-9. *Creating a Special-Purpose Function from a General-Purpose Function*

We want to have the ease of calling sum_squares_of_range but maintaining the power of funneling all of the logic through sum_range_with_transformation. The way to do this is with **currying**. Currying a function means that you are taking a general-purpose function and creating a special-purpose function from it by fixing one or more parameters to a constant value.

For instance, if we wanted to build on the program in Figure 14-3 to make a special function called sum_squares_of_range, we could add the code listed in Figure 14-9 to do it.

As you can see, instead of writing the sum_squares_of_range function from scratch like we did in Figure 14-1, we used sum_range_with_transformation as a building block to create our function. This allowed sum_squares_of_range to become a simpler way of writing sum_range_with_transformation with some of the parameters built in.

We can go a step further to define a function-generating-function where you create a custom summing function based on a transformation function. That sounds a little weird, but perhaps an example might help. The code in Figure 14-10 can be attached to the end of Figure 14-3 to produce a working program. In this example, the create_summing_function takes the transformation as its argument and returns a brand new function, which uses that argument as the last parameter to sum_range_with_transformation, so that it provides a really easy way to create new transformation functions.

14.5 Anonymous Functions

Functions are just values. As we learned way back in Chapter 8, you often don't even need to create variables to hold each intermediate value. Similarly, we don't always need to store functions in variables either.

Just as typing the number 5 produces the value 5, using the function keyword defines a new function. Let's look back at the code we wrote in Figure 14-10. Let's say we wanted to create a new summing function, but this time we want to raise the members of the range to the fourth power before summing them. Now, we could create a separate function to raise a number to the fourth power and then just use the technique in Figure 14-10. However, an easier way would be to skip naming the function altogether and define it when we call `create_summing_function`. The result would look something like Figure 14-11, which would be appended to the program you wrote in Figure 14-10.

```
var create_summing_function = function(transformation) {
   var summing_function = function(r_start, r_end) {
      return sum_range_with_transformation(r_start, r_end, transformation);
   };
   return summing_function;
}

var sum_cubes_of_range = create_summing_function(cube_number);

var result_cubes_currying = sum_cubes_of_range(3, 6);
alert("The sum of the cubes (using currying) is " + result_cubes_currying);
```

Figure 14-10. *Creating a Special-Purpose Function Generator*

```
var sum_fourth_power_of_range = create_summing_function(function(x) {
   return x * x * x * x;
});

var new_result = sum_fourth_power_of_range(3, 6);
alert("The sum of the range raised to the fourth power is " + new_result);
```

Figure 14-11. *Using Anonymous Functions*

As you can see, where in Figure 14-10 we used a named function for the transformation, here we are passing in the function directly. The function we are passing in has no name. It is defined and, rather than being stored in a variable, is simply passed as a parameter to a function. Functions that are defined within the code and not given a name are known as **anonymous functions**.

14.5.1 Review

In this chapter, we learned several advanced ways of creating and using functions. We have learned the following:

- Functions can be passed as parameters to functions.

- When a function takes another function as a parameter, it allows the function's processes to be tweaked.

- When two functions look almost the same except that they each perform a slightly different process, they can often be combined into one function that takes a function as a parameter.

- When a function takes a function as a parameter, it is known as a higher-order function.

- Functions can return other functions as values.

- Functions can create new functions to return as a value.

- When a function is created, it combines and stores both the code to execute and a link to the scope that it was created in.

- The link to the scope will be used as the parent scope when a local scope is created for each function invocation.

- If a computer programming language stores a link to the active scope for use as a parent scope in a function when it is created, it is said that the programming language has lexical closure.

- Currying is a process of defining new, specific functions from more generic or higher-order functions by prespecifying one or more parameters.

14.5.2 Apply What You Have Learned

1. Modify the counter program in Figure 14-8 so that it takes a starting value, allowing you to start your counter at any value you want.

2. Modify the counter program further so that you can also specify a "skip" value (i.e., progress the counter by more than 1 per call).

3. Modify the program in Figure 14-11 to perform another transformation. If you need an idea, try just doubling the values.

CHAPTER 15

Intermediate Objects

So far, we have created objects that just contain data. Objects that just contain data are sometimes known as **records**—they store data, but they don't *do* anything. In Chapter 11, we wrote functions that manipulated these records. If you want to perform an action (such as withdrawing funds from an account), you would call the appropriate function, and it would do what you want. This is a fine programming style and works well for many situations. However, as programs get larger and more complex, it is beneficial to make the functions that operate on the objects more tightly connected to the objects themselves.

In Chapter 11, we grouped together several related variables into a single object. This made several improvements to our code:

1. It used fewer variables since the values were all properties of one variable.

2. It allowed the related values to travel together to functions without having to pass them individually.

3. It made the code more understandable because the related values were packaged into a single unit.

15.1 Attaching Functions to Objects

Packaging together related values into an object like we did in Chapter 11 is known as **encapsulation**. However, encapsulation can be taken further by also adding functions to our objects. As mentioned in Chapter 11, these functions are called "methods." Methods are functions which are properties of objects, where calling the function from the object will pass the object to the function as an implicit parameter (i.e., not in the parameter list). We will start by making functions where the object is passed *explicitly* and then show how to pass the object *implicitly*.

© Jonathan Bartlett 2023
J. Bartlett, *Programming for Absolute Beginners*, https://doi.org/10.1007/978-1-4842-8751-4_15

Let's say that we had an object that represented a car. It will have two values—the number of miles traveled and the amount of gas left. Now, let's say we have a function that drives us ten miles. What needs to happen? Well, that function would increase the number of miles driven and decrease the amount of gas left.

Figure 15-1 has the code for such an object. As you can see, the `drive_car` function relates several different values—the number of miles traveled, the amount of gas left in the tank, and the car's gas mileage. Since the `drive_car` function is so tightly related to the car abstraction, it makes sense to just attach the function directly to the `my_car` object, like in Figure 15-2.

As you can see, we assign the function the same way that we assign the rest of the values. We could have also done it the long way by typing `my_car.drive = function() { ...}`, but this way is simpler.

So how do you call the function now that it is in the object? Well, all function calls that we have made in this book have been made by simply typing the name of the variable which holds the function (usually a global variable) and calling it by adding parentheses and listing the parameters to pass to the function. It is done the same way here. The only difference is that since the function is stored in the object rather than in a global variable, we have to access the function value as a property on the object.

So we would write the following:

```
my_car.drive(my_car, 50);
```

What advantages does this give us? Not many yet. However, one important thing that this accomplishes is to have fewer global variables since, so far, we have usually stored functions in global variables. Now the function is only stored *within* the car object. For our simple programs, this might not seem important, but, in large projects, the number of functions can grow to thousands. In those cases, keeping the set of global variables to a minimum is essential for sanity.

```
var my_car = {
  miles_traveled: 0,
  gas_left: 10,
  miles_per_gallon: 20
};
var drive_car = function(the_car, miles_driven) {
  the_car.miles_traveled = the_car.miles_traveled + miles_driven;
  the_car.gas_left = the_car.gas_left - (miles_driven /
    the_car.miles_per_gallon);
  if(the_car.gas_left <= 0) {
    alert("You ran out of gas!");
  }
};

drive_car(my_car, 50);
drive_car(my_car, 100);
drive_car(my_car, 200); // I'm out of gas!
```

Figure 15-1. *A Simple Car Object*

```
var my_car = {
  miles_traveled: 0,
  gas_left: 10,
  miles_per_gallon: 20,
  drive: function(the_car, miles_driven) {
    the_car.miles_traveled = the_car.miles_traveled + miles_driven;
    the_car.gas_left = the_car.gas_left - (miles_driven /
      the_car.miles_per_gallon);
    if(the_car.gas_left <= 0) {
      alert("You ran out of gas!");
    }
  }
};
```

Figure 15-2. *Attaching a Function to an Object*

Along the same lines, note that when it was a global variable, we named it `drive_car`. We gave it the longer name to prevent **name clashes**—where two functions accidentally get the same name. When you put functions in global variables, you usually have to give them very long names to prevent someone else from accidentally calling another function the same name. This is not the case when the function is stored on the object itself. Additionally, if the function is only attached to the object, we already know that it is operating on a car, because that is where we assigned it. Therefore, we shortened the name of the function to just `drive`, which makes the code clearer and easier to write.

One issue, though, is that the `drive` function looks a bit redundant. The code is calling the `drive` function on the object but is also having to pass in the object as a parameter. It turns out that almost every function you define on an object requires the data of the object to be present. Therefore, if you look up a function on an object using a property (i.e., `car.drive`), JavaScript has a way to implicitly send the object (i.e., `car`) to the function without having to make it a parameter. JavaScript has a special variable, always named `this`, which holds the object that was used to look up the function (if there was one). It is called `this` because it refers to "*this* current object that we are using."

Therefore, we can remove the parameter `the_car` from the function because it will be automatically passed in through the variable `this`. Taking advantage of the `this` variable, we can write our code as shown in Figure 15-3.

So, while most parameters to functions are *explicitly* passed to the function because we named them when we defined the function, the `this` parameter is *implicitly* passed to the function—it is not in the parameter list. Instead, JavaScript handles it automatically behind the scenes.

In object-oriented programming, functions which are defined on objects and make use of the `this` variable are often referred to as **methods** or also as **messages**. Unlike other languages, in JavaScript, the distinction between a function and a method is *only* in the way that you use it—if your function makes use of the `this` variable, it is a method.

You can also think of methods in terms of human language. The object is the subject, the method is the verb or command, and the function parameters are the direct object, adverbs, or other modifiers.

```
var my_car = {
  miles_traveled: 0,
  gas_left: 10,
  miles_per_gallon: 20,
  drive: function(miles_driven) {
    this.miles_traveled = this.miles_traveled + miles_driven;
    this.gas_left = this.gas_left - (miles_driven /
      this.miles_per_gallon);
    if(this.gas_left <= 0) {
      alert("You ran out of gas!");
    }
  }
};
my_car.drive(50);
my_car.drive(100);
my_car.drive(200); // Out of gas!
```

Figure 15-3. *Writing Functions for Objects Using* this

When we see my_car.drive(50), we should read it as "dear my_car, please perform your drive function using 50 as your parameter."

So far, we have seen that using functions attached to objects decreases the number of global variable names, leads to shorter function names, and makes programming a little more English-like.

15.2 Using Objects Productively

There are several reasons to use objects in your code. Because it follows the subject/verb/object pattern of language, it is much easier to understand code written in an object-oriented style. Therefore, by combining functions with their related data, you make your program easier to use and modify because the code is clearer.

Objects also help programmers separate code into clearly definable parts. This practice is known as **modularization**. By attaching functions to the objects that hold their data, you are not only programming the computer, but you are communicating to future programmers (and your future self) where the divisions between ideas within the code are. This allows a programmer to focus their thoughts and actions on relevant functions. If I know where all of the code that relates to my_car lives, I can easily find it and modify it. Because all of the functions surrounding my_car are defined near each other, when a change needs to be made, it is easier to find related functions which also need to be modified in tandem.

```
var magic_car = {
   miles_traveled: 0,
   drive: function(miles_driven) {
      this.miles_traveled = this.miles_traveled + miles_driven;
   }
};
```

Figure 15-4. *A New Object That Implements the Same Interface*

When you program larger programs, it is sometimes difficult to keep track of what is happening to the data throughout the program. If you remove a field or change how it is used, how will you know if you modified the rest of the code to use it correctly? By baking all of the code related to an object *into* the object itself, it is easier to find the places where changes need to be made when the code for an object is modified.

Programming is not just about making your programs work. You also must make them understandable and modifiable by both yourself and others. Thinking through what objects you need, what functions they need to work, and what pieces of data they need will help you make better objects which will help you both now and in the future. It will make your code more readable, understandable, and maintainable.

Object-oriented programming has more benefits, though, than just the fact that it makes your code easier to read and understand. Object-oriented programming allows you to use objects, not based on the data they contain but based on the functions they can perform.

We already have code that allows us to drive a car. Let's say that we invented a new kind of magic car that is not limited by gasoline at all. It can drive any number of miles that you want. Such a car can be implemented using code shown in Figure 15-4.

This object isn't nearly as complicated as our previous object, but that's not what I want to emphasize. Do you notice that this object *also* has a drive method? The function operates differently for this new kind of car, but it has the same name and takes the same parameters as the drive function on our other object.

This allows us to write functions and methods that take an object as a parameter without having to care exactly what the object is. In other words, if I have a function that needs to use the drive method, that function doesn't have to care *which* version of the `drive` method it is using. Whether it is a car or a magic car, as long as my function uses the `drive` method, then I can use the either type of object for the function.

15.3 Constructing Objects

Having a single object with a function attached does not give us a lot of progress. Most programs have lots and lots of similar objects. Building objects with a set pattern is known as constructing objects, and functions that construct objects are known as **constructors**. JavaScript has several different ways of constructing objects. However, since this is an introductory book, we will only look at one—constructor functions.

A constructor function is a function that is called with JavaScript's `new` keyword. Constructor functions, by convention, are named starting with a capital letter, so they can be readily identified as a constructor function. Let's say that I wanted to write a constructor for my car that takes the starting amount of gas in the car.

Such a function might look like Figure 15-5. Notice that we created the car by saying `new Car(50)`. What this did was create a new blank object and set it as the `this` object for the `Car()` function. We then called the `Car` function with 50 as the parameter. The `new` keyword, rather than relying on the function returning a value using the `return` keyword, instead returns the newly built object that was used in the `this` variable.

In this program, the `Car` function is a constructor. It works together with the `new` keyword to build a new object for use. The function doesn't *have* to start with a capital letter, but most JavaScript programmers follow this convention to make sure that it is clear which functions are supposed to be used as constructors.

In some programming languages, `Car` would be considered a **type** or a **class**. A class gives a programmer an expectation of what the object can do—what properties it will have, what functions it will have, and how they work together. This is somewhat similar to a constructor in JavaScript because the constructor sets up the initial properties and functions on an object.

```
var Car = function(starting_gas) {
   this.miles_traveled = 0;
   this.gas_left = starting_gas;
   this.miles_per_gallon = 20;

   this.drive = function(miles_driven) {
      this.miles_traveled = this.miles_traveled + miles_driven;
      this.gas_left = this.gas_left - (miles_driven /
         this.miles_per_gallon);
      if(this.gas_left <= 0) {
         alert("You ran out of gas!");
      }
   };
};

var car_with_lots_of_gas = new Car(50);
var car_with_little_gas = new Car(10);

car_with_lots_of_gas.drive(20);
car_with_little_gas.drive(1000000); // Out of gas!
car_with_lots_of_gas.drive(20); // This car still has gas!
```

Figure 15-5. *A Car Constructor*

This means that most objects that are made by a constructor will have similar properties and functions.

15.3.1 Review

In this chapter, we covered the basics of how to attach functions to objects. We have learned the following:

- Since functions are values, functions can be stored as attributes of objects just like other values.

- Attaching functions to objects reduces the clutter of the global namespace.

- If a function is called through an object, the object that the function was stored on is passed implicitly through the this parameter.

- Structuring code in this way makes software more readable because it follows the typical English subject-verb-object sentence structure.

- Functions that create and initialize new objects are called constructors.

- Constructors are typically stored in variables starting with uppercase letters to distinguish them from other functions.

- Constructors are usually named according to the type of object they are creating.

- Constructors are called using the new keyword.

- Using a constructor allows you to create a lot of similar objects with very little code.

15.3.2 Apply What You Have Learned

1. Create a constructor Rectangle which creates an object with base and height attributes.

2. Extend your Rectangle constructor to also have two methods: find_area() and find_perimeter() that give you the relevant answers. These should not have any parameters and only use the implicit this parameter. If you have forgotten your geometry, for rectangles, *area = base × height* and *perimeter = 2 (base + height)*. Be sure to test them to make sure they work.

3. Create a new constructor for a Circle that takes a radius as a parameter. It should also have find_area() and find_perimeter() methods. If you have forgotten your geometry, *area = π x radius²* and *perimeter = 2 x π x radius*. Be sure to test them to make sure they work.

4. Create a function called biggest_area that takes an array of Rectangle objects and tells the user what the biggest area was in the array, using the find_area() function.

5. If your `biggest_area` function only uses the `find_area()` function of the object, then you should be able to send it *any* object that implements a similar function. Since `Circle` objects also have a `find_area()` function, try interweaving `Rectange` and `Circle` objects into the same array. Since they are both supposed to respond the same way, they should both be able to be treated equivalently by the `biggest_area` function.

PART V

Programming Applications

In this part of the book, we will look at some basics of how an application works. We will look at modifying a page using JavaScript, accessing an external service, and even writing a simple service.

CHAPTER 16

Modernizing JavaScript

Before we get started in some of the details about how applications in the real world are written, I wanted to take a moment and introduce you to some modern features of JavaScript which are commonly used in modern applications. Note that the goal of this book is not to provide a comprehensive introduction to JavaScript itself but rather to use JavaScript as a jumping point for learning programming in general. Nonetheless, I wanted to take some time and introduce a few modernizations of JavaScript that have been introduced over the years which you are likely to run into if you read JavaScript code. None of these are radical departures, but they do make JavaScript a little easier to read and write.

JavaScript was originally written with a primary goal of being simple, easy to implement, and easy to learn. The basic ideas behind JavaScript are sufficiently simple that the author of JavaScript originally wrote JavaScript in only 10 days. However, as it has become more and more widespread as a programming language, additional features have been added on.

In this chapter we will look at some of the more commonly used additions to JavaScript that have been added over the years. Additionally, we will also hit on some older features that are important but haven't yet been discussed in the book.

16.1 Declaring Variables with let and const

The `var` keyword is what we have been using to declare variables so far in this book. As we have noted, when used outside of a function, `var` declares a global variable, and, when used inside a function, `var` declares a local variable that is scoped to the function it is contained in. However, `var` has some weird behaviors that need to be maintained for backward compatibility with older code, even though it probably isn't wise to use these behaviors.

© Jonathan Bartlett 2023
J. Bartlett, *Programming for Absolute Beginners*, https://doi.org/10.1007/978-1-4842-8751-4_16

First of all, the var keyword can occur *anywhere* in the function, and it still backward-applies to the usage of the variable previously in the function. If you declare a variable with var more than once, these all get bundled into a single variable declaration. Finally, being function-scoped is somewhat of a surprising feature, as most programming languages delineate scopes at the *block* level.

Because of these drawbacks, more recent iterations of JavaScript introduced the let keyword for declaring variables. Using let is very similar to var, with some important distinctions:

- The let keyword must occur *before* using the variable.

- Every time you use the let keyword, it declares an entirely new variable.

- The let keyword is block-scoped, not function-scoped.

- If you try to use let twice in the same scope for the same variable, it will generate an error.

The code in Figure 16-1 illustrates the differences. Following along will help you see the differences in how the two ways of declaring variables behave.

Another keyword for declaring variables is const, which stands for "constant." This works very similarly to let, except that, once assigned a value, the variable cannot have another value assigned to it. This is helpful in two ways. First, it enables optimizations within JavaScript that can make your code faster if you have code that needs to execute quickly. Second, and even more importantly, it helps you to remember which variables are actually varying and which ones are supposed to be left alone. The const keyword will remind you that this variable is only supposed to be assigned once, and, if you forget, the subsequent assignments to that value will yield errors.

The last lines of Figure 16-1 will give an error because the constant value is reassigned.

```
var x = 3;
var z = 3;

var myexamplefunc = function() {
  x = 4; // refers to the function-scoped x
         // (var is declared later)
  z = 4; // refers to the global z

  let y = 5; // creates a new y
  var x = 5; // declares that x is function-scoped

  if(true) {
     var x = 6; // just reaffirms the existence of x
     let y = 6; // creates a new y for this block
  }

  // x is 6 and y is 5
  window.alert("x is " + x + " and y is " + y);
}

myexamplefunc();

// x is 3 and z is 4
alert("x is " + x + " and z is " + z);
const myval = 3;
myval = 4; // Error
```

Figure 16-1. *Differences Between* let *and* var

In most modern JavaScript applications, let and const are preferred to var. We have used var primarily because it is more forgiving for beginners and reflects a lot of existing documentation on JavaScript. However, if you go further, you will probably see let and const quite a bit.

16.2 Destructuring Assignments

One thing that saves a lot of typing is what is known as a **destructuring assignment**. Let's say you have an array myary that has the value [23, 43, 5]. Now, let's say that you want to separate these values into the variables x, y, and z. Usually, you would do that like the following:

```
let x = myary[0];
let y = myary[1];
let z = myary[2];
```

However, destructuring allows us to tell JavaScript in a succinct way how to do the assignment. Here is the same assignment using destructuring:

```
let [x, y, z] = myary;
```

What this says is that we should expect that myary is structured in such a way that it looks like the left-hand side and that we should assign the variables accordingly. Any additional members of the array are ignored, and if there aren't enough members of the array, the variable will be filled with undefined.

This also works with objects as well. Let's say that we have an object that looks like this:

```
var myobj = {
    field1: "val1",
    field2: "val2",
    field3: "val3"
};
```

Let's say that we wanted to extract field1 and field2 into their own variable. This can be done as follows:

```
let { field1, field2 } = myobj;
```

If we wanted to rename field2 to be myotherfield, then we can write it like this:

```
let { field1, field2: myotherfield } = myobj;
```

Destructuring is very helpful when you want to extract several pieces of an object or an array without having complicated code. You simply mirror the left-hand side so that the variable you want to assign is in the same location that you are expecting on the right-hand side. You can embed arrays within objects within arrays and so forth.

As mentioned, this book is not intended as a complete JavaScript book, but I did want to let you know about some pieces of syntax that are both helpful and you are likely to see out in the wild.

16.3 Accessing Properties with Strings

One important feature of JavaScript that has been in there from the beginning is the ability to access properties using the string value for the name of the property. This allows usage of JavaScript objects as extremely flexible stores of data. To see what I mean, let's look at an example object.

```
var theperson = {
    name: "Jim",
    age: 20,
    hair: "brown"
};
```

Now, we already know how to access individual properties of this object using theperson.name or theperson.age. However, we can also ask the object for a property that is named by a string. If we want the name property, I can ask for it by doing theperson["name"]. By putting this on the left-hand side of an assignment statement, I can set a field in this way as well, whether or not it existed beforehand.

Because this is a string, I can use a variable as well.

```
var myfield = "name";
alert("The person's name is " + theperson[myfield]);
```

This means that a user can even say what field they would like to access.

```
var myfield = prompt("What field would you like to read?");
alert("The value of that field is " + theperson[myfield]);
```

This allows for a huge amount of flexibility in both the creation and usage of object fields. In fact, property names can actually be arbitrary strings and don't even have to be accessible in the "normal" syntax. For instance, I could set a field like theperson["some,;/field-+"]. If we tried to access that field using the normal method, we would get a syntax error. But it is a perfectly valid operation as a string.

There are many cases where it is useful to have an object serve as a random grab-bag of key-value pairs. Using objects in this way allows you to do this. In computer programming, objects used in this way are referred to variously as **dictionaries**, **hashtables**, **maps**, or **associative arrays**.

16.4 Function Syntax

So far we have declared functions by typing something like the following:

```
var myfuncname = function(param1, param2) {
    // Function body here
}
```

This syntax was chosen to emphasize the distinction between *creating* a function and *assigning a name* to that function. I think doing it this way helps make it easier to understand how creating and passing functions as parameters works (like we did in Chapter 14). However, there is a combined syntax that does both at once that is much more commonly used. The same snippet above, using this other syntax, looks like this:

```
function myfuncname(param1, param2) {
    // Function body here
}
```

However, modern JavaScript adds yet another way to create functions, which is known variously as **lambda functions** or **arrow functions**.[1] Creating the same function using lambda/arrow functions looks like this:

```
var myfuncname = (param1, param2) => {
    // Function body here
}
```

The meaning is (almost) the same, but it gets rid of the annoyingly long `function` keyword.

There are indeed some slight differences to regular functions, but usually they are unimportant. The main differences are as follows:

- Regular functions get another special variable we haven't talked about, known as `arguments`. This is essentially an array of all arguments passed to the function, which allows functions to be called with more arguments than are shown in the parameter list. Arrow functions do not have this special variable.

---

[1] The term "lambda function" comes from an early conception of computer programming known as "lambda calculus," which focused on creating functions dynamically using an operator known as the "lambda" operator. The term "arrow function" comes from the fact that the syntax uses the characters => which looks like an arrow.

- Arrow functions do not overwrite the `this` variable (see Chapter 15). If you want to inherit the current `this` variable being used, arrow functions will help out. If you want to make an object method, you should use the traditional syntax.

- Regular functions can be called with the `new` keyword to build objects (again, see Chapter 15). Because arrow functions do not work with their own `this` variable, you cannot use arrow functions in this way.

So aside from a few edge cases, arrow functions are basically identical to the syntax we've used so far. However, while it might seem trivial, the fact that arrow functions don't clobber the `this` variable comes in handy quite a bit. If you are writing a method inside an object and need a dynamically created function, you can choose a regular function or an arrow function based on whether or not you want `this` to be overwritten.

16.4.1 Review

In this chapter, we learned about additional syntax available in JavaScript. We learned the following:

- Variables can be declared with the `let` and `const` keywords for block scoping and slightly cleaner behavior.

- Variables declared with the `const` keyword should not be reassigned after declaration.

- Assigning variables based on complex object and array layouts can be greatly simplified through destructuring assignments.

- The arrow syntax for functions is more compact and convenient to write.

- The arrow syntax for functions does not overwrite the `this` special variable.

16.4.2 **Apply What You Have Learned**

1. Go through your old programs and rewrite them using `let` instead of `var`.

2. Look through a program and find a variable which was never reassigned, and use the `const` keyword for declaring the variable.

3. Rewrite a program that uses functions to use the arrow syntax.

4. Rewrite the function in Figure 11-5 so that it uses destructuring syntax to put the child's age in a separate variable.

CHAPTER 17

Working with Remote Services (APIs)

One of the most fundamental aspects of modern computer programming is writing a program that interacts with servers. JavaScript is primarily a front-end language, meaning that it usually deals with the interactions with the user. There is usually some database or other remote service somewhere where your data is stored, retrieved, or manipulated from. So how do you access these services?

Many if not most modern services are accessed via HTTP/HTTPS requests on the Web (go back to Chapter 3 to refresh yourself on HTTP). Essentially the servers are constructed so that the URL tells the server what data you want or want to modify, and the server responds appropriately. Therefore, by knowing what these URLs look like and what the server is expecting, you can construct URLs and HTTP requests to fetch, modify, and manipulate data on the server.

The specifics of the structure of the URLs and how they should be accessed via HTTP is known as an **application programming interface**, or **API**. APIs actually refer to any documented interface for programming another system. For instance, all of the standard JavaScript objects and functions (such as `alert`, `prompt`, `document`, etc.) are part of the JavaScript API.

However, for this chapter, when we refer to an API, we are referring to a remote service's documented interface over HTTP.

Many APIs cost money to use, but there is one API that is free now and almost certain to remain free in the future because you already pay for it with your tax dollars: NASA's Data API. This API provides a gateway to all sorts of data gathered and curated by NASA itself. The NASA API includes the following:

- The Astronomy Picture of the Day

- Satellite Imagery of the Earth

© Jonathan Bartlett 2023
J. Bartlett, *Programming for Absolute Beginners*, https://doi.org/10.1007/978-1-4842-8751-4_17

- Mars Rover Photos

- Mars Weather Service

- Much, much more!

You can find out general information about NASA's API at `api.nasa.gov`.

17.1 Getting an API Key

Most APIs need to know who you are. Or, at the very least, they need to identify the fact that you are a distinct individual. The reason for this is that, if you started abusing the platform (trying to hack into it, using too many resources, adding bad data, etc.), the person running the API needs to be able to cancel your access to the API.

For that reason, most APIs require at least a modicum of authentication. One way of performing this authentication is with an **API key**. Usually, an API key serves as both the username and the password for access to a site. Sometimes they need to be kept secret, sometimes not. Note, however, that *everything* that is delivered to a user on a web page (including your JavaScript) is visible to the user, so you don't want any of your *secret* access keys to be included in your JavaScript or in any file loaded into the browser by your JavaScript. In the case of the NASA Data API, it is perfectly fine to include your API key in your JavaScript files.

For doing these exercises, you will need to register your own API key. To do so, go to `api.nasa.gov` and fill out their form that says, "Generate API Key." This will return a very long string such as this (not a real API key):

`hgohi6oLOJLMZProclQIY2ku1lXebMHfMlxXQ94E`

You will need to copy that down so that you have it for the future. For all of the examples in this chapter, we will refer to this simply as `APIKEY`. So, wherever you see `APIKEY`, replace it with the value you received from NASA.

You can simply use your browser to try out your API Key. Go to the following URL and you will see information about NASA's astronomy picture of the day:

`https://api.nasa.gov/planetary/apod?api_key=APIKEY`

This is a particular URL that performs a predefined function intended to be used by another program. Such URLs are often referred to as **endpoints**. What we will be doing in this chapter is getting our JavaScript code to access and use this data.

17.2 JSON: The Language of Data

You might have noticed that the data in the URL we accessed in the previous section looked strangely familiar. You might have thought that it looked surprisingly like a JavaScript object. In fact, the data that this URL generates is in a format known as JSON, which stands for JavaScript Object Notation. It is a subset of JavaScript that is often used for transmitting data on Internet APIs.

Before JSON, the major format for Internet APIs was XML. XML is similar to HTML, but you can create whatever tags you want.[1] However, XML wound up being a lot more difficult to use than many people expected. Processing XML was simply a hard programming task that took too much time and was too error-prone.

With JSON, however, the data comes in *already ready to be put into a variable.* There is no real processing to do—it's just ready to go. Therefore, the whole step of reading and processing the data into a usable form can simply be skipped. JSON data is transmitted in a format that is already ready to be used in a program.

JavaScript provides two main functions for reading and writing JSON (though, as we will see, even this will wind up being largely unnecessary). To convert an object or array to JSON, simply use the `JSON.stringify()` function. This takes a JavaScript value as an argument and then returns a string which is the JSON-format version of the object.

The other function, which takes a JSON string and gives back the equivalent JavaScript object, is `JSON.parse()`. The following code shows these two functions in action:

```
var obj = {
    mykey: "myval",
    myotherkey: [1, 2, 3]
};
var str = JSON.stringify(obj);
console.log(str);
var newobj = JSON.parse(str);
console.log(newobj);
```

---

[1] In fact, HTML is essentially a set of tags within XML. There are some historical technical distinctions, and HTML is generally processed in a more forgiving way than XML, but, on the whole, you can generally think of HTML as being a set of tags in XML.

When this runs, it will first log to the console a *string* which contains the JSON representation of the object which should roughly match the JavaScript. The second log will be the object that is created from processing the JSON code. As a note of terminology, turning a programming language data structure into a transmittable or storable structure (like a string) is known as **serialization**, while taking the transmittable/storable structure and generating the programming language data structure again is known as **deserialization**.

17.3 Accessing the Network with JavaScript

Now that we know a little about the data structure being used, we can now look at how to load that data using JavaScript code. JavaScript provides two mechanisms for accessing the network. The older one is known as XMLHTTPRequest. You will see this with a lot of older code. The newer (and easier to use) one is known as the Fetch API, named after its primary function, fetch.

The Fetch API is easiest to describe with an example. So, to start with, we will simply fetch the information for NASA's Astronomy Picture of the Day and display the title to the user. Figure 17-1 shows the code.

This code starts with a called to fetch, passing in the URL that we want to fetch. However, the network doesn't always work immediately, but the fetch function returns immediately in case you had other things you needed to do. However, what the fetch function returns is known as a Promise. A promise is an object which encapsulates the idea of something that takes an unknown amount of time to process and for which we want to do something with the results. Here, we don't know how long it will take to transmit the data, but, once it is transmitted, we want to process it. A Promise has a function called then which gives the Promise a function to call when all of its processing is done. This function should take a single parameter, which is the result of whatever we were trying to do.

```
fetch("https://api.nasa.gov/planetary/apod?api_key=APIKEY").then(
    (response) => {
        response.json().then((jsonval) => {
            var title = jsonval.title;
            alert("The picture title is " + title);
        });
    }
);
```

Figure 17-1. *A Simple Example of the Fetch API*

In our code, we called then with a function that took one parameter, response, which is the response that we get back from communicating with NASA's web server. In order to get the JSON value of the response, we have to call the json function of the response, which will make sure we have all of the data and then, assuming it is in JSON format, will convert it to a JavaScript object. However, this too comes wrapped in a Promise, which requires that we call then and send it a function it can call when the data is all ready.

Finally, when our data comes in the parameter jsonval, we can access all of the fields we received. These are the same fields you observed when you accessed the URL yourself. We used the title field to display to the user. Feel free to try with other fields as well.

17.4 The Query String

A URL can have a **query string** appended to the end of it (also referred to as **search parameters**). A query string is a set of key=value pairs appended to the end of the URL which modifies the request. The pairs are each separated by an ampersand (&), and the whole of the query string is separated from the main URL by a question mark (?).

In fact, the URL we are hitting already has a short query string. Let's look at the URL again:

https://api.nasa.gov/planetary/apod?api_key=APIKEY

Notice there is a single key=value pair attached to the end of request following the question mark. The API also allows for other query parameters to be added as well. While the API has a number of keys that it supports for its query string (you can see more at api.nasa.gov), we will focus on one: date. This will give you the Astronomy Picture of the Day for that particular date. The API states that this must be given in a specific format, namely, YYYY-MM-DD. So, for August 3, 2009, the date would be formatted as 2009-08-03. The following URL incorporates this into the query string:

```
https://api.nasa.gov/planetary/apod?api_key=APIKEY&date=2009-08-03
```

Note that it may be tempting to manually construct these URLs from a string; there is a standard class called URLSearchParams that will handle this for you. To generate the preceding URL, you can do the following:

```
var query = {
    api_key: "APIKEY",
    date: "2009-08-03"
};
var query_string = new URLSearchParams(query).toString();
var full_url = "https://api.nasa.gov/planetary/apod?" + query_string;
```

Usually in computer programming it is best to use the supplied functions rather than try to do things yourself, because there are often small caveats and gotchas that are accounted for in the functions that you may not recognize. If you aren't thoroughly familiar with the format or protocol, or aren't really careful, you can wind up screwing things up badly and even causing errors or, worse, security problems. Therefore, when the format of something is going to be read by a computer, it is almost always best to use standard functions to handle them rather than try it yourself.

```
<html>
  <head>
    <script type="text/javascript"
                    src="apodquery.js"
                    defer="defer">
            </script>
  </head>
<body>
  <h1>Astronomy Picture of the Day Query Tool</h1>

  <p>
    What date would you like to view?
    Enter as YYYY-MM-DD.
  </p>

  <input type="text" id="dateinput" />
  <button id="thebutton">Go</button>

  <p>
    <img src="" id="theimage" />
  </p>
</body>
</html>
```

Figure 17-2. *Astronomy Picture of the Day Query Tool (HTML)*

17.5 Interacting with a Web Page

In this section, we will show how to use both the ability to read a URL and manipulate it with a query string to do a full interactive page using the Astronomy Picture of the Day. Here we will show a tool for querying the Astronomy Picture of the Day by date and it displaying that picture for you. Note that this will require that the user enter in the date as specified in the previous section (YYYY-MM-DD).

The HTML we will be using for this is shown in Figure 17-2. The corresponding JavaScript code is given in Figure 17-3.

```
// Connection points to the API
let endpoint = "https://api.nasa.gov/planetary/apod";
let mykey = "APIKEY";

// Connection points to the web page
let image_elem = document.getElementById("theimage");
let date_element = document.getElementById("dateinput");
let my_button = document.getElementById("thebutton");

var retrieve_picture_for_date = function(the_date) {
   let params = {
      api_key: mykey,
      date: the_date
   };
   let query_string = new URLSearchParams(params).toString();
   let full_url = endpoint + "?" + query_string;
   fetch(full_url).then((response) => {
      response.json().then((jsonval) => {
         image_elem.src = jsonval.url;
      });
   });
};

my_button.onclick = () => {
   let date_value = date_element.value;
   retrieve_picture_for_date(date_value);
};
```

Figure 17-3. *Astronomy Picture of the Day Query Tool (JavaScript)*

As you can see, this code has the same basic structure as Figure 17-1 but expands it in the following ways:

1. It is triggered by a click on an HTML element.

2. It pulls in an extra field from HTML.

3. It uses URLSearchParams to construct the query string.

4. It manipulates the HTML after completion.

You will find that a lot of programming on the Web consists of precisely these kinds of interactions.

17.6 A Few Other Bits to Note

Accessing web pages with URLs and query strings alone will get you far, but there is a limit to how much data you can pass through a URL. Because of this (and other reasons), there are other ways to pass data to a web server. There are a variety of HTTP **methods** (also called **verbs**) which HTTP supports. The standard one we have been using so far is called GET. The three other common ones are POST, PUT, and DELETE.

Whether and how these work depends entirely on the API, but the overall *goal* of having these different verbs is as follows:

- GET is for getting data that already exists on the server, specifically identified by a URL.

- DELETE is for deleting data that already exists on the server, specifically identified by a URL.

- PUT is for updating data that exists on the server, specifically identified by a URL.

- POST is for creating data that doesn't already exist on the server. The URL used here is generally the same URL every time you create something new.

Since PUT and POST are for sending data, they also support what is known as an **entity body** or **payload** which can be sent along with the request. There are a variety of ways in which this data can be encoded, but the two most common are either (a) the same format as the query string or (b) using JSON.

Along with your data, oftentimes when accessing remote APIs you also have to send specific HTTP headers (we learned a little about HTTP headers back in Chapter 3). One particular header is the Content-Type header, which most services require that you send with PUT/POST payloads describing how they are formatted (for reference, the Content-Type of a query string formatting payload is application/x-www-form-urlencoded and the Content-Type of a JSON payload is application/json).

The following is a simple example of using an HTTP POST method to a payload, just so you can see all of the pieces in place:

```
var myobject = {
    a: 1,
    b: "someval"
};
```

```
fetch("https://www.example.com/some_endpoint", {
    method: "post",
    headers: {
        "Content-Type": "application/json",
        "Other-Header": "My other header value"
    },
    body: JSON.stringify(myobject)
}).then((response) => {
    // Do something with the response.
});
```

For detailed information about how this all fits together, it depends entirely on the API you are accessing. This section just tells you what sort of things the API documentation will be referring to.

☞ A NOTE ON CORS

I wanted to take a moment to mention CORS to you. This is somewhat outside the scope of what this book is aiming for, but I thought I'd mention it before it causes you problems. CORS, which stands for "cross-origin resource sharing," is a browser security feature that allows a web server to tell browsers what website they are expecting traffic from. The idea is to prevent a browser window looking at one page to trigger actions on another website. Therefore, before making a request, the browser will "preflight" the request to the server to check and see if the request is coming from a valid source.

I mention this because, if you try to attempt to access an API but you keep on getting nothing but errors back, it is possible you are running into CORS errors. This is especially true if you are building your own API (which we will cover a little bit of in Chapter 18). You have to explicitly whitelist any host that you are receiving requests from that is not the same as the server that is hosting the JavaScript. Usually, if there is a CORS problem, the JavaScript console will mention either "CORS," "cross-origin," or "preflight" problems.

There are a lot of nuances involved here, but I mostly wanted to make you aware of the issue before spending days trying to figure out why something isn't working.

17.6.1 Review

In this chapter, we practiced accessing a remote JSON-based API with JavaScript. We have learned the following:

- Programmers use the term API to refer to the documented way to access functionality built by another developer or organization.

- On the Web, APIs are usually based on HTTP requests to specific, documented URLs.

- NASA has an easy-to-access API for public querying of NASA data, which can be found at `api.nasa.gov`.

- Many APIs have their accessed managed through an API key which contains the user's access credentials to the service.

- Many APIs use JSON, a format based on a subset of JavaScript, as the format for transferring information.

- JavaScript includes the `JSON.stringify` and `JSON.parse` functions to allow for converting back-and-forth from JSON strings to JavaScript objects.

- The standard JavaScript `fetch` function is used to make HTTP requests from JSON.

- The `fetch` function returns a `Promise`, which is then given a function which it should call when the data is ready.

- Additional data can be sent via HTTP using the query string, which is usually formatted with `key=value` pairs.

- HTTP has multiple methods which can be used for data access. The default method is `GET`, but there is also `PUT`, `POST`, and `DELETE`.

- The `PUT` and `POST` methods can take an HTTP entity body to allow for more data than may be supported by the URL alone.

- Using the fetch function, the programmer can also send additional HTTP headers as well.

- CORS is a security measure that is implemented by browsers to control which web pages have permission to access which HTTP endpoints.

17.6.2 Apply What You Have Learned

1. The Astronomy Picture of the Day also supports getting a count of random images instead of a specific date. Change the code in Figures 17-2 and 17-3 to leave out the input field, but just have a button which fetches three random images each time you push the button. Note that, here, the API will now be giving you back an array of objects, not just a single one. You might consider using console.log to display the results while you are still working on it, so you can see exactly what is being given to your code.

2. Modify the previous program so the user can enter how many pictures they want to view. Note that, for this one, you will need to dynamically add and remove <img /> tags based on the number of pictures the user requests.

3. Look through NASA's list of APIs. Look for one that you find interesting, and practice accessing it with your browser. Now write an interface with HTML and JavaScript for accessing this API.

CHAPTER 18

Writing Server-Side JavaScript

So far, we have written user interfaces, but we are only accessing *other people's* server-side code. In this chapter, we are going to take a very brief look at the other side of the equation and give you a quick taste of server-side programming. The goal of this chapter is not to even get you fully set up for doing server-side programming. That would require an entire additional book. However, I do think it is important for you to know at least a little bit about what goes on there.

18.1 Programming Languages

While the user-facing side of web programming (also known as **front-end** or **client-side** programming) is done almost exclusively in HTML and JavaScript, on the server (also known as **back-end** programming), JavaScript is actually much more rarely used. Additionally, programming languages are rarely used by themselves but are instead used along with **application frameworks** which automate many of the tasks which are required to do server-side programming. Note that there are also front-end application frameworks (such as React, JQuery, and Angular, just to name a few), but it is a lot easier to write front-end applications without a framework than it is to write back-end applications.

The following are some popular programming languages that are often used on the server, with the name of common application frameworks for them in parentheses:

- Go (Gin, Iris, go-kit)

- Python (Django, Masonite, TurboGears)

- Ruby (Rails, Sinatra)

© Jonathan Bartlett 2023
J. Bartlett, *Programming for Absolute Beginners*, https://doi.org/10.1007/978-1-4842-8751-4_18

- Java (Spring Boot, Quarkus)

- PHP (Laravel, Symfony, Zend, Wordpress)

- C# (ASP.NET)

- JavaScript (Express)

The list of languages (and frameworks for them) is nearly endless, each with their advantages and disadvantages. My recommendation (for your next book purchase) is to pick one that looks easy to start with. This will probably not be the one you stick with, but having early, easy wins helps you to get more familiar with how everything works. Sometimes complicated frameworks are necessary, but it is better to start with something simple, and that way you will gain the experience to know why it is the complicated frameworks need their complications.

For myself, if I'm trying to write something quickly, I write it in Ruby using the Rails framework. When Rails was first introduced, you could write the same applications as before using only 10% of the code previously required! Today, many of the features of Rails are adopted by other frameworks, but I still think that Rails makes it easiest to write server-side applications quickly.

Other than that, I usually write code based on the requirements of the company I work for. Most companies don't want to have to maintain a whole host of programs written in different languages, so they generally try to standardize on a few. This means that, on the whole, you will generally not be choosing the server-side language you work with, so you should prepare yourself for the fact that you will probably have to learn several through your career.

In this chapter, since we've taken the time to learn JavaScript already, we will do a short example using JavaScript and the Express framework.

18.2 Using JavaScript Outside of the Browser

Originally, you could only use JavaScript within a browser. However, since JavaScript became an almost universal language that every developer needs to know *something* about, eventually people decided that if it was so useful on the browser, why not on the server? Therefore, a group of developers took Google Chrome's open source JavaScript engine, removed it from the browser, and created Node.js (often just called Node), a non-browser-based JavaScript engine. You can download Node for your own computer by downloading it from nodejs.org. You will need to be on the command line to run the commands in this section. You can find a short introduction to the command line in Appendix B.2.

The following is a simple Node app, which just writes to the output. You can call this file myapp.js.

```
console.log("Welcome to Node!");
```

After you have installed Node, you can run this JavaScript file using Node from your command line by typing node myapp.js. The language features of Node are identical to standard JavaScript, but the browser-based features (such as alert, prompt, document, etc.) are missing, and some extra functionality is included.

18.3 A Small Web Service Using Node

Figure 18-1 shows an example of a small HTTP service written in Node (save it with the filename nodeserver.js). This service will listen on port 3000 (a nonstandard HTTP port) for requests, and then, no matter what URL is requested, it will send back JSON data with the requested URL and a message.

This code introduces one new language feature we haven't talked about yet—JavaScript **modules**. A module is a way for JavaScript to package up code that works as a unit. This code is only processed if the application requests it. The require function loads a JavaScript module, which can then be assigned to a variable which is used to access the contents of the module. Here, the HTTP-serving features are in a module called http, which is then loaded and placed in a variable of the same name. From here, http works just like an ordinary JavaScript object.

The http object has a createServer function. This function is given a function as a parameter, which takes a request object (what the browser sends) and a response object (which we will use to send our response) and then processes the request. This function will be called anytime someone accesses our server. Then, this server is told to listen for requests on port 3000. Port 3000 was chosen because some computers already have a service listening on the standard HTTP port, so we are using an alternate port that is likely to be free on all computers.

```
const http = require('http');

let server = http.createServer((req, res) => {
  let data = {
    requestedUrl: req.url,
    message: "hello"
  };
  res.statusCode = 200;
  res.setHeader('Content-Type', 'application/json');
  res.end(JSON.stringify(data));
})
server.listen(3000);
```

Figure 18-1. *A Small Web Service in Node*

You can run this code just by running node nodeserver.js on the command line.

This can be accessed with your browser by going to http://localhost:3000/ whatever. We are using http instead of https because HTTPS requires a lot of additional setup to use. localhost is a standard name that refers to the machine that the browser is on. The :3000 addition tells the browser to look at port 3000 instead of the standard port (80). Then the path is everything coming after (starting with the slash). The server function will respond to any path given to it.

18.4 Why We Need Frameworks

In this example, our server responded to *every* request by running the *same* function. If you have multiple endpoints, this can become problematic. Think about it this way—you will need to check the URL for every possible endpoint someone may be accessing and do a whole lot of if statements to figure out what function they should call. Thus, one of the standard features of a framework is to perform **request routing**. Request routing means matching URL endpoints with functions that should run them. Running a sequence of if statements isn't problematic for two or three endpoints, but most applications have *hundreds* of endpoints, at which point a more elegant approach is needed.

Additionally, your application will probably have data that you want to store somewhere. While you *can* store it in the filesystem (and there are functions that allow you to do that), this is generally considered bad practices for a number of reasons. Instead, data is generally stored in databases. However, the process of connecting to databases, querying them, and getting the data back to your application in a usable form is sometimes quite time-consuming. Therefore, these operations are likewise often assisted by frameworks.

Frameworks often have other features, too, like job scheduling (i.e., run a report at midnight and send it somewhere), resource management (make sure nobody is calling an endpoint too often), interfacing with other services, and prebuilt data manipulation functions. Because of all of these features, application developers usually opt for using full frameworks rather than just serving requests directly.

18.5 Making Your Service Available

It's one thing to run an HTTP server on your own machine, but, what you really want is to make it available to the world. I'm not going to tell you how to do that (again, that would be another book), but I can tell you about the basic steps required to do so.

- You need to rent a server from a hosting service. My favorite hosting service is Linode, but there are innumerable other ones available, such as Digital Ocean, Azure, Bluehost, InMotion, AWS[1], and Hostinger.

- You need to configure your server so that it runs the language and framework you have chosen.

- You need to install your application on the server.

- You need to make sure your application starts when the server starts.

- You need to register a domain name for your service.

- You need to make sure the DNS record for your domain name points to the correct IP address of your service.

- You need to register for, install, and maintain SSL certificates on your server to enable HTTPS connections.

As your service gets bigger, you need to look at making your service **scale** (i.e., run faster using more machines). For that I suggest my book *Cloud Native Applications with Docker and Kubernetes*.

---

[1] If you use AWS, you should use Lightsail, as it is a lot less complicated than their other offerings.

18.5.1 Review

This chapter covered a little bit about server-side development. We have learned the following:

- While front-end programming is primarily HTML and JavaScript, back-end programming can use any number of languages.

- Node.js is used to enable JavaScript programming in situations where there is no browser available.

- Modules are bundles of JavaScript functionality that can be requested and stored into a variable using the require function.

- Node.js comes with an http module that enables you to easily write HTTP service code.

- Application frameworks are needed for a variety of common tasks in HTTP services, such as request routing, database access, scheduling, and accessing other services.

- In order to make an application available to the public, many other steps are involved, including finding a hosting provider, loading your code onto a remote machine, and registering and setting up a domain name with the DNS system.

18.5.2 Apply What You Have Learned

1. Modify the code in Figure 18-1 so that it gives different messages for the paths /mypath1 and /mypath2.

2. Extend the web server so that you define a hashtable (see Chapter 16) where the key is the path and the value is the message to be sent. Use hashtable lookups rather than if statements to find the appropriate message.

3. Extend the previous approach further so that, instead of containing a string message, the value is actually a function to run, which is given both the request and response objects as parameters. Doing this is very similar to routing with an application server.

4. Look up several of the hosting providers mentioned in this chapter. What do they offer? How much does it cost? How is it priced?

CHAPTER 19

Conclusion

Congratulations—you have taken the first steps into the wide world of programming. This book introduced you to the basics of computers, the Internet, web pages, CSS, and JavaScript. However, this book certainly didn't teach you all there is to know about any of these subjects.

Hopefully now you have a basic feel for what it is like to write and run a program and the kind of thought-work required to make a program run successfully. Where you go from here is up to you. If you like websites, then you should dig deeper into the topics covered here—HTML, CSS, and JavaScript. Learning a JavaScript framework like React or JQuery might also be a good idea. Other than that, there are all sorts of specialized tools, languages, and techniques for programming different devices and applications. There are tools and languages for database systems, phone apps, e-commerce apps, games, microcontroller systems (tiny devices with small chips), and desktop applications. Each of these has its own specialized tools and languages.

Your first language, however, is usually the hardest. Once you get used to the idea of statements, loops, variables, and functions, then, even if different languages do things differently, you have already trained your mind to think in these terms. Learning JavaScript may have been challenging, but it should make your next language much easier.

Keep in mind that software development is very dynamic. A programmer spends much of his or her life staying on top of new languages, tools, and techniques that are continually changing.

You've got a good start. Now build on it.

© Jonathan Bartlett 2023
J. Bartlett, *Programming for Absolute Beginners*, https://doi.org/10.1007/978-1-4842-8751-4_19

APPENDIX A

Glossary

The following are the definitions of the bolded glossary terms used throughout the book, plus additional terms you are likely to run into when reading about programming. When a term has more than one usage, the context for the term is distinguished in parentheses.

absolute path An absolute path is a relative URL that starts with a slash. The slash indicates that the relative URL should ignore the path component of the base URL and just use the given path instead. For instance, if the base URL is www.npshbook.com/example/example.html, an absolute path of /test.html indicates the URL www.npshbook.com/test.html. See also *URL*, *fully qualified URL*, *base URL*, *relative URL*.

absolute URL See *fully qualified URL*.

accessor In object-oriented programming, an accessor is a method that accesses an object's internal properties. In object-oriented programming, it is usually recommended that code outside of the object's own code should not directly access an object's internal properties but use methods (called accessors) to retrieve the data. This allows object programmers to modify the way that their object's internal properties are stored in future versions of the object without adversely affecting other code. See also *mutator*.

anchor In a URL, the anchor is a piece of extra data that is passed to the web page through the URL. It is located at the end of the URL, even after the query string if there is one. The anchor starts with a hash symbol (#), and everything after the hash symbol is part of the anchor. Hashes were originally intended to reference a section within a page to allow browsers not just to open up to a

251

J. Bartlett, *Programming for Absolute Beginners*, https://doi.org/10.1007/978-1-4842-8751-4

specific page but also to automatically scroll to a specific section within the page indicated by the hash and marked in the HTML with `<a name="hashname"></a>`. Now it is also used as a generic means of passing in data, much like the query string. In JavaScript, the anchor is retrieved through `window.location.hash`. See also *URL*.

anonymous function An anonymous function is a function that is not given a name but is just used as a parameter in a higher-order function. See also *function, higher-order function*.

API See *Application Programming Interface*.

API Key An API key is a piece of data (usually a single string) which contains authentication information for an application to connect to an API.

application framework See *framework*.

application layer The application layer is the seventh layer of a networking system according to the OSI model. The application layer is defined by each individual application such as email, web browsing, or file transfer. The application layer is for the main purpose of the communication, with the other layers mostly just supporting this layer. See also *OSI model*.

Application programming interface An application programming interface (API) is a set of records, objects, functions, and classes which define the way that a programmer should interact with an existing system. An API is primarily a set of documentation of existing or new functionality and how a programmer can gain access to it. See also *documentation*.

argument See *parameter*.

arithmetic and logic unit The arithmetic and logic unit is the part of the Central Processing Unit that performs math and logic functions. See also *Central Processing Unit*.

array An array is a sequence of data values or records, usually all of similar types of data. Each element of an array is referenced by its position in the array, called the index, with zero referring to the first element. See also *data format, zero-based indexing.*

arrow function An arrow function is a shorthand way of defining functions without using the `function` keyword. Arrow functions are often used when generating new functions inside other functions or when passing functions as parameters. Arrow functions do not make use of the `this` object.

ALU See *arithmetic and logic unit.*

ASCII ASCII (the American Standard Code for Information Interchange) is a way of representing letters, digits, punctuation, and processing codes using numbers. Because computers only process numbers, ASCII allows a number to represent a letter or other mark on the screen. In ASCII, each letter is represented by exactly one byte. While ASCII has been largely superseded by UTF-8, UTF-8 is, for the most part, backward compatible with ASCII. To the extent that it is covered, ASCII is covered in this book because it is by far the simpler of the two systems, and ASCII is almost entirely compatible with UTF-8. See also *data format, Unicode,* and *UTF-8.*

assignment statement An assignment statement is a JavaScript statement that is specified by an equal sign (`=`). An assignment statement has an expression that yields a value on the right-hand side of the equal sign and a location to store the value on the left-hand side of the equal sign. An example assignment statement is `myvar = myothervar * 2;` See also *expression, syntax, right-hand side, left-hand side.*

associative array An associative array is a data structure which has keys (usually strings) where each key contains a corresponding value. Associative arrays do not usually place restrictions on the contents of keys or values. All JavaScript objects can function as associative arrays. When doing so, the keys become JavaScript properties.

attribute (HTML) In HTML and XML, an attribute is a setting used to modify or add additional information to a tag. While attributes have many purposes, one of the most common reasons for adding attributes is to add a `class` or `id` attribute that can be used for specialized styling using CSS. In the following markup, the `<p>` tag has the `class` attribute set to `important`: `<p class="important">Important text here</p>` See also *HyperText Markup Language, Extensible Markup Language, tag.*

attribute (object) In object-oriented programming, an attribute is a piece of data tied to an object. For instance, if an object represents a car, that object might have attributes for where it is located on the map, how much gas it has left, and what direction it is going.

back end The back end of a system is the code that is running on the remote server. This is usually responsible for the ultimate storage and processing of data. See also *front end.*

background (CSS) The background of an HTML element is the area painted behind the content, padding, and border of the element.

background (back-end programming) In back-end programming, something is running in the "background" if it is running in a separate process or thread other than the one that is processing requests.

base case In recursive programming, the base case is the condition that stops the recursion and returns a simple answer. Recursive functions are usually set up to reduce the problem to a simpler and simpler problem until an answer can be provided directly. This place/condition where an answer can be provided directly is the base case. Without a base case, a recursive function would never be able to stop and would generate an infinite loop. See also *recursive function, inductive case, infinite loop.*

base URL The base URL is the starting point for relative URLs. The base URL is usually set to the URL of the current document being viewed, but in HTML this can be adjusted using the `<base>` tag. See also *URL, fully qualified URL, relative URL.*

BBS See *bulletin-board system.*

binary The binary numbering system is a system that only uses 1s and 0s. The first few numbers of binary (starting with zero) are 0 (zero), 1 (one), 10 (two), 11 (three), and 100 (four). See also *decimal, octal, hexadecimal.*

binary digit See *bit.*

binary file A binary file, as opposed to a text document, is a file which is not readable in a text editor but requires a more specialized program in order to read and manipulate the file. See also *text document.*

bit A bit is a binary digit—either a 1 or a 0. In the binary number system, 1 and 0 are the only digits. Computers are able to work more easily with binary digits because they can be implemented using the presence or absence of electrical current. See also *byte, binary.*

block A block is a grouped sequence of statements. In JavaScript, blocks are indicated with opening and closing braces ({ and }). Blocks are used to designate the body of a function, a branch of an `if` statement, or the body of a loop. See also *control structure, function.*

boolean A boolean value is a true/false value. It is essentially a bit that is treated such that the 1 is true and the 0 is false.

border (CSS) The border of an element is the area surrounding the main content and the padding.

bug A bug is an error in the program.

built-in function A built-in function is a function that is a part of the programming system and doesn't need to be added by the programmer. A common built-in function used in this book is the JavaScript `alert` function, which displays messages to the user. See also *function.*

bulletin-board system A bulletin-board system was a popular method of computer communication in the days before the Internet. Basically, a computer would call a main computer over the phone lines, and the user would directly interact with the main computer on the other side. The user could leave messages and files for other users to pick up when they dialed in.

byte A byte is a sequence of eight bits and therefore has the ability to hold a number between 0 and 255. While individual bytes are rarely used in computer programs anymore, most quantities on computers are given in terms of bytes, such as the size of computer memory chips and hard drives. See also *bit, binary*.

Cascading style sheet Cascading style sheet is a text file format which specifies how HTML (or even XML) should be displayed to a user. It uses property lists to define what style should be used to lay out a block of text, and then it uses selectors to specify which tags go with which property lists.

CDN See *content delivery network*.

Central Processing Unit The Central Processing Unit (CPU) is the core of a computer which actually performs all of the data processing.

chip See *integrated circuit*.

class In object-oriented programming, a class is very similar to a type and is often used interchangeably. Types usually refer to single values, while classes refer to whole objects. Types are typically predefined by the programming language, and classes are generally defined by the programmer (with the exception of a few built-in classes). A class describes what properties are available on the *instances* of the class and what methods can be called on them. In JavaScript, objects don't really have classes, but they do have constructors, which serve a similar purpose of defining the attributes and valid functions of an object. See also *constructor, instance, object*.

CLI See *Command-Line Interface*.

client A client is a computer or software program which accesses the services of another computer across the network, called the server. See also *server*.

client-side See *front end*. See also *client*.

command-line interface A command-line interface (CLI) is a user interface that allows users to interact with the computer by directly typing commands and getting textual output on the screen. Most command-line interfaces have at least some amount of programmability, allowing users an almost unlimited flexibility in running system programs. See also *graphical user interface*.

command prompt In a command-line interface, the command prompt is the text that sits to the left of the blinking cursor. What the prompt actually says varies based on your computer's settings, but usually it has things like the name of the current directory, the name of the computer, the name of the current user, and then special character that indicates that you should start typing (typically either #, $, or >). See also *command-line interface*.

comment In computer programming, a comment is a section of text within the program that is used entirely for information for another human being reading the program. A comment is ignored by the programming language itself. For instance, if you had a piece of code that is complicated, you might include a comment to tell other programs (or yourself at a later date) why the code is so complicated and what you are trying to accomplish.

compression Compression is a process which reduces the size of a value (usually a string), usually by removing redundant information or finding simple patterns within the value.

computer A computer is a piece of hardware that uses programs called software to process data. It is called a computer because its operation primarily consists of computation. See also *general-purpose computer, special-purpose computer*.

concatenation Concatenation means combining by appending to the end and usually refers to sticking two strings together. For example, concatenating "hello" and "world" would get you "helloworld".

conditional expression A conditional expression is an expression which yields a true or false value. Conditional expressions are often used in control structures to determine which branch of code to follow or to serve as a control for a loop. See also *expression*.

console A console is a program that allows direct interaction with the programming environment. A console allows you to directly enter statements, and the console will evaluate and execute the statements immediately, yielding back the return value for you on the screen.

constructor In object-oriented programming, a constructor is a function that builds a new object instance of a specific class. In JavaScript, since there are no classes, the constructor itself fills the role of the class by setting up the properties and functions that a variable should have. See also *instance, object, class, object-oriented programming*.

container A container is a special type of virtual computer that can run under a standard operating system.

content When thinking about a document, the content usually refers to the actual data that a person sees, as opposed to how it is displayed. For instance, the content would include the text on a page, but would not include the font that the text is in, the line spacing, or any background images. See also *presentation*.

content delivery network A content delivery network (CDN) is a service which provides high-speed serving of non-changing (static) files.

content type A content type (also called a MIME type) is the format that a given piece of data is in. It is like a filename extension, but it is used for any stream of data, not just files. Content types are often used for data streams with multiple different types of data embedded in them, such as emails that contain attachments. Content types are specified with a general type and a more specific subtype, such as `image/png`, which means that it is an image (general type) and is specifically formatted as PNG image (the subtype). Webpages are of type `text/html`.

control structure A control structure is a statement or combination of statements that affect the sequencing of program statements. Control structures include function calls (which transfer the control sequence to the function), return statements (which transfer the control sequence back to the calling function), looping operations such as `while` and `for` (which repeat a given set of statements until a condition is reached), and branching operations such as `if` (which choose which path to operate based on a condition). There are other control structures, as well, which have more complicated functionality. See also *flow control statement, loop, function, syntax.*

control unit The control unit is the part of the Central Processing Unit that interprets instructions and directs the other parts of the CPU. See also *Central Processing Unit.*

CPU See *Central Processing Unit.*

CSS See *Cascading style sheets.*

currying Currying refers to the process of generating a function by specifying one or more parameters of another function. See also *higher-order function.*

data bus The data bus is a piece of hardware that manages communication between system components. For example, a data bus connects the Central Processing Unit to the computer memory. See also *Central Processing Unit, memory.*

data format A data format is a way to structure data so that other computer programs can read it. Since data is only a sequence of numbers, a data format defines the meanings of those numbers so that they can be used to convey information. See also *file format*.

data link layer The data link layer is the second layer of a networking system according to the OSI model. The data link layer deals with how the data on the physical layer will be divided and interpreted. It usually has a methodology for naming each local device (often called a MAC address). See also *OSI model, MAC address*.

data transformation A data transformation is a process of converting data from one data format to another. Oftentimes, there is more than one data format available for the same type of data. A data transformation converts between these different formats. Data transformations can also manipulate and summarize data into more usable forms. See also *data format, file format*.

data structure A data structure is a conceptual way of storing information. It is similar to a record, but a data structure can also refer to an entire set of different types of records that work together to accomplish a goal. See also *record*.

decimal Decimal is the numbering system that most people are used to using. It uses the digits 0–9 to make numbers. See also *binary, octal, hexadecimal*.

declaration A declaration is an instruction in a programming language that gives the language information about how to interpret other parts of a program. For instance, the declaration var x; is a declaration that tells the programming language that x will now refer to a variable. Other sorts of declarations can include what version of JavaScript is being used or, in HTML, which set of tags are being used. See also *doctype declaration*.

destructuring assignment A destructuring assignment is one where the left-hand side holds the variables in a structure which mimics their expected locations in a complex structure on the right-hand side. This allows for easier assignment of individual variables from complicated structures.

dictionary See *associative array*.

directory A directory (also called a folder) is a container for files or other directories usually used to keep files on a computer organized. In a URL, directories are indicated by slashes. For example, in the URL `www.npshbook.com/example/test.html`, the path is `/example/test.html`. This path refers to the `test.html` document in the `example` directory. See also *URL*, *fully qualified URL*.

DNS See *domain name system*.

doctype declaration: In HTML and XML, the doctype declaration specifies what type of document (i.e., what set of tags) is being processed. An HTML doctype declaration looks like this: `<!DOCTYPE html>` See also *HyperText Markup Language*, *Extensible Markup Language*.

Document Object Model The Document Object Model is an API (a set of objects, functions, and object classes) that describes how a programmer should interact with an HTML page. The Document Object Model was built to simplify and standardize this interaction not just within JavaScript but across multiple languages. That way, once you learn how to interact with web pages in JavaScript, your API knowledge can also be used in other languages that manipulate HTML. See also *API*, *class*.

documentation Documentation is any written documents or program comments that help navigate other programmers through a piece of code or a system. Documentation is important because most code will be handled by more than one person, so any information future programmers may need to update programs should be documented somewhere. Things that are especially important to document are the purpose of functions, the parameters used in a function, any global variables, and any surprise "gotcha" encountered while building the program or that may be encountered using the code or the program.

DOM: See *Document Object Model*.

Domain name system The domain name system (DNS) is a system that allows people to use friendlier names for computers on the Internet. Normally, each computer on the Internet is assigned an IP address, which is just a sequence of numbers. Not only are numbers hard to memorize, but these numbers can change if a computer is moved to another network. The domain name system allows user-friendly names such as `www.npshbook.com` to be used instead of the numeric IP address. The domain name system works behind the scenes to translate the hostname into an IP address for the computer to connect to.

domain-specific language A domain-specific language is a programming language that is geared toward a particular application (domain). Such programming languages often limit the programmer to a very few set of operations, and only some of them attempt to be Universal. A configuration file can be considered a domain-specific language of sorts. However, sometimes a domain-specific language is simply a general-purpose language with domain-specific features tacked on. See also *general-purpose computer*, *special-purpose computer*, *Universal programming language*.

DSL See *domain-specific language*.

element In HTML, an element consists of a start tag, an end tag, and all of the content and tags in-between them. See also *tag*, *start tag*, *end tag*, *markup language*, *HyperText Markup Language*.

encapsulation Encapsulation is a programming methodology in which access to read and manipulate data fields is only granted through functions or methods, never (or rarely) by direct access. The goal of encapsulation is to (a) make sure that fields are synchronized with each other, (b) make sure that all business and domain rules are appropriately followed concerning the data, and (c) make sure that the interface (the functions or methods) does not have to change even when the underlying data fields may change. For instance, a bank account might be encapsulated by giving the programmer no direct access to the account balance but giving methods to check the balance, deposit money, and withdraw money. In this way, it can ensure that if the programmer calls the functions to withdraw money, for example, all overdraft rules are appropriately applied rather than relying on the programmer to always remember to apply them. This also allows the implementation of these functions to change without drastically impacting other parts of the program.

encryption Encryption is a process that allows two parties to communicate without a third party listening in. It can also refer to a method of digitally signing a message to prove the identity of the sender.

end tag In HTML, an end tag marks the end of a block of content that is used for a specific purpose. An end tag looks just like a start tag but begins with a slash. So, if the start tag was `<p>`, then the end tag will be `</p>`. See also *tag, start tag, markup language, HyperText Markup Language.*

endpoint An endpoint is a destination URL for a specific API action or service. More generally, it refers to any specific location for a remote service.

entity In HTML and XML, an entity is a named character, symbol, or sequence of characters. Entities are specified by starting with an ampersand (&) and ending with a semicolon (;). For instance, `&copy;` is an entity that refers to the copyright symbol.

entity body For HTTP `PUT` and `POST` methods, the entity body is the main data stream which is sent to the service which passed separately from the URL. The format of the entity body should be noted in the `Content-Type` header of the request.

Ethernet Ethernet is the most prominent means of physically connecting two devices on a local area network. See also *data link layer, network, local area network.*

expression An expression is a combination of variables, literals, operators, and functions that yield a value in a single statement. For example, 2 + 3 * 5 is an expression, as is (myvar * 2) - myothervar and myfunc(myvar + 1). Individual literals and variables also count as expressions, too. Anything that can exist on the right-hand side of an assignment statement is considered an expression. See also *variable, literal, operator, function, assignment statement, right-hand side, syntax.*

Extensible Markup Language The Extensible Markup Language (usually referred to as XML) is a text-based markup language that is very similar to HTML with the primary difference being that there is not a predefined set of tags to use. Programs utilizing XML get to make up their own tags to match the type of data they are trying to convey. XML has the benefit of being more flexible than HTML, at a cost of needing different programs to be customized to understand each others' sets of tags. Many file formats today are simply predefined sets of XML tags. XML has stricter rules than standard HTML as far as how tags are formed, which makes it easier and faster to process. For example, there are cases where HTML allows start tags without corresponding end tags, while XML always requires end tags. HTML written according to these standards is sometimes called XHTML. All HTML in this book is also XHTML. See also *markup language, text document, HyperText Markup Language.*

extension See *filename extension.*

file format A file format is a way of structuring data on-disk so that the data can be read back by a computer program. A file format defines the types of data that can be stored within a file and how it is structured so that it can be read back. Since a file is only a sequence of numbers, there is no way to tell what the numbers are supposed to mean apart from the file format, which tells the program (actually, the programmer) how the sequence of numbers should be interpreted. See also *protocol, data format*.

filename extension A filename extension is a short code placed at the end of a filename which tells the computer what format the given file is in and, in some cases, what program should be used to open the file. The filename extension is separated from the main filename by a period. For instance, the filename `mydocument.rtf` has a filename extension of `rtf`, which means that the file is in Rich Text Format. Other common filename extensions include `docx` for word processing documents, `jpg` or `png` for image files, and `html` for web pages. See also *content type*.

firewall A firewall is a device or a program that restricts access to network resources, either on a single computer or across a network of computers. The firewall is meant to separate "outside" from "inside" communication, so as to limit what resources an outside network can access. Firewalls provide an additional layer of safety and security to computers on the "inside" of the firewall.

fixed-point number A fixed-point number is a computer-stored decimal number. It is called a "fixed point" because of the way it stores the number—it has a fixed number of positions to the right and left of the decimal that it can store. This makes the range of numbers it can cover smaller than that of floating-point numbers but makes the calculations more exact for the range that it covers. Fixed-point numbers are often used to store money amounts for that reason. See also *floating-point number*.

flash memory Modern computers phased out Read-Only Memory (ROM) for flash memory. Flash memory is like ROM in that it is not erased when the computer turns off but like RAM in that it can be altered. Flash memory is often used for computer bootup instructions as well as USB-based thumb drives. See also *Random-Access Memory, Read-Only Memory, Universal Serial Bus*.

floating-point number A floating-point number is a computer-stored decimal number. It is called a "floating point" because of the way it stores the number—the digits of the number are stored separately from the location of the decimal point. This allows it to store numbers that are very large or very small but sacrifices some amount of precision. See also *fixed-point number.*

flow control statement See *control structure.*

folder See *directory.*

for loop A for loop is a type of loop that includes some amount of loop initialization and control management. In JavaScript, it takes the form for(*initialization ; loop condition ; loop control*){*loop body*}.

It is basically a while loop that gives a specific area for loop control statements. An example for loop should illustrate the point for(var i = 0; i < 10; i = i + 1) { alert(i); }. This code will display each number from one through nine. The initialization creates the control variable and sets the value. The loop condition checks to see if the value is less than ten before executing the code. Finally, the loop control increases the control variable to go to the next number. You can put any statements you want for the initialization, condition, and control statements, but the ones in the example are fairly typical. See also *loop, loop condition, loop body, loop control variable.*

framework A framework is a set of tools (functions, objects, classes, etc.) which make programming certain types of systems more easily or enables more powerful features for a certain type of programming.

front end The front end of a system is the part that the user interacts with directly. On the Web, the front end is usually written in a combination of HTML, CSS, and JavaScript.

fully qualified URL A fully qualified URL (also called an absolute URL) is a URL that contains all of the information needed to access a remote document or service. As opposed to absolute

URLs and relative URLs, fully qualified URLs rely on no contextual information whatsoever in order to connect. A fully qualified URL usually includes the protocol, the server, and the document path. For example, `www.npshbook.com/example/example.html` uses HTTP as the protocol, connects to the server `www.npshbook.com,` and accesses the document at the path `/example/example.html`. When people discuss URLs, they are usually talking about fully qualified URLs. See also *URL, relative URL, network path.*

function A function is a sequence of steps that a computer can perform that is encapsulated as a single unit. Functions usually consist of a list of parameters, which serve as input to the function, a sequence of instructions, and a return value, which is usually where the result of the function is given. Functions are used for several purposes, including specifying a piece of code that can be run multiple times from different parts of a program and separating a program out into logically distinct components. See also *parameter, return value.*

function scope Function scope is the scope created by a function definition. Within a function, all variables declared using the `var` keyword get put in the function's scope as well as all of the function's parameters. These variables cannot be accessed by name anywhere outside of the function body. For more advanced programmers, if a function is declared *within* another function, it can access all of the variables in the enclosing function. Function scopes are actually created when the function starts executing. Therefore, if a function calls itself, each execution of the function gets its own unique copy of the scope. This will cause a separate copy of each variable to exist for each active function. See also *function, variable, variable scope, recursive function.*

general-purpose computer A general-purpose computer is a computer that can be loaded with software that can perform any possible calculation (within practical limits). See also *special-purpose computer, Universal programming language.*

global scope The global scope is a scope that is always visible to every function. See also *variable scope, global variable.*

global variable A global variable is a variable that is defined in the global scope and thus visible within every function, unless that function has a local variable of the same name. See also *variable scope, global scope, variable.*

graphical user interface A graphical user interface (GUI, pronounced like "gooey") is the typical type of interface we see on modern computers—heavy uses of icons, media, windows, and screen management, with interactions taking place primarily through an interactive device like a mouse. See also *command-line interface.*

groupware Groupware is a set of software applications that allow a user to interact with a group. Groupware usually includes scheduling and messaging applications that work together.

GUI See *graphical user interface.*

hashtable See *associative array.*

hexadecimal Hexadecimal is a numbering system that consists of the digits 0–9 as well as the letters a–f for an expanded list of 16 total digits. Hexadecimal is often used in computer programming because every two hexadecimal numbers represents a single byte. See also *decimal, binary, octal, byte.*

higher-order function A higher-order function is a function that either takes a function as a parameter or generates and returns new functions as a result. Higher-order functions are often difficult to grasp but, once understood, can greatly simplify many programming tasks.

hostname The hostname is the name of a computer or group of computers on the Internet. For instance, in the URL `http://`www.npshbook.com/, *http* is the protocol, *www.npshbook.com* is the hostname, and / is the path. This means that the URL will transmit to the computer or group of computers named by *www.npshbook.com* using the HTTP protocol and ask for the document /.

HTML See *HyperText Markup Language.*

HTTP See *HyperText Transfer Protocol.*

HTTP method See *HTTP verb.*

HTTP verb The HTTP protocol has several commands, called verbs, that it can receive. The two main verbs are GET, which is usually used to retrieve documents, and POST, which is usually used to transmit a form to the server.

hyperlink A hyperlink is a short piece of text in a digital document, which, when clicked, takes the viewer to another, related document.

HyperText Markup Language HyperText Markup Language (usually known simply as HTML) is a specialized markup language used for displaying documents on the Web. It uses tags to mark different pieces of content for different purposes. See also *markup language, tag, text document.*

HyperText Transfer Protocol The HyperText Transfer Protocol (HTTP) is the application layer protocol used on the Internet for transferring web content (web pages, images, etc.). When the data transfer is encrypted using SSL or TLS, the protocol is referred to as HTTPS. See *application layer, Transport Layer Security.*

identifier An identifier is a programmer-chosen name for a value. Most identifiers in programming languages refer to variable names, function names, or property names. Identifiers differ from keywords and operators, which are fixed, prespecified words that have a specific meaning in a language. Programming languages have rules for what makes a valid identifier, but usually any group of characters without spaces or special characters that start with a letter can be used an identifier. See also *variable, operator, keyword, syntax.*

IMAP IMAP (the Internet Message Access Protocol) is one of the application layer protocols used to retrieve email from an email server. See also *application layer, SMTP, POP*.

index An index is a number used in arrays and character strings to specify which item of the array or string you want to access. See also *array, string, zero-based indexing*.

inductive case In recursive programming, the programmer usually tries to redefine the problem into simpler and simpler problems with the same form as the original. For instance, in the `factorial` function, the factorial is represented in terms of the factorial of smaller numbers. The conditions that cause a recursive program to call itself with a simplified version of the problem are called the inductive case. See also *recursive function, base case*.

infinite loop An infinite loop is a loop in which the loop condition is improperly written, such that the loop body never stops executing. See also *loop, loop condition, loop body*.

information architecture For websites, information architecture refers to how web pages are organized and how users can navigate through the website. For computer programs, information architecture refers to how data is divided into data structures such as objects and arrays.

inheritance See *subclass*.

initialization Initialization is a term that refers to the beginning steps of a loop, program, or function, in which the programmer sets initial values to variables. JavaScript does not require that initialization happen at the beginning of a program or function, but it is usually good programming practice to do so. See also *loop initialization*.

input In computer hardware, input is anything that comes into a program from outside of the computer. Keyboards, mice, and hard drives are all examples of input systems. In computer programming, input can refer to anything that comes into a section of a program, even if it does not come from outside

the computer. For instance, the input of a function can refer
to external input (such as keyboards) as well as the function's
parameters and global variables. See also *input/output
system, output.*

input/output system An input/output system is a set of hardware
specifications for allowing devices to be added to computers. One
popular input/output system is the Universal Serial Bus (USB).
See also *USB.*

instance In object-oriented programming, an instance is an
object of a particular class. For example, I might have a class of
Car that describes the basic potential features of a car and then
thousands of Car object instances that are used to model traffic.
Each instance of the Car class has the properties and methods
that the Car class describes. JavaScript does not have classes, but a
similar concept is built through constructors. See also *object, class,
constructor.*

instruction pointer In machine language, the instruction pointer
contains the memory address of the next instruction to fetch and
execute. See also *machine language, memory address.*

integer An integer is a counting number—a number with no
decimal points.

integrated circuit An integrated circuit is a piece of silicon with
numerous transistors and other miniaturized semiconductors
packed into a small area. Integrated circuits may be as simple
as a few transistors wired together to make a timer or a few
billion transistors wired together to make a modern computer
microprocessor.

interface In object-oriented programming, an interface (also
called a protocol) is a list of related methods that an object or
class may implement that contribute toward a similar function
in non-similar objects. For instance, beds and cars have very
little in common, but they might both have a function called
getLocation() and setLocation(). If they both implemented

equivalently named functions to accomplish similar goals, then you could regard that as an interface. Defining interfaces allows people to write general code that allows the code to be used in a variety of circumstances with different kinds of objects so long as the objects each implement the same interface.

Internet The Internet is the worldwide conglomeration of networks operating under a standard set of protocols for locating and communicating with each other. See also *network*.

Internet Protocol The Internet Protocol (IP) is the network layer protocol used on the Internet for addressing devices and routing data to them. See also *network layer, Internet, TCP/IP, IP address*.

IP See *Internet Protocol*.

IP address An IP address is how a computer is identified on the Internet. The Internet Protocol uses the IP address to ensure that data arrives at the proper destination. See also *Internet Protocol, network layer*.

JavaScript JavaScript is a programming language that is widely used today to make web pages more interactive.

JavaScript library A JavaScript library is a prebuilt group of functions that can be loaded into your application. See also *framework*.

JavaScript console See *console*

keyword A keyword is a word that looks like an identifier but has a specific meaning in the given programming language. See also *identifier, syntax*.

L-value See *left-hand side*.

lambda function See *arrow function*.

LAN See *local area network*.

left-hand side In an assignment statement, the left-hand side refers to the code on the left-hand side of the equal sign (=). The goal of the left-hand side is to yield a storage location that can hold the value given in the right-hand side. Therefore, the left-hand side is interpreted differently than the right-hand side. On the right-hand side, myarray[0] refers to the *value* that is held in the first element of myarray. On the left-hand side, myarray[0] refers to the *storage location* that is the first element of myarray. Storage locations specified by the left-hand side of assignment statements are often called L-values. See also *assignment statement, right-hand side.*

lexical closure Lexical closure is the idea that functions that are defined inside of other functions have full access to the variables defined in their containing scope. Even if the containing function returns, if a function was defined inside that scope and returned from that function, the scope remains "alive" whenever the returned function is called.

library A library is a set of prebuilt functions, objects, and/or other programming tools that assists a programmer to accomplish specific tasks. For instance, many websites offer JavaScript libraries that provide functions that a programmer can call to retrieve data from their website.

link See *hyperlink.*

literal A literal refers to a value that is entered directly in a programming language as opposed to one that is given as input or calculated from other values. For instance, in the statement var myvar = 0;, the 0 in the program refers to the number 0 itself. Any value that is written directly into a program is considered a literal.

local area network A local area network (LAN) is a network of computers within a modest physical proximity that are all managed under a single administration. Most home and office networks are local area networks. See also *wide area network.*

local variable A local variable is a variable with a non-global scope. In JavaScript, local variables have function scope. See also *variable, global scope, function scope.*

loop A loop is a sequence of statements that are repeated. Loops generally consists of two logical components—the loop condition and the loop body. The loop body is the sequence of statements to be executed repeatedly, and the loop condition is a conditional expression that controls whether or not the loop continues repeating or is finished. See also *conditional expression, loop condition, loop body, loop control variable, for loop, while loop*.

loop body In a loop, the loop body is a sequence of statements that gets executed over and over again. In most types of loops, the sequence of statements executes until the loop condition evaluates to false. See also *loop, loop condition*.

loop condition The loop condition is a conditional expression that controls whether or not the loop body is executed. See also *conditional expression, loop, loop body*.

loop control variable A loop control variable is a variable that is used to gauge the progress of a loop and determine whether or not it is finished. A loop does not have to have a single loop control variable—sometimes a loop condition is controlled by a variety of conditions of several variables. However, most loops make use of a single variable to determine whether or not it should keep executing. Therefore, in order to avoid an infinite loop, it is important to make sure your loop control variable is modified properly in the loop body (or in the loop control in a for loop). See also *loop, loop condition, loop body, for loop*.

loop initialization Loop initialization is a term that refers to setting up the variables in order to execute a loop. In some forms of loops (such as the while loop), loop initialization is done manually, while in other loops (such as the for loop), at least part of the initialization is part of the loop syntax itself. See also *loop, while loop, for loop*.

MAC address The MAC (media access control) address is how a computer is identified on a local network (at the data link layer level). This is different than the IP address, which is how a computer is identified across a larger network such as the

Internet. Computers on the Internet typically have both a MAC address and an IP address. The MAC address allows a network card to quickly identify which packets of data belong to that network card without the complexities of understanding the Internet Protocol. See also *IP address, Internet protocol, data link layer, packet.*

machine language A machine language is the set of instructions that a computer is able to process natively. The three most common machine languages are the x86 platform (used by most desktop computers), the PowerPC platform (used by many gaming systems), and the ARM platform (used by many smartphones). Most programmers do not use machine language but, instead, use other programming languages that make the task of programming easier. See also *programming language.*

map See *associative array.* Additionally, a map can also refer to a function which does a transformation of values in an array using a specified transformation function.

margin (CSS) The margin of an element is the space outside of the border. The margin is considered the minimum amount of space between this element and the next, which means that margins are not added together, but the maximum of two touching margins is used for the space between two elements.

markup language A markup language is a text document that has certain codes written into it that tell a person or a computer program how to interpret each piece of text. Common markup languages are XML and HTML. See also *HyperText Markup Language, Extensible Markup Language.*

memory The memory of a computer refers to the data that is held in a computer. The memory is a sequence of storage locations, each of which holds eight bits (one byte) of data. It usually refers to Random-Access Memory, which goes away when the computer is switched off. See also *Random-Access Memory, bit byte, memory address.*

memory address The computer memory is simply a very large sequence of bytes. Each byte is given a number that refers to its position in the sequence of bytes. This number is known as a memory address. See also *memory, byte*.

message Another term used for *method*. It has a slightly different technical meaning, but they are usually used interchangeably.

method A method is a function that is attached to an object. In JavaScript, this is done by setting a property of an object to a function. When a method is called, the object that the function is attached to is passed as an implicit parameter to the function. In JavaScript, this is done by setting the special variable this to the object. See also *function, object*. A method can also refer to an HTTP method or verb. See *HTTP verb* for this usage.

microchip See *integrated circuit*.

MIME type See *content type*.

modem A modem (from the words "*mo*dulator" and "*dem*odulator") is a device that converts a digital signal to an analog signal for transmission over phone lines.

modularization Modularization refers to a practice in programming of separating out a program into simpler pieces, called modules. This helps to better organize the program, to reduce the amount of local complexity (since the units are thought of in more holistic and unified ways), to reduce the amount of global complexity (since the interaction points between the modules are better documented and understood), and to make the program more understandable (because you can reasonably understand the program at both a local level and a global level). Without modularization, oftentimes programs would have to be understood simultaneously at a broad and local level since there was nothing that partitioned the system into parts.

module In JavaScript, a module is a largely self-contained library of code which can be loaded upon request into a variable. It is a type of library that has special scoping rules that allow additional code isolation from the rest of the system. See also *JavaScript library*.

mutating function See *mutator*.

mutator In object-oriented programming, a mutator is a method that changes an object's internal properties. In object-oriented programming, it is usually recommended that all changes to an object's properties occur through mutators so that only the object is responsible for maintaining internal consistency. Otherwise, if an object needed two values to change together, and someone using the object only changed one of them, the object would be in an invalid state. Using mutators puts the burden of object consistency on the person who wrote the code for the object to begin with. See also *object-oriented programming, accessor*.

name clash A name clash is when a programmer accidentally uses the same name for two different things (usually variables). Depending on the programming language and the way it occurs, this either can prevent the code from running (because the language can't distinguish between the two uses of the name) or causes data corruption (because two parts of the code are using the same location for different things). See also *variable*.

network A network is a group of computers that are connected together so that they can send data to each other. See also *Ethernet, local area network*.

network layer The network layer is the third layer of a networking system according to the OSI model. The network layer deals with moving data between different physical network segments. The most common network layer protocol is the Internet Protocol. See also *OSI model, Internet Protocol*.

network path A network path is like a fully qualified URL but without the protocol specified. It is also like a relative URL, but relative only to the protocol of the base URL. A network path is indicated by starting with two slashes (//). For instance, the URL `www.npshbook.com/example/example.html` has a network path of `//npshbook.com/example/example.html`. Network paths are often used when a document can be accessed by more than one protocol and you want all of the links using the same protocol. For instance, if a document can be accessed via either HTTP or HTTPS (using `http:` or `https:` as the protocol), using network paths for links will keep the session in the same protocol as was used to access the original document. See also *URL, fully qualified URL, base URL, relative URL.*

nil See *null*.

null Null (also called nil) is often used in programming languages to represent an empty value. In JavaScript, you can set values to `null` if you don't know what the value is. It is similar to `undefined`, except `undefined` is usually assigned by the system itself when a variable has not been set to anything. In other words, `undefined` is used by the JavaScript language when it doesn't know what the value should be, and `null` is used by programmers to specify that they don't know what the value should be. `null` and `undefined` are equal when compared using `==` but not equal when compared using `===`. Most programming languages don't have separate values for undefined and null values. In other programming languages, null is defined as the number zero. See also *undefined*.

null-terminated string A null-terminated string is a way of implementing strings such that the last value is a sentinel (usually the null value) signaling the end of the string. JavaScript strings are not null-terminated (JavaScript stores the count of the characters instead), but null-terminated strings are seen on a number of programming languages. See also *string, null, sentinel.*

object An object is a data structure that can contain both regular data and functions. In JavaScript, although every value is technically an object, objects usually refer to custom-defined objects that contain multiple values.

object-oriented programming Object-oriented programming is a method of programming where data records and related functions (called methods) are encapsulated together into units called objects. See also *class, subclass, interface, instance, object, accessor, mutator, constructor attribute, property.*

octal Octal is a numbering system that only uses the digits 0–7. It is commonly used in computers since each octal digit represents exactly three bits. See also *binary, decimal.*

opcode The word opcode stands for "operation code." In machine language, an opcode is part of a machine instruction. It is a number that refers to what process the CPU should perform with the instruction. The CPU uses the opcode to know what operation to perform. The opcode is combined with other operands to form a complete machine instruction.

operand An operand is a value that is operated on by an operator. In the expression 2 + 3, + is the operator, and 2 and 3 are operands. Operators are like parameters to built-in functions. See also *expression, operator.*

operator An operator is a symbol or keyword in a programming language that tells computes a value. For instance, + is an operator that adds two values, and == is an operator that compares two values and yields true or false based on whether they are equivalent. See also *operand.*

OSI model The OSI model is a way of thinking about the different needs of a communication system broken out into independent layers. The OSI model is what, for instance, allows wired and wireless computers to interoperate on the same network despite having very different ways of physically connecting to the network. The OSI model divides the needs of a network communication system into seven layers which can each act independently of the others. See also *physical layer, data link layer, network layer, transport layer, session layer, presentation layer, application layer.*

output In computer hardware, output is anything that goes from the computer to a device outside of the computer. Your monitor, speakers, and hard drive are all examples of output systems. In computer programming, output can refer to anything that is the result of a section of a program, especially its return value, and any global variables that it modified. See also *input/output system, input, return value*.

packet A packet is a piece of a communication sent as a unit across the network. When sending or receiving data, the operating system or network can decide to break up the transmission into pieces called packets and send each packet individually. The destination computer then reassembles the packets into their proper order before sending them on to the destination program.

padding (CSS) The padding of an element is the area just outside the content area but before the border.

parameter A parameter is a value that is given to a function for processing. In JavaScript, for instance, the function call `alert("hello there");` has one parameter—the string `"hello there"`. In JavaScript, each parameter is assigned to a local variable for the duration of the function.

parent directory On a computer, files are organized in a hierarchy of directories. If a file is in a given directory, the parent directory is the directory that the given directory is located in. For instance, if a file is in the directory `/example1/example2/myfile.html`, the directory that the file is in is `example2`, and the parent directory of `example2` is `example1`. See also *director*.

parse Parsing is converting specially formatted text from a simple string to something easier to manipulate as data. For instance, the string `"25"` can be parsed into the number 25, and the string `"2016-03-01"` can be parsed into a date.

payload The payload of a request is the "main data" being transferred. In HTTP `PUT` and `POST` requests, the payload usually refers to the entity body. See also *entity body*.

peripheral A peripheral is an external device attached to the computer such as a mouse, keyboard, or monitor. Most peripherals today use USB to connect. See also *Universal Serial Bus, input/output system.*

physical layer The physical layer is the lowest layer of a networking system according to the OSI model. The physical layer deals with the physical wires between devices or, in the case of wireless communication, the necessary physical requirements of the space. See also *OSI model.*

pica In typography, a pica is a size that is $\frac{1}{6}$ of an inch. See also *typography.*

point In typography, a point is a size that is $\frac{1}{72}$ of an inch. See also *typography.*

POP POP (the Post Office Protocol) is one of the application layer protocols used to retrieve email from an email server. See also *application layer, SMTP, IMAP.*

presentation When thinking about a document, the presentation usually refers to the way that data is displayed on a page, not the content itself. The presentation refers to fonts, colors, borders, backgrounds, placements, spacing, and other visual effects that are not directly tied to the text or data being presented.

presentation layer The presentation layer is the sixth layer of a networking system according to the OSI model. The presentation layer allows for the adjustment of the message before being sent to the application. Two common uses of this are encryption and compression. The TLS protocol, for instance, is a presentation layer protocol for encryption used on many websites. However, oftentimes the presentation layer is bundled into the application layer. See also *OSI model, application layer, TLS, SSL, encryption, compression.*

program stack See *stack.*

programming language A programming language is a method of conveying instructions to a computer in a way that is easier for programmers to use than the machine's native machine language but that is still precise enough to be translated into the computer's own machine language. See also *machine language*.

property (CSS) A CSS property is a setting that can be changed, such as `font-size` or `padding-left`.

property (object) An object property is a value that is set on an object. The property name is the name that the value is referred by, and the property value is the actual value stored. For instance, if we had an object called `myobj`, then the statement `myobj.myprop = "myval";` would set a property named `myprop` on the `myobj` object to the value `"myval"`.

protocol (networking) A protocol is a system of conventions used to facilitate communication or usage. In ordinary life, a common protocol is shaking hands when greeting someone or saying "hello" and "goodbye" on the telephone. On computer systems, protocols allow components and software built by independent groups to work together by sharing the same conventions. For instance, there are a number of different web browsers available for browsing the Web, but they are all able to do so successfully because they all follow a standard protocol for exchanging information with the website.

protocol (object-oriented programming) See *interface*.

query string In a URL, a query string is a set of extra data that is passed to the web page through the URL. If a URL has a question mark within the URL, everything after the question mark is considered part of the query string. Query string data is usually expressed as `key=val` pairs separated by ampersands (&). In JavaScript, the query string can be accessed in JavaScript through `window.location.search`. See also *URL*.

RAM See *Random-Access Memory*.

Random-Access Memory Random-Access Memory (RAM) is the typical type of computer memory. It refers to memory that can be both read from and written to. The RAM of a computer is wiped when it is turned off or rebooted. See also *memory, Read-Only Memory*.

Read-Only Memory Read-Only Memory (ROM) is a special type of computer memory that is usually only available for reading. For instance, the instructions that help a computer boot up used to be held in ROM-based memory. Today, flash memory is usually used for this purpose. ROM, since it is read-only, is not wiped when the computer is turned off.

record A record is a set of named, related values that are stored together. For instance, a record about a person could have their name, age, and hair color. In JavaScript, records are created using objects. See also *variable, object*.

recursive function A recursive function is a function that calls itself. Recursive functions are used when the method to solve a problem involves figuring out the answer from a simplified set and then expanding that set. As an example, the factorial function takes a number and multiplies it by all numbers below it until it gets to 1. This means that `factorial(5)` could just be written as `5 * factorial(4)`, and `factorial(4)` can be written as `4*factorial(3)`. Each step of the factorial simply comes up with a factorial of a smaller number until it gets to 1. The 1 is called a base case, which means that it is answered directly instead of recursively. In the factorial function, the factorial is coded to simply return the answer 1 for the base case of 1. Recursive functions are possible because each time the function is called, it gets its own stack frame—its own set of parameters, local variables, and return location. This allows each invocation of the function to have its own working scratch pad of information which doesn't interfere with the other invocations of the functions that are active at the time. See also *stack, stack frame, base case, inductive case*.

refactor In computer programming, refactoring refers to the process of rewriting how a computer program works, usually in order to make it more comprehensible, less error-prone, or more flexible for future expansion. Refactoring usually involves separating out different core components that had been previously linked together. For instance, when HTML was broken out into separate languages for content (HTML), presentation (CSS), and interaction (JavaScript), this was an instance of refactoring.

relative URL A relative URL is a partial URL that uses the current base URL as the starting point for the URL. In URLs, directories are separated by slashes (/), and the relative URL starts in the same directory as the base URL. For instance, if the base URL is `www.npshbook.com/example/example.html`, then a relative URL of `test.html` would refer to `www.npshbook.com/example/test.html`. A directory of `..` refers to the parent directory so a relative URL of `../test.html` would refer to `www.npshbook.com/test.html`. If a relative URL starts with a slash, it becomes an absolute path. See also *URL, fully qualified URL, base URL, absolute path, directory*.

request routing In an HTTP server, request routing refers to sending an HTTP request to the appropriate function based on the request properties such as the request path and the HTTP method.

reserved words In a programming language, a reserved word is a name that cannot be used as a variable name, usually because it already has special importance to the programming language. In JavaScript, for instance, `if` is a reserved word.

responsive (CSS) In HTML and CSS, a responsive page is a web page which looks good across a number of different screen sizes. This is often achieved by using special style sheets which enable/disable different elements based on screen size or change the page layout for certain sizes.

return value In a function, the return value is the final value yielded by the function. In JavaScript, the return value is specified in the function using the `return` keyword, which also returns control back to the code that called the function. The return value can be used as a value within an expression, assigned to a variable, or ignored. See also *function, expression, variable.*

right-hand side In an assignment statement, the right-hand side refers to the code on the right-hand side of the equal sign (=). The goal of the right-hand side is to yield a value that can be stored to the location specified in the left-hand side. See also *assignment statement, left-hand side.*

ROM See *Read-Only Memory.*

router A router is a device which determines which network a given packet of data should be sent to. On the Internet, routers work by looking at the destination IP address and deciding which network is most likely to have the destination IP address.

scale An application that scales is one whose performance improves by adding additional resources (such as additional computers). In an unscalable application, adding resources does not improve the speed or throughput of the system.

scope See *variable scope.*

Secure Sockets Layer See *Transport Layer Security.*

search parameters See *query string.*

sentinel A sentinel is a special value that tells a program that it has reached a special place in the data (such as the end). Oftentimes the null character (ASCII 0) will be used to mark the end of a sequence of letters. See also *data format, ASCII.*

serialization Serialization is the process of transforming an object in a programming language into a data stream that can be sent remotely or stored. Deserialization is the opposite process—converting a data stream into an object in a programming language.

server A server is a computer or a group of computers which provide a service to other computers on the network. Computers who connect to the server are usually called clients. See also *client*.

session layer The session layer is the fifth layer of a networking system according to the OSI model. The session layer deals with starting and stopping a conversation between computers. See also *OSI model, Transmission Control Protocol*.

SMTP SMTP (the Simple Mail Transfer Protocol) is the application layer protocol used to send email out on the Internet eventually winding up on the destination email server (it may have to be sent through more than one server to get there). This is a different protocol than the one used by a user to receive email from their email server, which is usually POP or IMAP. See also *application layer, POP, IMAP*.

special-purpose computer A special-purpose computer is a computer whose computational abilities are limited to specific types of computational operations and specific ways of combining them. See also *general-purpose computer*.

SSL The Secure Sockets Layer. See *Transport Layer Security*.

stack The stack is the part of computer memory that holds the call-specific information of all active functions. The stack usually holds things like parameters, local variables, and the point in the code to return to when the function is finished. Think of it as a scratch pad for active functions. It is called a "stack" because every time a function is called, the information for the new call (newly created local variables, the parameter list, and the location where we left off the last function) is placed "on top of the stack." Then, when the function is finished, that information is pulled off of the top of the stack to let the previous function continue running. See also *stack frame*.

stack frame The stack holds information about all active function calls currently in progress. A stack frame is the information for a specific function call. The stack frame usually holds information like function parameters, the location in the code to return to when the function is finished, and the local variables being used by the current call of the current function. See also *recursive function.*

start tag In HTML, a start tag marks the beginning of a block of content that is used for a specific purpose. Start tags are wrapped in angled brackets so that they can be recognized by the computer as being a tag. For instance, a tag marking the start of a paragraph looks like <p>. See also *tag, end tag, markup language, HyperText Markup Language.*

string A string is a defined sequence of displayable characters. In JavaScript, strings are designated by enclosing them in double or single quotes (" or '). Each character in a strings is usually encoded using either ASCII or a Unicode-based system such as UTF-8 or UTF-32. See also *null-terminated string, Unicode, ASCII, UTF-8, UTF-32.*

syntax In any file format or computer programming language, the syntax of the language refers to the pieces of the language that can be included and how they can be validly combined. For instance, in JavaScript, the syntax includes the different keywords (such as if, for, function, etc.), the different literals (such as numbers, strings, etc.), other parts of the language, and how they can be combined together to create a valid program. Syntax only refers to whether or not a computer can successfully understand the program. It does not refer to whether or not the computer successfully performs the function desired.

subclass In object-oriented programming, a subclass is a class whose default properties and methods are "inherited" from another class, known as the superclass. Inheritance allows specialized classes to be built quickly and easily from existing classes while allowing any functionality to be overridden as needed. See also *class, object-oriented programming.*

superclass See *subclass.*

tag In a markup language, a tag is a marker that indicates a specific usage for a piece of text. In HTML specifically, a tag is written using angled brackets with a start tag at the beginning of the content block and an end tag at the end of it. Tags indicate the start and end of pieces of content used for a specific purpose. For instance, the <h1> tag is used to mark level-1 headings, such as this: <h1>This is a Level 1 Heading</h1> See also *markup language, HyperText Markup Language, start tag, end tag.*

TCP See *Transmission Control Protocol.*

TCP/IP TCP/IP refers to the combined usage of the TCP and IP protocols as the foundation for communication on the Internet. See also *Transmission Control Protocol, Internet Protocol.*

text document A text document is a file that consists entirely of displayable characters, usually encoded in ASCII or UTF-8 (see Appendix D for more information on ASCII and UTF-8). Text documents can be edited using any standard text editor. However, text documents may also be specialized (such as HTML web pages) and have specific requirements for their format. In such cases, it is usually the user's responsibility to make sure that the document follows the proper requirements. See also *binary file.*

TLS See *Transport Layer Security.*

transport layer The transport layer is the fourth layer of a networking system according to the OSI model. The transport layer deals with breaking up data into packets, making sure that each packet is delivered appropriately, and making sure they are assembled in the right order on the other side. See also *OSI model, packet, Transmission Control Protocol.*

Transport Layer Security Transport Layer Security (TLS) is the most common presentation layer encryption method on the Internet. It is the successor to the previous Secure Sockets Layer (SSL) protocol. See also *presentation layer.*

Transmission Control Protocol The Transmission Control Protocol (TCP) is the protocol used on the Internet for the transport layer and the session layer. It is in charge of starting and stopping transmissions as well as making sure data arrives intact on each side. See also *transport layer, session layer, TCP/IP*.

Turing-complete programming language See *Universal programming language*.

type A type describes the set of valid values and available operations of a variable. Types are usually predefined by the programming language, though there are exceptions. See also *variable, class*.

typography Typography is an aspect of visual design that focuses on the way that words are laid out on a page.

undefined A variable or property is undefined if no value has been set for it. It literally means "no definition." See *null* for a fuller description.

Unicode Unicode is a system for representing all of the languages and writing of the world digitally. Unicode specifies over 100,000 characters/symbols. Unicode specifies a number for each character but does not specify how the computer represents that number. Other standards, such as UTF-8 and UTF-32, define how those numbers are represented on the computer. See also *UTF-8, UTF-32, ASCII*.

Uniform Resource Locator A Uniform Resource Locator (URL) is the standard method for identifying web content. For instance, www.npshbook.com/ is the URL for accessing this book's website, and www.amazon.com/exec/obidos/ASIN/0975283863 is the URL for buying a previous book of mine, *Engineering and the Ultimate*. See also *protocol, hostname, path, query string, anchor*.

Universal Serial Bus Universal Serial Bus (USB) is a specification for an interface that allows many different types of hardware to be plugged into a computer and used with minimal setup. See also *input/output system, peripheral*.

Universal programming language A Universal programming language (also called a Turing-complete language) is a programming language that can represent the entire gamut of computable functions (within practical limits of memory and time). Universal languages are *not* Universal because they have an advanced computation set—in fact, you can make a Universal language just with basic arithmetic and comparison operators. Universal languages are universal because they contain sufficient control structures (looping, function calls, if statements, etc.) to build new computable functions out of any starting set of operators. Universal languages are all equivalent in the computations that they can perform, though they may not be equivalent in other ways, such as input and output mechanisms and ease-of-use for particular applications. See also *domain-specific language, general-purpose computer, special-purpose computer, control structure.*

URL See *Uniform Resource Locator.*

USB See *Universal Serial Bus.*

UTF-32 UTF-32 is another character encoding based on Unicode. This encoding uses four bytes per character.

UTF-8 UTF-8 is a popular character encoding based on Unicode. It is widely used because of its backward compatibility with ASCII. Because Unicode specifies over 100,000 characters, it takes more than 1 byte to record each character. However, ASCII only stores one byte per character. In order to combine these two standards, the first bit of the byte (which is unused in standard ASCII) is set to 1 if the character needs more than one byte to hold it. This makes all ASCII files work in UTF-8 settings, but it means that it is harder to find the nth character of a string because you have to check each letter to see how many bytes it takes up. See also *data format, Unicode, ASCII, string.*

variable A variable is a named location (named by an identifier) in a computer program that is used to store a value. In JavaScript, variables are created either by declaring them as parameters in a function or by using the `var` keyword. Variables, as their name indicates, can vary by being assigned different values throughout the program. See also *syntax, identifier*.

variable scope A variable's scope refers to the places in a program that a particular variable can be accessed. Two common scopes in JavaScript are *global scope* and *function scope*. For instance, a variable in function scope cannot be directly accessed outside of the function itself. See also *global scope, function scope*.

verb See *HTTP verb*.

virtual private network A virtual private network (VPN) is a system that bridges together computers and networks across the Internet to act as if they were all on the local network. This is usually used for data security where the local area network allows for access to more secure resources than are available across the Internet. Therefore, it brings certain computers and networks into the local area network to share those resources.

von Neumann architecture The von Neumann architecture refers to the idea of putting both the program and the data it is operating on into the same memory. This allows for far more flexibility in the way that machines are built and used.

VPN See *virtual private network*.

WAN See *wide area network*.

whitespace Whitespace refers to any nonprinting character such as regular spaces, the end-of-line character, and tabs. In HTML and XML, all whitespace is treated together as if it were a single space. This is done because the writer of HTML does not know the screen size that the document will be displayed on and cannot rely on the spacing in the output matching the spacing in the document. Therefore, document authors are supposed to use tags and style sheets instead of whitespace to ensure proper spacing. See also *text document, HyperText Markup Language, Extensible Markup Language*.

wide area network A wide area network is a network that connects two local area networks that are geographically distant from each other. See also *local area network*.

while loop A while loop is a type of loop that takes the form `while(` *loop condition* `) {` *loop body* `}`. The loop condition is evaluated *before* each iteration of the loop body. If the loop condition is true, it executes the loop body. If the loop condition is false, the loop body is skipped and the program goes to the next statement. The loop is evaluated over and over again until the loop condition is false. See also *loop, loop condition, loop body*.

widget A widget is a generic term for a somewhat self-contained user interface element. A text field is a widget. A drop-down list is a widget.

Wi-Fi Wi-Fi refers to the most prominent protocol used for attaching a device to a wireless network. It is similar to Ethernet, but using radio waves. See also *Ethernet, network, local area network, data link layer*.

XHTML See *Extensible Markup Language*.

XML See *Extensible Markup Language*.

zero-based indexing Most computer programming languages (including JavaScript) start their array indexes at zero. This means that the first value of an array has an index of zero. This also means that the last value in an array has an index of one less than the length. So, for an array with four items, the first index is zero (as always) and the last index is three. This method is called zero-based indexing. This is different than mathematics, which uses the number 1 to refer to the first element of a set of values. See also *array, index*.

APPENDIX B

Operating System and Browser Specifics

JavaScript is a great programming language to learn because it can be used on any modern computer, using any browser. However, there are some minor differences between computers and operating systems so that things might look and work a little bit differently depending on which computer you use. When the main chapters reference a technique or a feature that is more system-specific, this appendix gives you additional context and information so that you are more likely to be able to find it on your computer.

However, there are hundreds of different systems and system configurations, and I can't possibly list them all in this book. All of the different versions of Windows (7, 8, 10, 11, etc.), Mac (Catalina, Big Sur, Monterey, Ventura, etc.), and Linux (Red Hat, Ubuntu, CentOS, etc.) have slightly different ways of doing things. Therefore, this appendix will cover just a few representative systems, which should give you enough background information to find the right setting on your own system. If you still have questions on how to do this on your own system, hopefully this appendix will give you the right context and ideas for what you need to ask someone about, either in person or in an online forum.

You will find that developers often wind up with their computers set up much differently than the average user. The reason for the difference is simple—ordinary users want all of the messy details hidden from them. Programmers, on the other hand, *use* the messy details to accomplish tasks. The average user wants to know *less* about what is going on behind the scenes, but programmers need to know *more*. Therefore, the defaults, made for the average user, focus on hiding technical information. Programmers tend to adjust all of their settings to show all of the gritty details.

© Jonathan Bartlett 2023
J. Bartlett, *Programming for Absolute Beginners*, https://doi.org/10.1007/978-1-4842-8751-4

B.1 The Browser Location Bar

The location bar of your web browser is at the top of the window, usually at the center or the left (see Figure B-1). For most web browsers, the location bar also doubles as a search bar. You can use the location bar to directly type in or view a URL, or if you enter in something that doesn't look like a URL, the browser will try to use a search engine (like Bing or Google) to search for the terms you typed.

However, many location bars have stopped actually displaying your complete location and hide several important details. Some browsers show it all; some browsers hide the protocol (i.e., `http`); some browsers hide everything but the domain name (i.e., `www.example.com`). Therefore, you should know how to get the location from the location bar if it doesn't show it automatically.

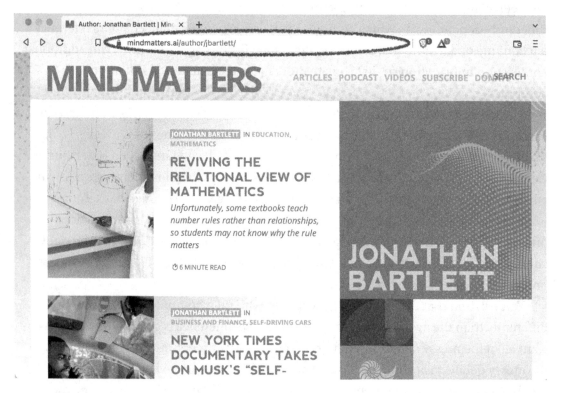

Figure B-1. *Finding the Location Bar*

In most browsers, even if the whole URL is not displayed, if you copy and paste the URL to a different document, it will paste the *full* URL. If you want to see the full URL displayed while you browse, several browsers have options for that. In Safari, for instance, if you go to the "Safari" menu, then click "Preferences" it will open up a dialog box. Under the "Advanced" settings, there is a checkbox that says "show full website address." If you click that, it will display much more of the URL. It still hides the protocol, but it will show you the rest. In Chrome and Brave, in "Preferences," under "Appearance," there is a "Always Show Full URLs" option that you can select.

B.2 Getting to the Command Line

The command line is a program that presents you with a screen that is similar to a pre-1990s computer screen—just lines of characters and a cursor where you can type. There is no mouse interaction and no pretty pictures—just you, your keyboard, and a bunch of text on the screen. The command line works like this: your cursor starts blinking next to a bit of text called the command prompt (it usually ends with #, $, or >). It is waiting for your command. After you type in a command, the computer runs it and spits the output to the screen. You know it has finished because you will see another command prompt as the last line of text.

Sometimes, if the command you run is interactive (such as `telnet`), the program itself will ask you or allow you to type responses or to control it in some way while it runs. You will know when it is finished because you will get another command prompt.

The command line can be a programmer's best friend. It allows a much more direct access to the computer than any other interface. Rather than wading through screen after screen of options and choices, the command line gives you instant access to the computer's resources. In addition, command-line programs tend to give you more information about what is going on than their more graphical counterparts.

A lot of people are intimidated by the command line because it gives you no prompting and no help. But that is also what makes it powerful. Programmers often make their programs easy to use by limiting the user's options. In those cases, it is the program that tells the user what to do, and the program tries to prevent the user from doing anything out of the ordinary. The command line, on the other hand, obeys your commands. It doesn't tell you what to do; it doesn't even make suggestions. It just does what you say. That is a little scary, but it is also empowering.

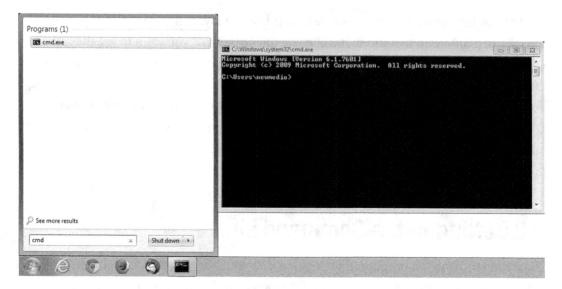

Figure B-2. *Getting to the Command Line in Windows*

After using getting a command line, you might also take a look at Appendix C.

B.2.1 Getting to a Command Line in Windows

Windows is the hardest operating system in which to find a working command line. In every Windows version, Microsoft attempts to bury the command prompt a little deeper, and the command line tools are buried even further down. In Windows, the command line is a program called cmd.exe. When you hit the start button, you can usually search. Typing in cmd will usually bring up the program that you want (see Figure B-2). An updated command line in Windows is known as powershell.exe and has more features, but is not always installed.

B.2.2 Getting a Command Line on a Mac

The Mac makes it much easier to get a command prompt. They hide the command prompt so that unwary users don't accidentally stumble over it. However, if you know where it is, it is not hard to find. To find it on most versions of MacOS X, first go in to the "Applications" folder, and find the "Utilities" folder. Within the "Utilities" folder, there is a program called Terminal.app. If you double-click that program, it will open up a command line for you.

B.2.3 Getting a Command Line on Linux

For most people using Linux, getting a command line isn't much of a problem. Most Linux users live on the command line. If you don't, somewhere on your desktop, there is some menu item that says "Terminal" or "Console" or "SH" or "TTY" or "Prompt." If it has an icon, it probably looks like an old green-screen computer. That will be your command line.

B.3 Using a Text Editor

A text editor is a program that edits documents which are stored as one long string of text (for more information about text strings, see Chapter 4). A text editor *is not the same as a word processor*. A word processor certainly includes long strings of text, but it also includes other things, such as formatting features (underline, bold, italic, font family, font size, etc.) and non-text elements (such as images). Historically, word processing files have been binary files. This means that the formatting functions were not described using text, but using raw numbers, since that is the normal way that computers operate on data. Because those files contained raw numbers (as opposed to text-encoded digits), they cannot be properly displayed in a text editor, which treats the entire file as one long string of characters. A **text document** is a document which *can be viewed* as simply a long string of text. Some file formats, such as HTML, include formatting instructions *as text* within the document. These files can be opened up with a text editor (which shows the bare formatting instructions themselves) as well as on a special viewer (a browser in the case of HTML), which would show the formatted version of the file.

There are numerous text editors available, each with their own advantages and disadvantages. However, one stands out as being relatively easy to use, flexible for a huge variety of circumstances, able to grow with you as a developer and works on every platform—*Visual Studio Code*. I would suggest that you download and use the *Visual Studio Code* editor (often referred to as *VS Code*). This editor is free to download and use and can really make everything easier. If you don't already have a text editor you like, I would suggest you try *Visual Studio Code* first.[1]

However, you can also work with the tools you already have installed on your operating system. I want everyone to know that programming doesn't require a bunch of extra tools but that, on modern computer systems, your operating system already ships with everything you need to get started. Therefore, each of the following section tells you how to get to your system-installed text editor. But I would still recommend that you use *Visual Studio Code* instead.

B.3.1 Getting Windows Set Up Properly

The first thing that you should do before editing text documents with Windows is to turn file extensions on. As described in Section 4.5, files use *filename extensions* to tell the user and the operating system what format the data is in. Unfortunately, in order to make it "easier" on nontechnical users, Windows often hides these extensions and just uses them internally to show the user an icon for the file format. This makes it difficult for building text files of various formats. We often need to modify the extension to tell the operating system what format we are writing in and to know precisely what the format of the file we are looking at is. Thankfully, Windows has an option to allow displaying of filename extensions. It works slightly differently in different versions of Windows, but the idea is the same.

1. Click on the Windows "Start" button.

2. Click on the "Control Panel" button.

3. Open up "Appearance and Personalization."

4. Click "Folder Options" or "File Explorer Options."

5. Click on the "View" tab.

---

[1] Despite the similarity in name (and despite also being published by Microsoft), this program has no real connection to Microsoft's *Visual Studio* development environment. *Visual Studio* is geared toward writing Windows-oriented applications, while *Visual Studio Code* is a programmer's text editor that can be used for just about any project on any operating system. I personally use *Visual Studio Code* whether I am on a Mac, Windows, or Linux, for just about every programming project. It's free and it is easy to use.

6. Under "Advanced Settings," look for the option "Hide extensions for known file types" and make sure the checkbox is *not checked*.

7. You also might want to find the "Hidden files and folders" option and select "Show hidden files, folders, and drives." This isn't needed for this book, but I didn't ever know a programmer who didn't use that setting.

Now you will be able to see the filename extensions in Windows!

B.3.2 Using a Text Editor in Windows

The text editor that comes standard in Windows is called *Notepad*. You can find it in the menus, or simply search for it in your search bar.

Once you have the program open, you can use the file menu to create, open, and save text documents. Be sure to pay special attention to the file extension you use to save documents. The operating system will use this extension to choose the program used to open the file. Generally, if you save a file with an extension other than `.txt`, you will not be able to open it back up in Notepad by double-clicking the file from the File Explorer. Instead, you will have to open Notepad first, and then choose "Open" from Notepad's menu to load the file.

When you save files, be sure to set the file extension appropriately. Use `.html` for HTML files, `.css` For CSS files, and `.js` for JavaScript files. The encoding should be set to either ANSI or UTF-8. See Figure B-3.

B.3.3 Using a Text Editor in Mac OS

The text editor that comes standard in Mac OS is called *TextEdit*. However, TextEdit also acts as a word processor, so it is important to keep in mind which mode it is in! We will discuss how to switch modes shortly. If it becomes too complicated, I would suggest just downloading and using *Visual Studio Code*.

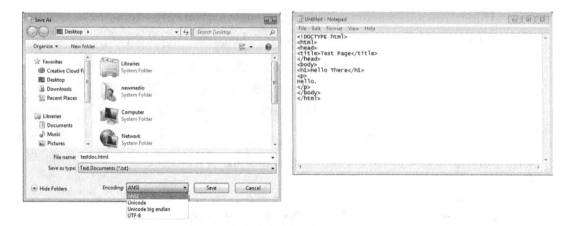

Figure B-3. *Saving an HTML File with Notepad*

To open up TextEdit, you can just click on the Spotlight Search icon and type in "textedit." Clicking on the TextEdit icon will open up the application. You can also get to TextEdit through the Finder, by going to "Applications" and clicking on "TextEdit."

When TextEdit first starts, it is acting like a word processor, not a text editor. If you are in TextEdit, and it has a formatting bar (with buttons to do bold, italic, etc.), you are in the wrong mode. When opening text files with TextEdit, be sure to check the "Ignore Rich Text Commands" checkbox in order to open the file as a text file. If you get the formatting bar, you are in the wrong mode, and you must close and reopen the file.

When creating new files with TextEdit, you can easily switch from word processing mode to text editing mode if it starts you in the wrong mode. Just click on the "Format" menu, and then click "Make Plain Text." Your document will now be treated as a text document. You can perform this action anytime before your first save without causing problems.

You can also set TextEdit to do text editing by default. To do that, go into the "TextEdit" menu, and then click "Preferences." Under the "New Document" tab, set the format to be "Plain Text." Under the "Open and Save" tab, check the checkbox that says "Display HTML files as HTML code instead of formatted text."

When you save files, be sure to set the file extension appropriately. Use .html for HTML files, .css For CSS files, and .js for JavaScript files. Also note that to open a text file, be sure to open up TextEdit first, and then open the file. Double-clicking the file itself may open it up in some other application, such as your browser.

B.3.4 Using a Text Editor in Linux

Since there are so many different distributions of the Linux operating system, I cannot describe how each of them works, so I will cover Ubuntu. Text editing is a staple of Linux usage, so finding a text editor should not be a problem on any Linux distributions. Some popular text editors include Atom, Gedit, and Kate. If you do not already know how to use these, do not try to use Vi or Emacs if they are options. They are both powerful programs but take a lot of time to learn to use—even just how to open and save a file!

In Ubuntu, to open up a text document, click "Applications" and then "Accessories," and then click "Text Editor" (or it may be called "gedit"). This will open up the Gedit editor.

When you save files, be sure to set the file extension appropriately. Use `.html` for HTML files, `.css` For CSS files, and `.js` for JavaScript files. Also note that to open a text file, be sure to open up your text editor first, and then use your text editor to open the file. Double-clicking the file itself may open it up in some other application, such as your browser.

B.3.5 Text Encoding Problems

Sometimes our text editors come up with some interesting surprises. The most common one is the text editor being set to write out using a different character encoding. Be sure, in the "Save" dialog boxes, that, if there is a character set option, it is set to either "ASCII," "ANSI," or "UTF-8" (see Figure B-3).

Also, **be sure that any autocorrect features or auto-quoting/smart quoting features are turned off**. In programming languages, if the language wants a double-quote character (i.e., "), the fancy curved quotes aren't going to work (i.e., "). However, some text editors or settings will auto-replace one for the other. If that is happening to you, find the setting that is doing it, and switch it off!

To switch off smart quotes on the Mac's TextEdit program, go into the "TextEdit" menu and click "Preferences." The setting should appear under "Options." Turn off all of the smart quoting, smart dashing, and spell-correcting features when programming.

B.4 Interacting with a Web Page in Developer Mode

It comes as a surprise to people first learning HTML that they can easily see the HTML, CSS, and JavaScript code of any website. But, in fact, it is true, and it is true for a simple reason—in order for you to be able to *use* the web page, you have to *receive* it first. In addition, every major browser has the ability to show you the things that it downloaded.

For some browsers, you may have to enable a "developer" mode in order to use these tools. To turn on the developer tools in the Safari browser, for instance, go to the main "Safari" menu and find the "Preferences" menu under that. This will open up a dialog box with several tabs. Click the "Advanced" tab. Toward the bottom, there will be a preference that says, "Show Develop menu in menu bar." Check that box, and then close the dialog box. You will notice a new menu for Safari—the "Develop" menu.

Once the developer mode is turned on, most browsers behave relatively the same for HTML, CSS, and JavaScript inspection. The following screens are from the Brave (and Chrome) browser but should work almost identically for all of them.

B.4.1 Viewing the Source

Browsers offer two different ways to view the source. The first way is to view the source *as initially downloaded*. In order to do this, once you are on a web page, first click the "View" menu; then click the "Developer" submenu; next click "View Source." This will pop up a new window or tab with the source code to the page as it was downloaded.

However, JavaScript can also modify the page while you are looking at it. Therefore, browsers also give you a way to view the HTML of the page *as it appears now* and allow you to interact with it and modify it. This tool is much more interactive and has many more features than the "View Source" menu option.

To make use of this tool, right-click (or control-click on a Mac) anywhere on the contents of the web page. This will open a context menu. Toward the bottom, click the "Inspect" menu item. This will bring up the web page as a tree of elements (see Figure B-4). This view is the way that the browser itself thinks of the code. If your window looks different, be sure the "Elements" tab is selected.

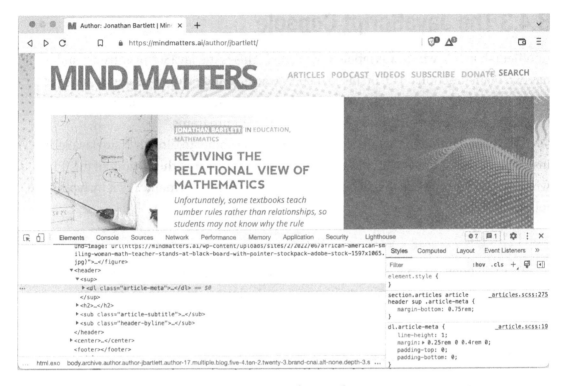

Figure B-4. *Viewing the Source Interactively on Chrome*

B.4.2 Interacting with the Source

Now that you are viewing the source code, you can actually click an HTML element in the inspection window, and the browser will highlight that element in the display. Additionally, after selecting the element, if you double-click it, you can modify it, or, if you delete it, it will be deleted from the page. Don't worry—this doesn't modify the site (or even the local files). This merely modifies the browser's current copy of the HTML.

Additionally, to the right, you can see that the styles that are applied to the currently selected element are shown. You can add or remove CSS styles from this window manually to see how they look.

B.4.3 The JavaScript Console

Another tab in this window is labeled "Console." This is the JavaScript console, and it has two main functions. The first is to display warning and error messages that occur when processing or interacting with the web page. These are usually network errors or JavaScript errors or logging messages from JavaScript programs.

The second function that the console gives is the ability to directly issue JavaScript instructions that interact with the window. There is a cursor at the bottom of this window, and you can use this to type any valid JavaScript statement. Try it by typing the following code:

```
alert("Hello");
```

This will open up an alert window on the page. Any valid JavaScript can be entered here. It's great for doing simple experiments or playing around with a web page.

B.4.4 The Network Tab

The network tab displays all of the network activity done by the current web page. If it loaded CSS, JavaScript, graphics, or anything else, that activity appears in the Network tab. You can click each item in this tab and get additional details, such as what URL was requested, what headers were sent, what was received, etc.

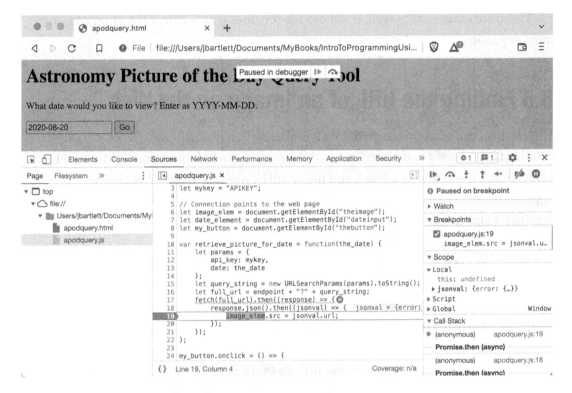

Figure B-5. *Interactively Debugging a Program*

B.4.5 The Sources Tab

The sources tab gives you access to the JavaScript debugger. A debugger is a tool that allows you to stop the program at any point, look at all of the values, and step through your program a single step at a time to identify problems in your code.

The sources tab will show all of the JavaScript you have loaded. You can click one of the files, and then click a line number to add a "breakpoint" in your code. Then, when JavaScript tries to run that line of code, it will stop and let you inspect what is going on.

Figure B-5 shows an example program in the debugger.

The right-hand side, under "Scope," shows the currently active variables. Under "Call Stack," it shows you the functions that were called to get your program to the current point (see about the stack in Chapter 13). When you are done inspecting, you can remove the breakpoint (if you don't want to stop there again) and hit the "play" arrow button to get the program running again. The other buttons allow you to go through the code slowly to see what is happening.

There are other tabs as well, but these are the ones you will be interacting with the most as you learn to work with web pages.

B.5 Finding the URL of an Image on the Web

Finding the URL of an image on the Web is actually really, really easy. In nearly every browser, all you need to do is to find the image you want to look at and right-click it (use control-click if you are on a Mac), and there will be a menu option that allows you to copy the address of the image to your clipboard. In Brave and Chrome, the menu option is called "Copy Image Address." Note that we don't want to copy the image *itself*, just the URL (which Chrome calls its *address*).

Once you copy the image URL, you can paste the address anywhere you like using control-v on Windows or command-v on a Mac.

When using Safari, Brave, and Chrome, you can also open up the image in a new window or tab using the menu titled "Open Image in a New Tab." Then, you can see the image all by itself and copy the URL from the address bar of the browser.

Every once in a while, you will find images that you can't right-click on for an image URL. This is usually either because the image is a background image (this trick only works for foreground images) or because they are using a nonstandard method of displaying the image. You might be able to find the URL of this image by right-clicking it and doing and "Inspect," but you would have to do some digging in the HTML to find the image. Nonetheless, there are innumerable images on the Web whose URLs are available just by right-clicking the image.

B.6 What to Do When a Program Doesn't Work

Every programmer has experienced it. You typed in a program, tried to run it, and then *nothing happens*. What went wrong?

I can't diagnose every problem you will have, but I can give you a short checklist of things to look for. There are some basic mistakes that are made over and over again, and I can hopefully cover them here.

If you put in a program, and the program did not work at all, or it did not work the way you wanted it to, here are some basic things to check:

1. Did you save your file as a text file with the proper extension? If your text editor has a formatting toolbar (with bold, italic, etc.), you are probably not saving your file as a text file. Convert your file to text mode and then save it (see Section B.3). Also be sure that you have file extensions turned on (see Section B.3.1). If file extensions are off, even if you specify a file extension, it will add a new, hidden file extension that you don't want.

2. Did you type in the program correctly? Computer programs are very sensitive, and *every character matters.* Changing one little character can be the difference between a successful and an unsuccessful program. Did you put in semicolons, or did you accidentally type a colon instead? Did you misspell a variable name somewhere? Did you get both the opening brace and the closing brace? Any mistake like this will cost you your entire program. Check carefully. After a while, it becomes second nature. I can now look at a page of code and spot such errors immediately. That comes with experience—for now, you have to hunt and check everything.

3. Did your text editor substitute in curly quotes for your regular quotes? Some text editors think you are typing a document and want to make your text fancy. When you type in a regular double-quote ("), they will auto-substitute curly quotes ("). This causes programming languages to go bonkers because they are very definite about the characters they are looking for. If your text editor is doing this, see Section B.3.5.

4. Open up a JavaScript console (see Section B.4.1). Are there any error messages displayed? If there are, you can click the filename and it will show you where in your file the error occurred. Also, you can search the Internet for the error message to get help.

5. If your program runs a little before it stops or if it runs but runs wrongly, you can often figure out what is wrong by adding in a lot of `alert()` messages in your code, so you can follow its progress. You can use `alert()` to display not only messages but also the contents of variables. This allows you to identify exactly what is going on in the code.

6. Check your value types. One of the most common programming errors is to forget what type of value is stored in a variable. For instance, any time you get a value back from a `prompt()`, it will be a string. If you wanted a number, you need to *convert* it to a number first (using `parseInt` or a similar function).

7. Check your loops. If your program has a loop, you have to be sure that there is some way to get out of the loop. If there is not a condition that allows it to exit, then you have not properly programmed it. Also be sure that the things you want it to do *every* time are *inside* the loop body and the things that you only want to happen once are *outside* the loop body.

8. Search engines are your friend. As a programmer, I always have a search engine open, and check the Internet to see if someone is having a similar problem.

9. Find a friend. Preferably, find a friend that has done some programming before. No matter what, you will each find mistakes that the other one didn't see. Two heads are better than one.

APPENDIX C

The JavaScript Toolbox on Docker

Before reading this appendix, be sure you know how to access the command line (details provided in Appendix B.2). The information in this appendix applies primarily to performing the examples in Chapter 3. The problem is that, to perform those exercises, you need your computer set up in a certain way.

In order to avoid having to get your computer set up in a specific way, we are going to instead use a tool called Docker to essentially download a small but complete, configured operating system to your computer and then run the commands inside that operating system. That way installing these tools has minimal impact on your system, but the tools work exactly as expected since they are running in their own mini-operating system.

Note that, since all of this is just for the examples in Chapter 3, you can also feel free to ignore this appendix and simply imagine those examples working. It's not as fun, but if you are having headaches installing everything, it might be worthwhile to skip it instead.

In order to get started, you first need to download and install Docker from `docker.com`. While there is a paid version of Docker available, you do not need any paid features for the examples in this book. Note that, on Windows, depending on your version, Docker may ask you to do some special configurations to get it up and running. Simply follow the instructions that it gives you during installation.

Once Docker is up-and-running, you can go to your command line (see Appendix B.2) and start using it. I have a computer image that is already set up to run the examples in Chapter 3. To start using it, simply run the following command:

```
docker run --rm -it johnnyb61820/jstoolkit
```

309

The first time you run this, it will start by transferring the operating system image from Docker Hub. After that, it will start a new virtual computer running this operating system (known in the Docker world as a **container**). It will give you a prompt that looks something like this:

```
root@5f166a25178a:/#
```

From here, you can type in the commands given in Chapter 3, and they should work correctly. Type exit on a line by itself to exit the container, or just close the window.

For more information about Docker and containers, see my book *Cloud Native Applications with Docker and Kubernetes*.

APPENDIX D

Character Encoding Issues

D.1 A Short History of Character Encodings

In computer programming, the problem of how to represent character strings (i.e., lines of text) is an ever-present issue. Generally, a string of characters is represented by an array of numbers, where each number represents one character (letter, digit, punctuation mark, etc.) of text. The problem then becomes a question of which numbers represent which characters. If every program had its own way of converting numbers to characters, it would be nearly impossible for two programs to communicate. If one program used the number 6 to mean the letter F, but another program used 6 to represent a comma, trying to get those two programs to talk to each other would require code to translate the number from one system to another, which would be a lot of work. In addition, if every programmer had to solve this problem for their own program, that would take a lot of effort for every program that deals with character strings (which is basically every program).

Therefore, early on in computer programming, standards were developed for representing character strings. Not only was ASCII developed early in computing, but the standards were already in place before computers existed, thanks to telegraph lines. The telegraph was a machine used in the 1800s and early 1900s for sending and receiving messages over long distances. It worked by sending short and long pulses over long wires. If you see Morse code printed out, it usually uses dots for the short pulses and dashes for the long pulses. For instance, the letter A is represented as . - in Morse code, and the letter X is represented as - . . -. In Morse code, the more common letters have shorter codes, and the less common letters have longer codes, making it easier for a telegraph operator to type messages.

© Jonathan Bartlett 2023
J. Bartlett, *Programming for Absolute Beginners*, https://doi.org/10.1007/978-1-4842-8751-4

In the mid-1800s, engineers developed the automated telegraph, which allowed users to type on typewriter-like machines. However, variable-length codes, which were great for manual telegraph operation, made these machines difficult to implement. Therefore, they developed a new code, called the Baudot code, which had a fixed-length character size. Eventually, the need for lowercase letters, punctuation, and other similar needs led to other codes with more expansive alphabets. In the 1960s, ASCII was developed as a further expansion and standardization for telegraph systems. Another standard, called EBCDIC, was developed for IBM mainframes based on the punch card system of early computers. However, EBCDIC has pretty much been completely superseded by ASCII and Unicode. ASCII gained wide use in computers both because it was already an international standard and because it fit nicely in the 8-bit byte that was popular in computers.

D.2 Unicode and International Character Sets

The ASCII system, however, is far from perfect. Its primary problem is that it only represents characters from the English language. As more and more countries started using computers, each of them had their own language with their own alphabet! Even more, some of the alphabets had more than 255 characters in them, and so they could not be represented by a single byte. In the beginning, some tried to accommodate for this by using extensions to ASCII or by using a separate character set for each language. However, as the importance of multilingual documents grew, the limitations of these approaches became clear, and the need for a universal code that contained all characters from all languages became evident. Therefore, a larger list of characters had to be made in order to encompass all of the world's alphabets.

This list of characters is called **Unicode**, which currently has over 95,000 characters! Unicode assigns a number to each character for reference, but does not by itself specify how those numbers are to be encoded. For instance, the UTF-16 standard uses two bytes for every character, but the UTF-32 uses four bytes for every character. They all represent the same Unicode numbers, but they accomplish that in different ways.

When Unicode was developed, most files were still written using ASCII. A way was needed to bridge the gap between ASCII and Unicode. Therefore, developers created an encoding of Unicode, called UTF-8, which looks like ASCII and uses single bytes for common English characters, but it uses multiple bytes for non-English characters. This allowed easier migration between older programs that only understood ASCII and newer programs which wanted to support users from every country. If your document only used English characters, it was identical whether it was encoded in ASCII or UTF-8. The differences only came when you ventured into other character sets. UTF-8 is less efficient for processing, but its ability to interoperate with older programs has made it the default in many applications. JavaScript uses UTF-8 for its encodings by default.

D.3 An Abbreviated ASCII Table

Because ASCII is still popular and is the same as UTF-8 for English characters, this book provides a list of ASCII character codes in the following. These are also important for some of the programs in Appendix E. The following list contains ASCII codes in decimal, octal, and hexadecimal. If the meaning of an ASCII code in enclosed like <this>, it is a non-printable character, such as a tab, a carriage return, or a control sequence. Control sequences are used to embed extra communication information in a string of text that is not used for user display, such as a record separator, or to mark the end of a transmission. The lesser used ASCII codes are skipped in the following table.

Decimal	Hexadecimal	Octal	Meaning
0	00	000	<null>
9	09	011	<tab>
10	0a	012	<line feed>
13	0d	015	<carriage return>
30	1e	036	<record separator>
31	1f	037	<field separator>
32	20	040	<space>
33	21	041	!
34	22	042	"
35	23	043	#
36	24	044	$
37	25	045	%

(continued)

Decimal	Hexadecimal	Octal	Meaning
38	26	046	&
39	27	047	'
40	28	050	(
41	29	051	)
42	2a	052	*
43	2b	053	+
44	2c	054	,
45	2d	055	-
46	2e	056	.
47	2f	057	/
48	30	060	0
49	31	061	1
50	32	062	2
51	33	063	3
52	34	064	4
53	35	065	5
54	36	066	6
55	37	067	7
56	38	070	8
57	39	071	9
58	3a	072	:
59	3b	073	;
60	3c	074	<
61	3d	075	=
62	3e	076	>
63	3f	077	?

(continued)

Decimal	Hexadecimal	Octal	Meaning
64	40	100	@
65	41	101	A
66	42	102	B
67	43	103	C
68	44	104	D
69	45	105	E
70	46	106	F
71	47	107	G
72	48	110	H
73	49	111	I
74	4a	112	J
75	4b	113	K
76	4c	114	L
77	4d	115	M
78	4e	116	N
79	4f	117	O
80	50	120	P
81	51	121	Q
82	52	122	R
83	53	123	S
84	54	124	T
85	55	125	U
86	56	126	V
87	57	127	W
88	58	130	X
89	59	131	Y

(*continued*)

Decimal	Hexadecimal	Octal	Meaning
90	5a	132	Z
91	5b	133	[
92	5c	134	\
93	5d	135	]
94	5e	136	^
95	5f	137	_
96	60	140	`
97	61	141	a
98	62	142	b
99	63	143	c
100	64	144	d
101	65	145	e
102	66	146	f
103	67	147	g
104	68	150	h
105	69	151	i
106	6a	152	j
107	6b	153	k
108	6c	154	l
109	6d	155	m
110	6e	156	n
111	6f	157	o
112	70	160	p
113	71	161	q
114	72	162	r
115	73	163	s

(continued)

Decimal	Hexadecimal	Octal	Meaning
116	74	164	t
117	75	165	u
118	76	166	v
119	77	167	w
120	78	170	x
121	79	171	y
122	7a	172	z
123	7b	173	{
124	7c	174		
125	7d	175	}
126	7e	176	~

APPENDIX E

Additional Machine Language Programs

If you enjoyed the machine programs in Chapter 5, this appendix has a few others you can try. If you are really brave, you can even try to write one of your own!

E.1 Multiplying Numbers

Since this machine does not have a multiply instruction, multiplications have to happen by repeated addition. Therefore, this program will take two numbers and multiply them together by repeated addition. The numbers that are multiplied will be in memory locations 61 and 62, and the result of the multiplication will be stored in location 63.

Figure E-1 shows the program.

0	1	2	3	4	5	6	7
22	0	61	22	1	62	20	2
8 0	**9** 20	**10** 3	**11** 0	**12** 20	**13** 5	**14** 1	**15** 21
16 4	**17** 1	**18** 37	**19** 4	**20** 3	**21** 65	**22** 33	**23** 4
24 133	**25** 2	**26** 0	**27** 133	**28** 3	**29** 5	**30** 64	**31** 15
32 0	**33** 25	**34** 63	**35** 2	**36** 0	**37** 0	**38** 0	**39** 0
40 0	**41** 0	**42** 0	**43** 0	**44** 0	**45** 0	**46** 0	**47** 0
48 0	**49** 0	**50** 0	**51** 0	**52** 0	**53** 0	**54** 0	**55** 0
56 0	**57** 0	**58** 0	**59** 0	**60** 0	**61** 8	**62** 4	**63** 0

Figure E-1. *Machine Language Program to Multiply Two Numbers*

This program stores the first number in register 0 and the second number in register 1. The program works by repeatedly adding the number in register 0 the number of times specified in register 1. Register 2 holds the results so far, and register 3 holds the number

319

© Jonathan Bartlett 2023
J. Bartlett, *Programming for Absolute Beginners*, https://doi.org/10.1007/978-1-4842-8751-4

of times we have performed the addition so far. Register 4 is used for holding comparison values. Register 5 holds the number 1 so we can add it to register 3 after each repetition.

E.2 Writing to the Screen

This program introduces a new piece of hardware—the screen. This screen will be based on really old types of screens—old-school text terminals. If you haven't seen them, they are like typewriters. No graphics, no windows, just text on the screen.

The way the screen will work is that the screen will read the last row of numbers in the computer memory page (memory locations 56–63) and display a single line of text based on those numbers. Each number will represent one letter to be displayed on the screen, based on the ASCII code for the letter (see Chapter 4 and Appendix D for more on ASCII codes). In addition to the standard codes, we will also treat the number 0 as a blank character. So, if the last line of the computer memory was 72, 69, 76, 76, 79, 0, 0, 0, the screen would say HELLO. At the end of step 8 (i.e., the end of each instruction), if any of these numbers have changed, the screen should update what it is displaying.

So, for our first program with displays, we will simply read the number in memory location 55. If it is greater than 100, we will write out the word Big onto the display, and if it is less than or equal to 100, we will write the word Sm to the display (I had to abbreviate "Small" to make the code fit).

Figure E-2 shows the program.

0		1		2		3		4		5		6		7	
22		0		55		20		1		100		37		0	
8 1		**9** 81		**10** 27		**11** 0		**12** 20		**13** 2		**14** 83		**15** 25	
16 56		**17** 2		**18** 20		**19** 2		**20** 109		**21** 25		**22** 57		**23** 2	
24 0		**25** 0		**26** 0		**27** 20		**28** 2		**29** 66		**30** 25		**31** 56	
32 2		**33** 20		**34** 2		**35** 105		**36** 25		**37** 57		**38** 2		**39** 20	
40 2		**41** 103		**42** 25		**43** 58		**44** 2		**45** 0		**46** 0		**47** 0	
48 0		**49** 0		**50** 0		**51** 0		**52** 0		**53** 0		**54** 0		**55** 0	
56 0		**57** 0		**58** 0		**59** 0		**60** 0		**61** 0		**62** 0		**63** 0	

Figure E-2. *Machine Language Program to See if a Number Is Big or Small*

E.3 Writing a Number to the Screen

Now, in all of the arithmetic that we have done, we have ended up with a number that we have stored in memory. However, if we were to copy that number to the screen, we would get weird results because the screen would think that it was an ASCII code for some other letter. For instance, the result of the first program in this appendix was 32. If we copied the number 32 to the screen area, it would look up what the value of ASCII code 32 is, and it would find out that it was a blank space! Therefore, we would see nothing on the screen.

So, if we had a number, how would we display it on the screen? Well, look at the ASCII codes. The digits go from 48 to 57. If it was a single-digit number (i.e., less than 10), then we could simply add 48 to the number and that would be the answer. For multi-digit numbers, it is more complicated because we would have to repeatedly divide by 10 for each digit.

However, for this program, we are just going to do the single-digit case. We are going to load a single-digit number from memory location 55, convert it to its ASCII code, and write Val: X to the screen, where X is our digit.

Figure E-3 shows the code.

0	1	2	3	4	5	6	7
22	0	55	20	1	48	133	0
8 1	9 25	10 61	11 0	12 20	13 2	14 86	15 25
16 56	17 2	18 20	19 2	20 97	21 25	22 57	23 2
24 20	25 2	26 108	27 25	28 58	29 2	30 20	31 2
32 58	33 25	34 59	35 2	36 20	37 2	38 32	39 25
40 60	41 2	42 0	43 0	44 0	45 0	46 0	47 0
48 0	49 0	50 0	51 0	52 0	53 0	54 0	55 7
56 0	57 0	58 0	59 0	60 0	61 0	62 0	63 0

Figure E-3. *Machine Language Program to Display the ASCII Code of a Number*

E.4 Going Further

Now that you know how machine language works, you might try writing your own program using this simplified system. The first thing you might try is combining the multiply program with the program to display a number and try to display the result on the screen (although it will only work if the answer is a single digit). The possibilities, though, are limitless, though your imaginations will probably require more than an 8x8 grid for memory.

If you enjoy this sort of programming, you would probably enjoy assembly language programming, which is similar to machine language except that instead of writing out the number of the opcodes, you would write out an abbreviated opcode name instead. My book, *Learn to Program with Assembly Language*, gives a broad overview of assembly language programming on modern computers and shows how various programming language techniques are implemented at the lowest level. In addition, while the machine language we are dealing with here was invented as a learning tool, *Learn to Program with Assembly Language* covers a real machine—the x86-64 family of processors.

While most programmers never need to program in machine language anymore, my hope is that doing these exercises will have accustomed your mind to the computer's way of thinking, which will help you be a better programmer in *any* programming language.

Index

A

Absolute path, 79
Absolute URL, 79, 80
alert function, 111, 114
alert() messages, 307
Altair, 12
Anchor, 23
Anonymous functions, 205–206
appendChild method, 165, 166, 174
Apple I, 12
Application frameworks, 241, 246
Application-layer protocols, 22, 23
Application programmer, 22
Application programming
        interface (API), 173, 175
    access network, JavaScript, 232, 233
    APIKEY, 230
    CORS, 238, 240
    DELETE, 237
    entity body/payload, 237
    GET, 237
    HTTP, 229, 237, 239
    interaction, web page, 235, 236
    JSON, 231, 232, 239
    NASA API, 229, 230, 239
    POST, 237
    PUT, 237
    query string, 233, 234
Arguments, 226
Arithmetic and logic unit (ALU),
        46–49, 54, 61
Arithmetic and Logic Unit sheet, 49, 52, 54

Arithmetic opcodes, 62
ARPANET, 13
Arrays, 37
    elements, 151
    index numbers, 151
    JavaScript, 150
    largest_age function, 153
    largest value, 152
    mixing objects, 154–156
    ordered sequences of values, 150
    products, 160
    programs, 151–154
    sequences of data, 159
Arrow functions, 226, 227
Artificial intelligence, 10
ASCII codes, 38, 311, 313, 320, 321
ASCII system, 312
Assembly language
        programming, 322
Assignment statements, 109, 130
    expression, 122
    functions, 122
    sample, 121
    variable, 121
Associative arrays, 225
Astronomy Picture of the Day, 229, 230,
        232, 233, 235, 240
Astronomy Picture of the Day Query Tool,
        235, 236
Attributes, 75, 76, 85–87, 89, 95, 96, 108,
        149, 163, 217
Automated telegraph, 312

© Jonathan Bartlett 2023
J. Bartlett, *Programming for Absolute Beginners*, https://doi.org/10.1007/978-1-4842-8751-4

Printed in the United States
by Baker & Taylor Publisher Services